Guiding K-3 Writers
to Independence

The New Essentials

Patricia L. Scharer & Gay Su Pinnell

■ SCHOLASTIC

New York · Toronto · London · Auckland · Sydney
Mexico City · New Delhi · Hong Kong · Buenos Aires

We dedicate this book to teachers whose
efforts ensure that their students not only
learn to read and write, but also become
lifelong readers and writers.

Cover design: Jorge J. Namerow
Interior design: LDL Designs
Acquiring Editor: Lois Bridges
Production Editor: Carol Ghiglieri

ISBN-13: 978-0-439-88449-5
ISBN-10: 0-439-88449-7
Copyright © 2008 by Patricia L. Scharer and Gay Su Pinnell
All rights reserved. Published by Scholastic Inc.
Printed in the U.S.A.
2 3 4 5 6 7 8 9 10   40   14 13 12 11 10 09 08

CONTENTS

INTRODUCTION

Guiding K–3 Writers to Independence: The New Essentials emerged from our work with Literacy Collaborative® and Reading Recovery® at the Ohio State University. Literacy Collaborative is a research-based school-reform initiative with the goal to raise literacy achievement in K–6 classrooms. Literacy coordinators train for seven to eight weeks at a university or district training site to become a school-based staff developer and coach for either primary (K–2) or intermediate (3–5/6) grades. (Visit www.literacycollaborative.org for more information about how to become part of the Literacy Collaborative network.) Reading Recovery teachers work for approximately half their day designing and delivering instruction to those first-grade students having the greatest difficulty learning to read and write. The goal is to accelerate each student's progress to average reading and writing within 20 weeks. (Visit www.rrosu.org for more information.) Both literacy initiatives provide intensive staff development for teachers, teacher leaders, literacy coordinators, university trainers, and administrators. In combination, these professionals provide a comprehensive system for supporting literacy and language learning across the years of the elementary school.

The chapters in this book were written by Literacy Collaborative and Reading Recovery professionals who have extensive experience in classrooms and as staff developers. The content in this book is informed by our work in classrooms with teachers and students who are learning about themselves as readers and writers. In contrast to educational initiatives that provide scripted, teacher-proof materials, our work celebrates each teacher as the expert decision maker charged with supporting the literacy development of each learner in the classroom. To do this requires that teachers continuously refine their skills for observing students and planning instruction to meet individual needs. It is our hope that this book will contribute to teachers, staff developers, and administrators as they continue to fine-tune their instructional programs supporting students as readers and writers. Each chapter ends with "Suggestions for Professional Development" that include ideas for study groups, seminars, staff development, or learning with a friend. You can find an additional study guide at www.lcosu.org. Appendices at the end of the book offer lists of children's literature and frequently asked questions that can be important resources for teachers as they use the ideas in this book with their students.

Readers will find a quartet of themes across the chapters in this book based on what we have learned through our work on numerous literacy projects over the past 25 years. The first theme is the assumption that all children and adults can and should be writers. We can recall a time when young children's writing was confined to copying from the chalkboard or filling in blanks on a worksheet. Our definition of writing is "a lifelong learning experience that begins with preschool as young writers create messages that are meaningful through picture and print." The writers in each classroom must also include the teacher who writes for a range of purposes, often sharing with students the challenges and successes experienced during the writing process.

The second theme is emphasizing the important role of oral language in linking thought processes with print. We recognize the importance of instructional contexts in which children talk with their peers and teachers about what they are reading and writing. Children's literature is central to those conversations, leading to a deeper understanding of the literary aspects of texts and also an appreciation of the writer's craft that can support students' own writing.

The third theme is that writing instruction should not be confined to a particular grade level or time of year. Rather, writing instruction takes place across a range of instructional contexts, each contributing in unique ways to students' abilities as writers.

Finally, this book assumes that teachers are instructional decision makers charged with becoming expert at both noticing their students' needs and planning to meet those needs in ways that support achievement in both reading and writing. Writers are created through daily opportunities to write, lessons that meet the needs of the class, and opportunities to celebrate students' efforts as they write.

This book's first section, "Getting Started: The Basics of a Quality Writing Program," sets the stage by taking readers into classrooms from kindergarten to grade 3 to see the writing process at work across the grades. Chapter 1, by Barbara Joan Wiley, offers a photo-essay of classrooms from kindergarten through grade 2, helping readers to "picture" writing instruction in the younger grades. Laurie Desai then describes the teaching and learning of writing in a third-grade classroom in Chapter 2. The voices of experienced teachers of writing are led by Barbara Joan Wiley in Chapter 3 as they explain how writing workshop supports the writers in their classrooms.

In the second section, "Building a Community of Writers," the chapters begin with Gay Su Pinnell and Irene Fountas's discussion of the role of oral language in writing instruction followed by the introduction of a new concept—Community Writing—by Andrea McCarrier in Chapter 5. Marsha Levering's chapter, "Becoming a Writer by Noticing the World," continues the discussion of how teachers can support young writers by helping them talk and write about their surroundings. The last chapter of this section reminds us that writing is more than getting down the first draft. In Chapter 7, Kecia Hicks encourages writers to celebrate the effort to look critically at our writing as well as at determining what's needed to make revisions that strengthen the quality of the message.

The importance of "Connecting Reading and Writing" is the focus of the third section. Gay Su Pinnell and Irene Fountas begin this section by describing the range of opportunities students have to write about what they are reading in ways that support their growing abilities as writers. In Chapter 9, Patricia Scharer turns the lens to picture books by exploring how teachers and students can analyze these texts to learn about a writer's craft. The next chapter, by Justina Henry, explores how learning the story structures found in the personal narratives children hear and read can help young writers tell their own stories. This section concludes with a description of a school-home project involving KEEP BOOKS®, inexpensive "little books" designed by educators at the Ohio State University, that children can read in school and take home to keep. In this chapter, John McCarrier and Gay Su Pinnell team to discuss how John's work as a KEEP BOOKS author serves as a model for teachers to share their own writing. (For information about KEEP BOOKS visit www.keepbooks.org.)

"Meeting the Needs of Individual Learners," the fourth section, centers on how assessment and instruction merge to support the individual needs of young writers. Chapter 12, by Sherry Kinzel, provides an overview of writing assessment and draws particular attention to the importance of conversations between teachers and writers. The case study of Jesse by Rauline Morris in Chapter 13 is a fitting example of how teachers can move writers from reluctance to enthusiasm within a quality writing program that centers on students' individual needs. This section concludes with Emily Rodgers' chapter on the importance of providing writing instruction for students who struggle as a way to support their growth as both writers and readers.

The final section is a set of resources to help teachers in "Taking Action" while planning their writing program. Lynda Hamilton Mudre's "Fifteen Ways to Help Young Writers" offers a succinct way to think through important aspects of writing instruction in the primary grades. The final chapter, by Lynda Hamilton Mudre and Gay Su Pinnell, focuses on handwriting, a skill some might argue is often neglected. Their approach to handwriting ensures appropriate attention to this skill as a way to foster fluency as a writer and clarity for the reader without compromising attention to the writing process. Six appendices round out this book with bibliographies, frequently asked questions, and teaching ideas.

Patricia L. Scharer   *Gay Su Pinnell*

Section I

Getting Started: The Basics of a Quality Writing Program

Getting Started: The Basics of a Quality Writing Program sets the stage by taking readers into classrooms from kindergarten to grade 3 to see the writing process at work across the grades. Chapter 1, by Barbara Joan Wiley, offers a photo-essay of classrooms from kindergarten through grade 2, helping readers to "picture" writing instruction in the younger grades. Laurie Desai then describes the teaching and learning of writing in a third-grade classroom in Chapter 2. The voices of experienced teachers of writing are led by Barbara Joan Wiley in Chapter 3 as they explain how writing workshop supports the writers in their classrooms.

CHAPTER 1

Writing Workshop: A K–2 Photo Journal

by Barbara Joan Wiley

One afternoon, I was to videotape kindergarten teacher Andrea Waselko's classroom as part of my research project that documents what good teachers do. I was late, and I walked into the classroom during writing workshop. As I set up my camera, I was struck by how industrious the children were—they were all busy writing. This scene reminded me of a conversation I had recently had with a friend, Susan Lear. She told me she had just attended an in-service, offered in her school district and given by an educational consultant, whose topic was, "Raising Test Scores for All Children." The consultant said she could tell who in a classroom would achieve by watching the children for five minutes and noting which ones had their "chins to their chests." The idea was that children who can attend, who have focused attention, are the ones who will be successful. How do Andrea and other good teachers make writing workshop an effective context in which teachers can initiate and support children to be independent writers who are focused and industrious?

This chapter documents with words and photos the definition and structure of writing workshop, and describes how to create a supportive environment for writing.

Following a Structure for Writing Workshop

Writing workshop is the time of day in a classroom when children write independently on topics they choose themselves. Teachers support their students' writing by teaching mini-lessons, conferring with individual writers, and interacting around children's writing. Typically, writing workshop begins with a five- to ten-minute mini-lesson, moves to a time for writing, and then ends with sharing time.

The greatest amount of time is spent as the students independently write while the teacher confers with students as needed. Sharing lasts from five to ten minutes (see Figure 1-1).

Mini-lessons may focus on (1) procedures, (2) strategic actions or skills, or (3) writers' craft. The procedural mini-lesson focuses on something that writers need to know, such as where to find sharpened pencils and extra paper. A strategic or skills-related mini-lesson may focus on how to spell a frequently misspelled word, such as *said* or *because*, or on the strategy of saying a word slowly more than once to hear more sounds in it. A craft mini-lesson focuses on ways writers choose words such as using exciting words or adding dialogue. At times, especially in kindergarten, the element of interactive writing becomes the mini-lesson. For example, in January, kindergarten teacher Kecia Hicks noticed that many of her students were writing so quickly that they were forgetting to put in spaces. So, Kecia conducted an interactive writing lesson in which the community retold the story of *Old Black Fly*, a book by Jim Aylesworth, with a teaching focus about including spaces between words (see photo below).

As the children write in writing workshop, the teachers confer with children who need help. For instance, kindergarten teacher Andrea Waselko first makes sure that everyone has something in mind to write about. Then, she makes a point of conferring with her low-progress writers as they begin to write independently. Her conference becomes a guided

FIGURE 1-1. Writing Workshop: Time Allotments

writing lesson that helps them to achieve more than they could have written alone. For example, she might say, "What story do you want to write today? Say that sentence again so that you will remember it. What is the first word? Say it slowly. What sounds do you hear? Write them down."

Teachers analyze one-fourth of their students' independent writing each day and jot down their findings. Teachers also make a point of getting around to every student regularly, so that they are familiar with their students' changing strengths and needs and can use this information effectively. This helps them determine which students need a conference. For example, a teacher might help a student decide what kind of dialogue to add to a story and discuss how to set it off with punctuation. Teachers also keep notes on the conferences they have to inform later teaching decisions. Clearly, these conferences are not conducted haphazardly; they are conducted for a reason.

From this mini-lesson, Kecia's students moved directly to writing at their tables with the reminder to "Remember spacing; it makes it easier to read what you have written."

Guiding K-3 Writers to Independence

A few children are asked to share their work at the end of the writing workshop. The teacher invites these specific children to share for a reason, such as because they have successfully tried what was taught in the mini-lesson and the teacher wants to highlight this achievement so that other students will take it on. In this way, sharing time becomes another powerful time for teaching. For example, one day, Andrea asked John to share because he had a two-page story, and her mini-lesson had been about how authors can write more by rereading what they wrote the day before and then adding text to the original writing. When John is finished reading, Andrea responds, "Thanks, John. I notice that you've written more and that your story is so much more complete than it was before. Did anyone else try adding to their story?" Sharing time is also a time in which class members celebrate their friends' writing with responses such as "I think" or "I wonder" or "I appreciate." Additionally, at sharing time, students might ask to share because they want help. They might want to know how to make confusing sections clear or they may need ideas to formulate satisfying endings.

Creating a Supportive Environment for Writing Workshop

Writers write best when they have everything that they need close at hand. A good writing center is like the dashboard of a fine car—everything that may be needed is provided. In the case of writing workshop, this means everything from sharpened pencils to a variety of paper. Resources that may be needed are also readily available, from name charts to word walls to dictionaries (see Figure 1-2).

Teachers provide materials that are most supportive to the writers in their classrooms. Appropriate materials are scaffolds. A scaffold helps students do more than they can do alone. For example, the type of pencil offered can be a scaffold. Emergent writers need to be taught to cross out rather than erase, because erasing takes too much time and destroys paper. So, they should be offered pencils without erasers on the end. Transitional writers, on the other hand, use erasures and crossing out effectively, so they can be offered pencils with erasers. All writers, however, are encouraged not to erase extensively, so that they can return to their original thinking when there is a need.

FIGURE 1-2. Writing Center

WRITING CENTER

Materials that are housed in a writing center reflect the current needs of the students in the room. Writing centers for emergent writers are full of many kinds of writing materials such as pencils, markers, and crayons, and a variety of paper—some white, some colored, some with lines, and some without (see Figure 1-3).

Early writers need a variety of writing materials as well as

FIGURE 1-3. Emergent Writing Center

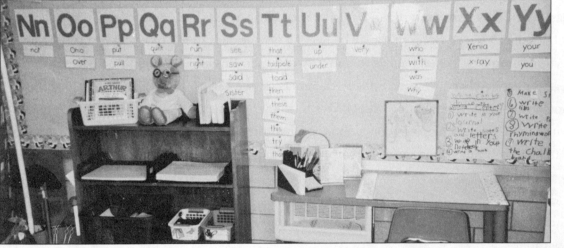

FIGURE 1-4. Early Writing Center

picture dictionaries, premade blank books, staples, and rulers (see Figure 1-4).

As children take on writing, the writing center becomes well stocked with all of the supplies a writer might need, from dictionaries and thesauruses, to papers, and pencils, and pens (see Figure 1-5).

FIGURE 1-5. Advanced Writing Center

WORD WALLS

Word walls (Cunningham, 1995) change, both throughout a school year and across grade levels. For example, the word wall in a kindergarten classroom might start in September as a group of high-frequency words the class has learned by tracing letters with crayons (see Figure 1-6). Later, it may become a chart titled "Words We Have in Our Heads" (see Figure 1-7). Later still, it may become a group of words displayed alphabetically across a wall in the classroom (see Figure 1-8).

Emergent and early writers can be more fluent writers when they carry the resources they need to spell around with them in their heads. The teaching foci for these writers will be to (1) accumulate a core of known words and to (2) say words slowly and write down the sounds that you hear. Too much emphasis on searching the room for the spelling of unknown words teaches dependency.

"Word walls in a first grade classroom are living things that are added to and taken away from as the need arises," states Al Amore, a primary teacher. "For example, when all of the children in my classroom knew how to spell a word without looking then the word was ceremoniously 'retired' from the word wall," he continued. "That's about when I put a chart of 'Kindergarten Words' up in the ABC Center [see Figure 1-9] and later a

FIGURE 1-6. Word Wall of High-Frequency Words

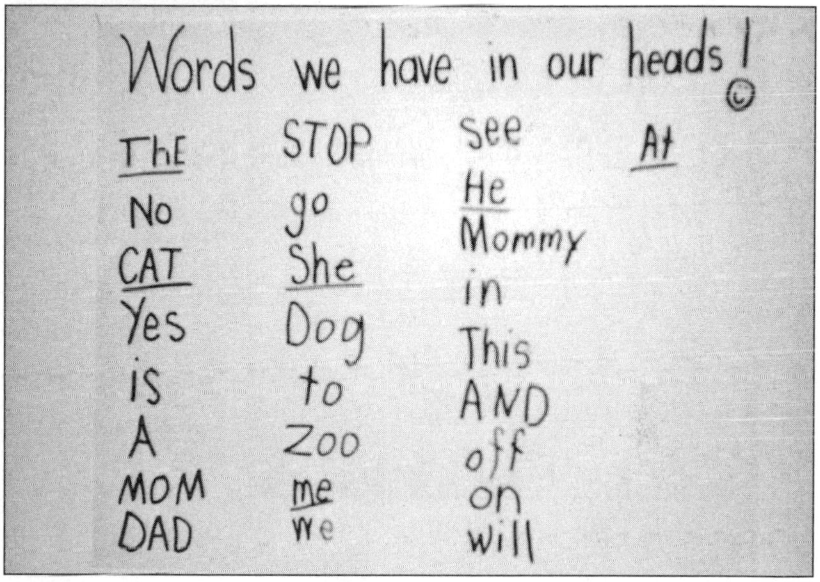

FIGURE 1-7. Word Wall in a Kindergarten Classroom

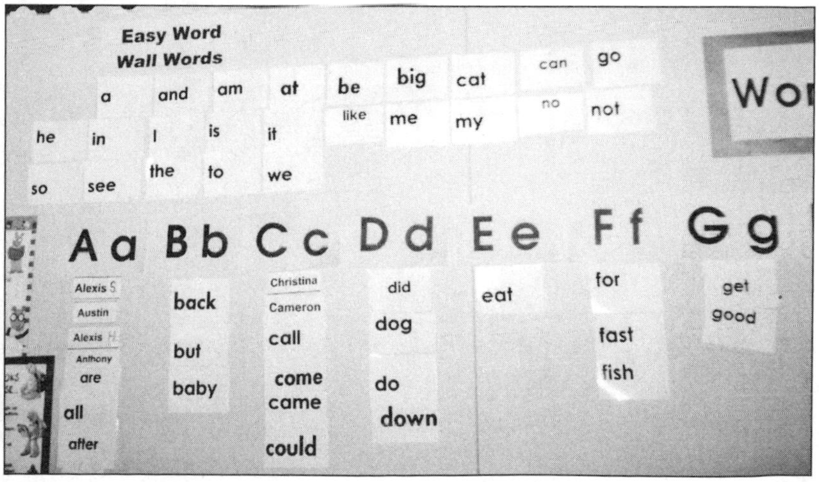

FIGURE 1-8. Word Wall Arranged Alphabetically

'We Can Read 100 Words' chart [see Figure 1-10]. When children are writing many personal narrative stories, the word wall needs to contain such words as *father, mother, cousin,* and *friend.* As children begin to write longer pieces with greater details, they will begin needing words like *because* to aid their writing."

In second grade, when children begin to keep a Think Book in which they write

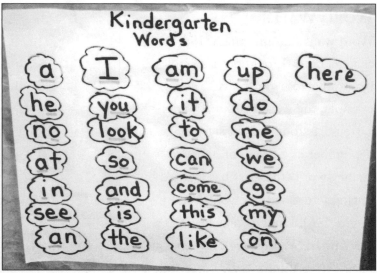

FIGURE 1-9. Word Wall of Kindergarten

FIGURE 1-10. Word Wall of 100 Words

their responses to books, social studies projects, or science experiments, words such as *appreciate, observe,* and *result* might appear on the word wall (see Figure 1-11). Second- and third-grade transitional writers need words that relate to their content area reading—words such as *evaporate, vitamins,* and *communities.*

NAME CHARTS

Name charts help students make connections between what they know and what they need to know. For example, if they are trying to spell the word *bread,* they can connect it to *Brandon*'s name to identify the first two letters. It is important to consider clarity, format, and position when making and using name charts (see Figure 1-12).

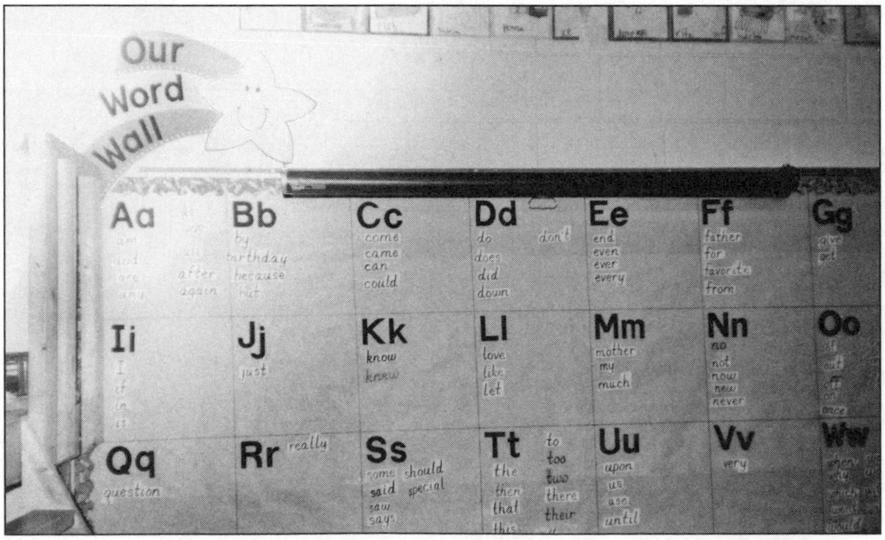

FIGURE 1-11. Advanced Word Wall

Guiding K-3 Writers to Independence

Guidelines for Making and Using Name Charts

- Let the children have a part in making the name chart. For example, in kindergarten, create the name chart with the children offering their own teacher-written names to be glued to the chart.

- Write names in large, clear, black print using markers.

- Place name chart within pointing distance of the literacy easel.

- Place small versions of the name chart in strategic places around the room (e.g., in plastic frames on tables, in the writing center, in writing folders).

- At first, you may need to consciously force yourself to refer to the name chart as a resource. Later, its use will become a natural part of your instructional repertoire. At the same time, the children will be initiating the link.

- Consider how the name chart may change appearance and use over time in relation to the students' needs (see photos).

- Using names is powerful, because children are learning through analogy to move from known to unknown and go beyond the information given.

Whatever form these resource charts take, they need to be available to support the children in the room to do just a little more than they can do alone.

Figure 1-12. Guidelines for Making and Using Name Charts

In a kindergarten class, the names might be printed in large manuscript letters on cards that can be moved in and out of a pocket chart with a picture of the child attached (see Figure 1-13).

In some classes the children's first names are grouped alphabetically; in others, they are not.

In a first-grade class, there may be one chart with only first names, one with only last names, and one with first and last names (see Figures 1-14 and 1-15).

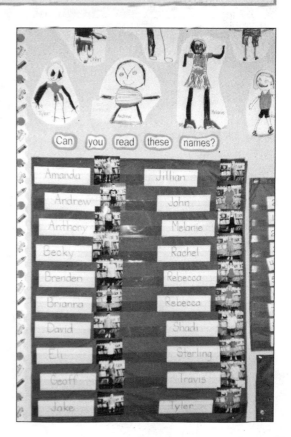

FIGURE 1-13. Kindergarten Name Chart

Name charts are displayed in a variety of places in the classroom.

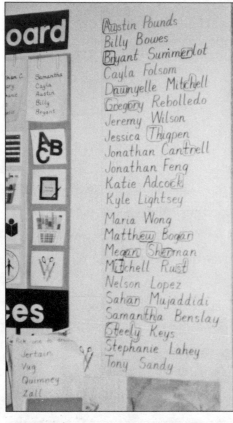

Austin Pounds
Billy Bowes
Bryant Summerlot
Cayla Folsom
Daunyelle Mitchell
Gregory Rebolledo
Jeremy Wilson
Jessica Thigpen
Jonathan Cantrell
Jonathan Feng
Katie Adcock
Kyle Lightsey
Maria Wong
Matthew Bogan
Megan Sherman
Mitchell Rust
Nelson Lopez
Sahan Mujaddidi
Samantha Benslay
Steely Keys
Stephanie Lahey
Tony Sandy

FIGURE 1-15. First and Last Name Chart

FIGURE 1-14. First Name Chart and Last Name Chart

FIGURE 1-16. Name Chart on Classroom Door

FIGURE 1-17. Name Chart on Bulletin Board

Guiding K-3 Writers to Independence

WRITING PAPER

Think about the type of paper you offer the children for writing. If the children are just beginning to write and use a huge amount of time and effort to form letters, then give them unlined paper. If the children can easily form letters but are having a difficult time keeping their lines straight on the page, then you may want to introduce a paper with baselines as a scaffold for the children. If the children are beginning to write more and more text at one setting, then you may want to offer them lined tablet paper rather than story paper, which provides 50 percent of the page for writing and 50 percent for illustration.

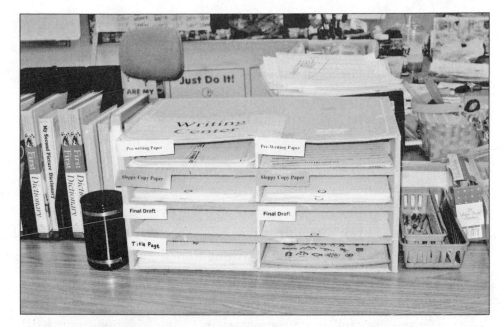

FIGURE 1-18. Writing Paper for Writing Workshop

If the children are taking on the writing process that moves from explaining, to drafting, to editing, to publishing, then they appreciate paper that addresses their needs (see Figure 1-18).

When teachers monitor the instruction and materials they provide their students so that they reflect what the children are currently learning, then the instruction and accompanying materials support young children's advances in literacy—and they are helpful and used! It is this type of responsive structure within a supportive environment that creates a context that, in turn, encourages literacy growth and achievement through focused attention, industrious students, and "chins to chests."

Suggestions for Professional Development

Working with your colleagues, use the following ideas to help all of you reflect on how you see yourselves as writers.

1. Ask everyone to think about the following questions and respond by quickly writing their thoughts for each.
   - How did I learn to write?
   - How do I feel about writing?
   - How often do I write?
   - Why do I write?
   - What kinds of things do I write?

- Do I consider myself a writer? Why or why not?
- Have my writing habits changed over the years? If so, how and why?
- What would I change about myself as a writer?

Share at table level and then with the whole group. What insights does this give us about the teaching and learning of writing?

2. Ask each participant to write a ten-minute story about himself or herself.

3. Have everyone work with a partner to role play conducting a writers' conference concerning a piece of personal writing. (You can use the writing from the suggestion above.) Use the following questions as criteria to help you determine what this writer needs.
   - Does the story make sense?
   - Does the story follow story structure, including an introduction, a description of something that the character wants, obstacles that get in the way of the character getting what he or she wants, a turning point, and resolution?
   - Is the language powerful?
   - Is the writing conventional?

Then, ask the partners to switch roles. Afterward, discuss what you learned about conferences as a writer and as a teacher. Ask participants to rethink, revise, or edit their pieces of writing in the next five minutes, applying what they learned in their conference. Have one or two teachers share their writing with the whole group, and ask the audience to respond. What was learned? How did the writers feel during the conference? While revising? What are the implications for writing instruction? ⬿

CHAPTER 2

Writing Workshop in Third Grade: A Visit to Journey's Classroom

by Laurie Desai

In Journey Swafford's third-grade class, student-authored poems such as Brandon's are not unusual. Journey's students are a community of writers. They know that during writing workshop they will talk about writing, share their writing with each other, conference with the teacher, and most importantly, write. They write for an extended period of time each day, and they not only look forward to that time, but demand it. These students are eager to write, share, critique, revise, and edit. In short, they want to go about the job of being writers.

How did Journey achieve this sense of a writing community in her classroom? Her class included a diverse group of students, including those with special needs and those used to excelling, and it was Journey's expectation that all her students would "join the group." She acknowledged what each student brought to the table, was excited by their gifts, and welcomed each and every one into the writer's club. And by year's end, when the students held their Authors Café, they all were writers and all had a piece of

> **Dreamer**
>
> Dreamer let your
> dreams sing you a
> lullaby one that
> will guide you to the
> stream that
> never ends where
> the river
> dances on the river
> bank where the
> fireflies glitter
> in the night
> sky and all
> dreams run free
> — Brandon

A writer engaged in his craft.

writing they were proud to share with their peers, their parents, and the other teachers in their building. As Journey says, "It wasn't just about the content of the pieces, but it was the value in the process of the writing, it was the joy."

Journey's classroom is a warm and inviting space. Bookshelves line the walls and are filled with baskets of books categorized by author, genre, series, award

A well-stocked writer's corner.

winners, and class favorites. The children's desks are arranged in groups allowing peers to work with each other and support each other's growth. A futon serves many purposes. It flanks a carpet where community meetings occur on a daily basis, and it is often filled with readers and writers looking for that perfect spot to make meaning, whether in their reading of others' writing or the composing of their own writing. The walls are covered not with prepackaged teacher materials, but with the students' own carefully edited and illustrated work, and with the charts they have co-constructed with their teacher to remind them what good readers and writers do as they engage in their craft. Poetry anthologies are prominently displayed. A writer's corner gives students access to all the tools a writer needs—special paper, pencils, tape, scissors, glue, and references, such as dictionaries, thesauruses, and books about the writer's craft. Most importantly, populating this room is a group of happy, eager students who want to share the books that serve as inspiration for their writing, and want to share and talk about the pieces they are in the process of composing.

Composing is the essential component of the writing workshop. As Donald Graves's pioneering work demonstrated, published authors engage in a daily process of writing, revising, and conferring. Writing is often, but not always, a solitary task. Writers discuss ideas and share drafts with others. They refine their writing through conversations with their peers and the subsequent revision of their work. They keep folders and notebooks filled with ideas for current and future writing projects. They continually focus not just on the present task but also on future projects. Writers are voracious readers; they read as writers focusing not only on the story, but also on the craft of writing. They are observers of life—their own as well as the lives of others. Events of mammoth proportions, as well as the tiny, seemingly insignificant details of ordinary life, are seeds for their thinking and their work. Writers observe, question, and hypothesize as they use their pens to create and re-create the world around them. Writing workshop allows the third graders in Journey's room to immerse themselves in that same process as they "join the group," and become writers themselves.

In this chapter, I describe writing workshop in Journey's third-grade classroom, and draw examples from a year of observations. I explore how Journey structured her workshop, began the year, dealt with the needs of a diverse group of children, and engaged them all in the process of writing as they explored the demands of a variety of different genres. No picture of a classroom is complete, however, without the voices of the children involved in the classroom. So, included throughout this chapter are the voices of Journey's students as they reflect on the process they engaged in as writers in her writing workshop.

The Structure of Writing Workshop

Just as many published authors structure their writing day, allowing them a guaranteed time and place to engage in the composing process, so, too, do children benefit from an expected schedule for their writing time. Journey scheduled her writing workshop for the same time each day and had a predictable structure to the hour-long workshop. She began with a writer's talk and mini-lesson, allowed the bulk of the workshop time for independent writing and conferring, and then ended the workshop with group share and evaluation.

A writer's talk is the teacher's opportunity to give the students a quick snapshot of a writer, the writer's work, or the writing process engaged in by the writer. In a two- to three-minute time frame the teacher can bring an author's craft to life, allowing students to use the authors as mentors and to realize that their own processes are similar to those of published writers. These talks are one component of

helping the students feel that they are each a member of the writing community. In fact, Journey did such a good job of establishing that community that when she spoke in a writer's talk of the way Ralph Fletcher maintained his writer's notebook, her students took credit for that idea, and noted that Ralph Fletcher used the same kind of notebooks that they did. Listening to the students, it was clear that they

Talking about the writer's craft.

believed that they had developed a technique that Fletcher had chosen to copy.

Mini-lessons, as their name suggests, are short, concise lessons given by the teacher to meet the current needs of the students. They can help students learn the procedures of writing workshop (management), develop a sense of the way writers work, or learn about the

Writing is thinking.

conventions of writing such as spelling, grammar, or punctuation. Journey periodically reviews her students' writing, looks at her course of study, and develops mini-lessons based on what she noticed her students needed to inspire them and to improve the quality of their writing. For example, noticing that her students were having trouble writing effective titles for their writing projects, Journey developed a series of mini-lessons on how to develop the title of a piece of writing so that the reader wants to read more, because the writer hasn't given away the whole story in the title.

During the 35 to 45 minutes of independent writing, Journey allows her students to engage in the process of writing. Her students know that during this time they are to be quiet and are to be writing. At times they focus on a particular genre and all the students write similar pieces, but at others the students are free to write in the genre that best fits the project and the message they want to convey. During this time, Journey conferences with her students either individually or in small groups with similar needs. Her goal is to help students better understand the process of writing, always remembering that it is her job to aid the writers and not fix the particular pieces of writing in which they are currently engaged. While Journey wants her students' writing to be exemplary, she also knows that the children need to be able to apply what she is teaching not only to their current piece of writing, but to any piece they might write in the future. So, when Journey squats down to be at eye level with a student, and asks in her quiet but intensely interested voice, "How's it going today?" she wants to know what lessons that student is currently able to apply, and how she might guide that student to take on a new writing challenge that can be explored in the current piece, but mastered over time. A daily block of writing ensures that this focus on process rather than product will allow her students to engage in the writing process.

Journey always ends her workshop with a chance for the students to come back to the carpet and share with their peers the work they have done during writing workshop. This happens in many ways. On some days, two or three students are asked to read their current pieces to the whole group, while on others, the students share quietly in pairs. Often, Journey asks a student to share how she was able to successfully apply a mini-lesson to her current writing project. However the sharing occurs, Journey makes it clear to the students that they are sharing because she understands that writing is hard work, that she values their efforts and celebrates their successes, and that they are part of a community of writers, all of whom are engaged in a similar process.

A Visit to Journey's Classroom

On a day in early spring, Journey's writing workshop was alive with fresh air and excited students. The students were eager for writing workshop to start. Students were working on their own projects, each with a different topic, and each tackling different genres, but all were eager to begin writing. Gathering on the carpet and on the futon with their writer's notebooks in hand, the students talked with each other about their projects. Many wanted to share their writing with the whole class, and some just wanted a friend to listen to the piece being read aloud.

Journey began the workshop by talking about Carl Anderson. She began, "Carl Anderson is a writer that I have been reading who teaches teachers about writing." She went on to explain that his work had helped her become a better teacher, because he had helped her to think about how to help students as they revised their writing. Today, she wanted to share one of his ideas and have them try it out. Anderson had suggested that the writer's notebook was a great spot to experiment with a piece of writing. For example, if writers weren't happy with the lead they currently had for their piece of writing, they could try out several others in their writer's notebook. Journey went on to explain that she wanted the students to try out this idea when they went back to their seats.

A few days before, she had given them a "seed" for their writer's notebook. She had asked them to write a poem that started with "I Am" and talked about themselves. To try out Anderson's idea, she asked them to go back to that poem, find a line that they thought could use some work, pull it out of the poem, put it at the top of a fresh page, and tinker with it. She told the students that they could change their word choice or how they had arranged the words. She suggested that they might want to eliminate some unnecessary words. The choice was up to them, but she wanted to see the line written in three ways in their notebooks. She went on to explain that they didn't have to use any of the ideas, because they were the author and could make their own choice of which line worked best in the piece. However, she noted that often, once you had played around a bit, you found something that you liked better than what you had originally written.

To illustrate that point, she asked Brandon if she could talk about some of the revision choices he had made as he was working on the poem that appears at the beginning of this chapter. Journey had copied his original piece and his most recent version on chart paper and was explaining to the class some of the choices in words and format that he had made. Brandon, however, as the author of the piece, felt that Journey was not accurately representing his thinking. So, Brandon took over as the expert, explaining why he changed a word or two and how he had made his decisions. Since the class truly appreciated his poem, his explanations went much further in helping the class understand the value of revision than anything Journey might have said.

Returning to their seats, the students all found their poems, read and reread, selected a line, and began to struggle with the task of revision. The students knew that after they had completed this task they could return to their current piece of writing. The students were at different points in the revision process, but Journey could quickly scan the writing process chart and determine who was ready for a final draft conference, who might need help with starting a new piece, and who was working on editing or revision. Journey noted the two students who needed a final draft conference and added them to her list of students with whom she wanted to meet. She had reread her students' current projects the night before, and she knew which students needed some teacher support. A couple of students she planned to talk with individually. One was spending too much time on a current project and needed some help narrowing his focus. Another would benefit from a short conversation, because Journey knew from experience that this student needed to talk about her writing plans before she actually put pen to paper, and wanted to be sure to give her that opportunity early in the workshop. Finally, four students needed more than the mini-lesson to really be able to think about revision. Journey planned to bring them together for a guided writing lesson.

As the students quietly wrote, Journey met independently with those students she had identified earlier and then quickly gathered her guided writing group. She asked the students to bring their writer's notebooks to the back table, and joined them with her own notebook in hand. Journey knew that she had a group of "reluctant revisers" with her, and thought that perhaps they might find a way into the process by tinkering with something fairly basic like a title. She asked them to turn to their "I Am" poems as she turned to hers, and explained that while she liked her poem, she didn't think her title would really capture her readers. She showed the students some other possible titles that she had considered and written in her notebook, and as a group they discussed the advantages and disadvantages of each and helped Journey to select a new title. She then asked them to take on the same task themselves and to think about several titles

Children with similar needs in a guided writing group.

for their own poems. As they worked, Journey left the table to meet with one of the students needing a final draft conference and then returned asking the students to share with her and each other. Benefiting from the lesson and their peers, the students were successfully able to work on and revise their titles. Journey sent them back to their individual projects as she finished conferencing and talking to several students about their revisions. It was a busy but productive 45 minutes.

The students quickly returned to the carpet for a final five minutes of sharing. They talked with each other about their revisions. Journey had selected two students from her conferences to share with the whole group, because she knew "they could add to the conversation about revision in a productive way." She also made sure to include a student from her guided writing group to share his work with titles, because she wanted to "build in some attention and reinforcement for his willingness to take the risk."

The Writer's Notebook

At the beginning of the school year, Journey's students weren't able to write for 35 or 40 minutes at a time. Nor were they able to easily self-select topics that were of interest to them. And, while many of her students had been engaged in the writing process in the past, they still needed to learn about the demands of a wide range of genres, and were still learning much about the craft of writing. How did Journey begin developing the writing workshop structure we just read about? She began by asking the students to keep what many published authors have talked about and maintained themselves—she asked the students to keep writer's notebooks.

Knowing that third graders believe that writing has to be about something big like a family trip, a visit to a local amusement park, or a new family pet, Journey began the year by helping the students realize that writing doesn't have to be about a major event. Writing can come from the smaller, simpler aspects of students' lives. She helped them to find the significance and the importance in their own experiences. Journey also helped them to develop their writing muscles by having them gradually write more each day, as they discovered topics they cared about and things they wanted to say.

To do this, she started by having them "plant seeds" in their notebooks during independent

Students "plant seeds" in their writer's notebooks.

writing time. She gave her students open-ended prompts to write about; prompts which allowed students to think about their own lives. They began by drawing a picture of themselves and then writing about how they were given their name or nickname; making a list of their favorite books, favorite foods, and favorite movies; writing about a significant event; writing about a special object from their childhood; and explaining the origin of family expressions. The students were encouraged to glue favorite pictures or mementoes into their notebooks and to write about them. Students spent time outside sketching favorite spots and explaining why those spots mattered to them. They walked the halls of their school looking for things they hadn't noticed before and then came back and wrote about their observations. They were beginning to look at their world like writers do. And while they were doing this, they were sharing their observations with each other. Journey was reading their notebooks and commenting, not just as a teacher, but as a fellow writer and observer. After hearing their teacher's and their peers' ideas and thoughts, the students were adding ideas to their own notebooks, recognizing that inspiration can come not only from themselves, but from others. They not only were becoming writers, they also were becoming a writing community.

Once Journey was sure that the notebook had become something that mattered to her students not just because it contained school work but because it contained their life work, she asked that the students take home the notebooks and spend ten minutes writing each night. While for the most part her students self-selected topics to write about, Journey also helped to guide them as they got started. Her students wrote about movies they had watched, family events they had attended, and the ride home on the bus. They wrote about fights they had had with siblings, the presents they wanted for birthdays, and who was their current best friend. Sometimes they wrote fantasy stories or poetry, and added a chapter or verse each night.

In short, they filled their notebooks with pieces of themselves, with things that mattered to them, with the reality of their lives. After spending three to four weeks at the beginning of the year working in their notebooks, it is no wonder that the students had no trouble finding a topic when it was time to move from the notebook to the process of writing. Journey allowed her students the time and privilege of rereading what they had already written, thinking about what really mattered to them, and selecting a topic that they wanted to expand and to take through the writing process. They were ready to write because they had been writing more and more each day, and because they were writing about something they had already thought about and that mattered to them.

The Writing Process

As a teacher of writing, Journey respects the final products her students created, but values most the process involved in their creation. She works hard to create a writing community in her classroom where her students write, revise, edit, and share their work with others. For visual support, Journey posts a writing-process chart that includes all the steps she believes to be important to the composing process.

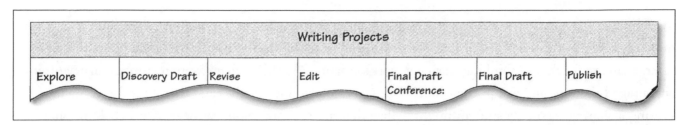

Writing Projects						
Explore	Discovery Draft	Revise	Edit	Final Draft Conference:	Final Draft	Publish

Figure 2-1. Writing Process Chart Header

Recognizing that students move at different paces and that with any given piece some need more time working on one spot than on others, Journey asks that they move their names on the chart as they move through the process. Thus, with a quick glance at the board, Journey can see where each of her students is in the writing process at any given time. The process chart is more than a management tool, however; it serves as a guide to the steps involved in the creation of a piece of writing (see Figure 2-1).

Journey's writing process chart.

The students begin by exploring their lives in their writer's notebooks and returning to that thoughtful contemplation whenever they need to recharge their batteries and begin a new piece of writing. They move from that exploration to a discovery draft. In a discovery draft the students write quickly and get down as many ideas as they can. The job is not to censor their thinking, but to get down all of their ideas and thoughts about the topic. Once the ideas are on paper, the students begin the hard task of revising. It is here that they employ the craft of writing as they determine the piece's focus; decide on its genre; work on writing an interesting lead and satisfying ending for it; and decide which details are necessary to include for reader understanding and which can be eliminated. During the revision process students also focus on word choice, sentence variety, and organization. Once revision is finished, the students engage in the editing process as they make sure that they have followed the correct mechanics and conventions. At this point, the students are ready for a final draft conference with Journey. Before the conference, she asks that they reread their piece one more time to ensure that they have carefully thought about their message and their audience. During the final draft conference, a piece of writing is discussed with the teacher to make sure it reflects the student's best ability to think, revise, and edit, and is then given back for revision and editing, or preparation of a final draft. Not all pieces are published, but those that are will go through another teacher edit and then be completed using whatever special paper and format are appropriate.

The exciting part of the writing process for Journey is that it is not always linear. She finds that it is a more organic process than that. While each step needs to occur during the creation of a piece, there is often a circling back or rethinking during a work's creation. As the students were revising, Journey often encouraged them to go back to their notebooks to explore an idea further and then to revise some more. During a sharing session, a student might realize that more information was necessary to help his audience to understand his piece, and this also resulted in more revision. Sometimes as a student was editing, a new idea or even a new format came to mind. Later in the year, students revisited pieces that they thought were final drafts, but that instead became seeds for a new piece of writing or were tackled using a different genre. Through the use of the writing process the students learned what every published author knows well—a piece of writing is never finished. With more time and more experience, any piece of writing can serve as inspiration for something new.

"Life" Topics

On any given day Journey's class can be found writing about a wide range of topics. Logan loves dinosaurs and wrote about them in his notebook, in expository pieces, and even in his poetry. Marissa wrote often about her dog Snowflake, who had died. Hannah and Will are both Harry Potter fans and that love inspired much of their writing. Heaven is fascinated by puffer fish and uses them as the topic for her investigation. Tyler's poem about Dollywood, an amusement park where everyone had been, was a class favorite.

Each of the students in Journey's class had explored a wide range of genres as dictated by her course of study, but each had also developed pieces in genres that felt appropriate to the content. Journey's writing workshop had not only allowed this to happen, it had encouraged it. Journey's development of a writing community allowed the children to find their writing interests and share them with each other. The students weren't just writing for the teacher; they were writing for themselves and for each other. They weren't just writing about school topics; they were writing about life topics. So revision, while still a difficult task, was something the students tackled enthusiastically because they were thinking of their audiences and of the message they wanted their readers to understand. They listened when Journey talked with them, and they tried to take on new aspects of the writer's craft. They knew that they would share their writing and that they would get responses from their teacher and their peers.

In Conclusion

Journey's students have indeed become members of the writer's club. Given the expectation that they would write every day, given a teacher who valued the process of writing, and given the gift of writing about topics that really mattered to them, these children flourish as writers. The children are eager to write and to share their writing with others, their teachers, their peers, and their families. They eagerly prepare for their year-end Author's Café, celebrating their year of writing by selecting the piece they most wanted to share, revisiting that piece a final time to make any necessary revisions, and practicing to read their pieces aloud to a large group of teachers, families, and friends.

Nikki is one example of the many students in Journey's class. She wrote all year about her brother Scott. There seemed to be thousands of ways that he found to annoy her, and she wrote about most of them. Scott's actions were real to her, and as is the case for many siblings, they mattered to her. When it was time to select a piece to share during Author's Café, Nikki knew exactly which one she wanted to share. She wanted to select a piece that her audience would appreciate. And she did. Her peers had enjoyed the piece, and many of them understood her dilemma with Scott and eagerly related to it. After Nikki had finished reading her piece during the Café, Scott, who was five, stood proudly in front of the audience with a huge smile on his face and told everybody that he was Scott and that his sister wrote about him being " 'noying." What better outcome for a third-grade writer than a receptive audience and a topic that resonated not only with those listening, but with the subject of the piece?

The children in Journey's class are engaged in a process that acknowledges their strengths, supports their growth, and celebrates their success. Each successfully became a part of a community of writers.

Suggestions for Professional Development

1. Work with your colleagues to create a series of questions based on their professional readings that can help them reflect on their classroom organization. These questions could include:
   - How is your classroom organized to be conducive to a writing workshop?
   - How are the desks and tables organized in ways that support writing?
   - Where can students comfortably engage in writing and conferring?
   - Where can students meet as a whole group?
   - How are supplies organized to help students engage in the writing process?

     When the list is complete, ask teachers to consider the questions and set two goals for strengthening their classroom environments.

2. Have teachers work together as a group or grade level and generate a list of favorite authors. Ask each teacher to research one author by checking Web sites, memoirs, and books, and then use this material to develop information sheets that could support an interesting writer's talk. Each talk should be less than five minutes and include information such as how the author gets ideas, uses techniques for revision, or manages time for writing. Finally, ask each teacher to share the information sheets with the other teachers. ❧

CHAPTER 3

Getting Writing Workshop off to a Good Start: Building on the Counsel of Teachers

by Barbara Joan Wiley

It was June, and the sunshine was streaming through the wall of windows in Patti Miller's grade 1 classroom, illuminating 25 children diligently working. At the teacher's signal, their heads lifted, and cries of "No!" "Not yet." "Do we have to?" echoed through the classroom in response to the teacher's comment that it was time to stop writing workshop.

Only a second earlier all of these young students' eyes had been focused on the papers on their desks, hands rapidly writing, minds actively thinking about the stories they were telling. Now it was time to stop.

Patti thought, "If this is the worst thing that happens to them this year, then I've done my job well! I have created a classroom of eager, budding authors. How exactly did I do it? What made writing engaging for these children?"

She reflected on the year of work with her students and hypothesized that it was because she taught according to how she believed children learn. "I know that children learn best when they are excited about what they are doing and when the task is not too easy or too hard," she said.

This chapter shares information regarding how Patti and other primary (kindergarten through second grade) teachers believe children learn and how they use this knowledge to teach writing by conducting writing workshops in their classrooms. Writing workshop is a time in the school day, from about 20 minutes in kindergarten to one hour or more in second grade, when children are writing independently and teachers are helping them become better writers by including them in an active workshop of mini-lessons, conferences, and sharing time. In this chapter the teachers explain how they launch, structure, and provide appropriate materials for their writing workshops.

The Theory and the Practice: How Children Learn and How Teachers Teach

"I believe children learn through teacher support," Patti says. In practice, this means that as children change, teachers change their instruction. The idea is that learning occurs when children work in their zones of proximal development—that is, when a more capable other assists them to do more than they can do alone (Vygotsky, 1934). Once a task is learned by a child, the teacher needs to "up the ante" by making the task change in difficulty or become more complex so that learning can continue to occur. Teachers scaffold learning by periodically monitoring their students' progress through the use of formal and informal assessments to find out what the students know and what the students need to know. Then, they provide appropriate instruction that will teach the students what they need to know next. In a sense, the teacher's mind is always thinking: (1) What do they *know*? (2) What do they *need* to know next? and (3) How can I *teach* them what they need to learn next?

According to Patti, "The key is that as children shift in their ability, teachers shift in their teaching." These shifts occur over time in all aspects of the writing workshop as children learn routines, take on the skills and strategies of writers, and investigate the craft of writing. Every time they learn something, they incorporate it into their repertoires, and are then ready to take on new learning.

As Patti pondered the answers to her questions regarding making writing engaging for children, she thought about how she and other teachers she knew had launched the writing workshop, followed a structure for the workshop, and supported the students' writing by providing appropriate materials.

Getting Writing Workshop off to a Good Start

The beginning of the year is a crucial time in which teachers think about how they might best introduce the instructional context of writing workshop. They know that what is valued in a community is what is learned there so they are careful in choosing their language. They ask themselves a series of questions: "How might I launch my writing workshop so that I emphasize what makes a difference?" "What makes a difference and why?" "Are my words saying what I want them to say?" "Is my language explicit enough that the children can understand what I say?"

In this chapter, we'll hear from three teachers who have a wealth of experience in successfully implementing writing workshop: Andrea Waselko (kindergarten), Kate Bartley (first grade), and Shelley Gilbert (second grade).

Andrea Waselko's Kindergarten: The Definition of Story

I begin and end the year helping my students define *story*. When my students write, I want them to be working on something that matters—a story from their lives, not words about rainbows or hearts. I begin teaching the meaning of story on day one by telling a story from my life.

As the children gather around me, sitting on the rug, I talk about how my dog Spencer had become sick over the weekend.

I have a dog and my dog's name is Spencer. Spencer had a problem on Saturday. In the middle of the night I woke up and it was very, very dark. All I could see was my clock and it said three o'clock. Then I heard the sound that had woke me up. Cough! Cough! Cough! Spencer was coughing. He was sick and he coughed all night. He kept me up and I didn't sleep at all! Then in the morning I took him to the doctor. Spencer got some medicine. I'm hoping that tonight when I get home from school he'll be feeling better.

Andrea Waselko and her kindergarten class.

Then, I ask about three children to tell their stories, either standing by my chair or sitting on the rug. The important thing is that they are talking!

CHRISTIAN: My friend, their dog, one of them got out of the fence and got into the road and they died and a car ran over them.

SAMANTHA: My dog peed on the floor and we didn't know what happened but she died that's why.

ASHLEY: My Aunt Lisa and Uncle Ben got cats. One cat is mine and one cat lives there. There was a party and they stayed in the basement because they were scared.

Then, I write my story as the children watch. I compose a sentence, say words slowly to hear sounds, and link sounds to the name chart. That day I wrote, "Spencer got sick." Next, I send the children off to the tables to write their stories. They have three directions to follow. First, they are to write their first and last names on their papers. I have individual sentence strips with their names printed on them that they get and copy from a bulletin board at the back of the room. Next, they draw a picture. Finally, they write the words to go with their pictures. Often at this time of year their words are random—like letters, or strings of letters (see Figure 3-1). Soon children are documenting some beginning and/or ending sounds (see Figure 3-2).

FIGURE 3-1. Child's Writing—September 6   FIGURE 3-2. Child's Writing—November 20

> My dad took me to school.

When the children have finished, I share one or two papers. I am careful to appreciate the way they have followed directions and comment on the content of their stories. For example, I might say, "Anthony did a beautiful job. Let me show you. Here at the top is his story and he used pencil for his story and crayons for his picture. His story is a happy story about animals."

As the year progresses, writing workshop takes on a predictable structure that the children grow accustomed to. These routines move from mini-lesson, to conferring, to sharing. First, I give a five- to ten-minute mini-lesson. During a mini-lesson I demonstrate a principle related to conventions or craft of writing. For example, I might teach about how writers write all the way across a page from left to right before they return to the left again to write their next words. In a craft mini-lesson, I might teach how writers reread what they have written to help them think about what needs to come next in their story. But always, before I send the children to the tables to write, I ask a few children to tell their stories. This time for storytelling lasts all year long. If a few children can't think of anything to write, I talk with them on the rug before they go to the tables.

As they write, I confer with the children about their story, often asking them to tell their story aloud as a support to move them from speech to print. As I listen to them talk, I am thinking about what they need to strengthen their story. For example, if their introduction needs to be fleshed out, I might ask about missing information like: "When did this happen?" "Who was with you?" or, "Where were you?"

After they finish writing, I share two or three students' stories. My responses to their stories help them to clarify their understanding of what a story is. I believe that this clarity helps them to become better writers. For instance, I might say, "Remember, we're writing stories that have happened to us. Not things that are going to happen but things that we have already lived. That's what Zachary did." Or, I might help them to build their definition of story by clarifying what is not a story: "Going to the bus stop is not a story, but going to the bus stop when the bus doesn't come and you don't know whether or go home or stay waiting is a story."

By the end of the year, my students are writing pages of print. Their stories are so exciting that I can hardly wait to read what they have to say (see Figure 3-3).

My students have begun to think as writers. They know that a list of "I like…" sentences is not a story. They know that writers have things happen to them and these things become their stories.

FIGURE 3-3. Child's Writing— End of Year, April

> My brother throwed a football and I said, "No, no, no!" The football touched my leg.

Kate Bartley's First Grade: Telling Our Stories

I'm a storyteller. I always have been and I always will be. By the end of the year my students know as much about my life and me as I know about theirs. I begin teaching writing by telling an engaging story. My classes have always seemed to love the one I tell about false teeth and shaving cream (see Figure 3-4).

I want my students to know that they are telling a story to an audience and it is their responsibility to captivate their listeners by sharing real-life stories and telling them with

Kate Bartley discusses a chart with her first-grade class.

panache! At times, my stories become interactive as my students interject their ideas or questions.

When I am finished, I "think aloud" about how I might title my story. "Let me think, my story is about camp and about shaving cream. I'll call it 'My Camp Story' because it's a story about a fun trick that happened to me while I was camping."

By selecting a generic title, I am making it easy for my students to connect to my story and in so doing have a topic that they can write about. I then begin a chart entitled "Topics We Can Write About." I write, " 'A Camping Story' by Mrs. Bartley" as the first title on the chart.

In the days that follow, I retell my story or

FIGURE 3-5. Jessica's Story

False Teeth and Shaving Cream

When I was a little girl every summer I'd go to church camp.

One special summer, I had a counselor named Hammy. He was a big tease. He used to chase us around with his false teeth in his hand. "Chomp, chomp, chomp," he'd call as we ran away screaming. "Got ya," he'd yell when we were caught. We were both scared and excited at the same time. It got so bad that we would try to avoid him.

One night we decided to get him back. Three of us sneaked into his room and stole his false teeth from the glass by his bed.

Hammy spent the next morning looking for his teeth.

That afternoon we handed him back his teeth. We said, "Ha, ha we finally got ya back." But, ours was not the last laugh.

As we climbed into our bedrolls that night we screamed bloody murder. Our toes were touching something cold and clammy. "It's shaving cream," Hammy yelled. "Got ya." We laughed and he laughed. We cleaned up the mess and fell asleep dreaming of chomping teeth and clammy cream.

FIGURE 3-4. False Teeth and Shaving Cream Story

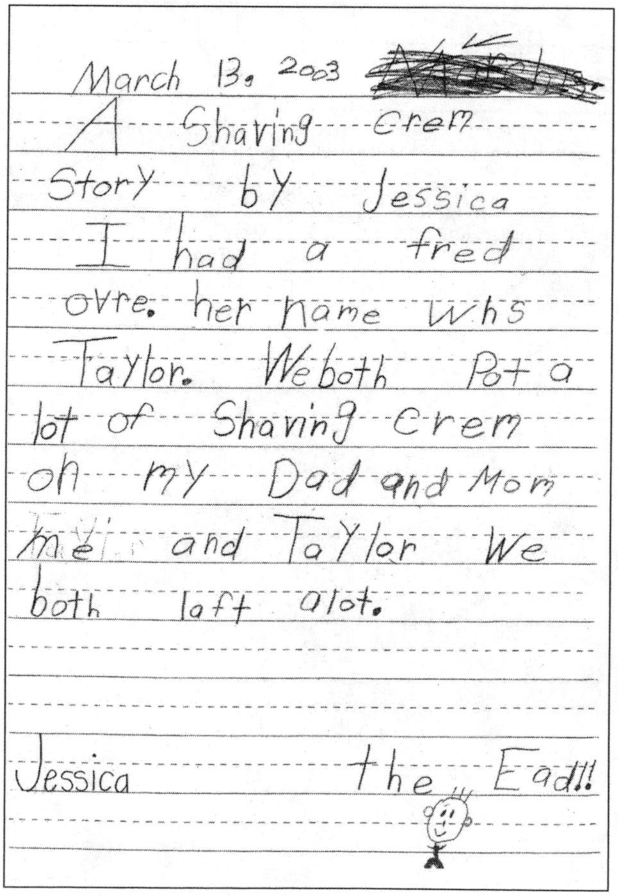

tell a new one. Soon, I have a student tell her story, and then we select a generic title that I add to the list. After a while, the students are telling the majority of stories and I become a listener of their storytelling. As the children hear their friends tell stories and add their titles to the chart, they get ideas for stories of their own. Soon, we are all telling baby stories, or grandparent stories, or broken bone stories! (See Figure 3-5.) We are learning that we all have stories to tell and that they are similar to but also different from someone else's.

Early First-Grade Experiences That Support Writing

1. I read aloud lots of good personal narrative stories such as *Owl Babies* by Martin Waddell.

2. The children and I retell some of our favorite stories.

3. I model storytelling by telling about something interesting from my own life.

4. I encourage different children to share their oral stories over several weeks.

5. I involve the children in a shared experience, such as looking for the classroom's lost hamster. We tell our story over and over again so that we will remember it.

6. The children and I write the story about our shared experience together (for example, *How We Lost and Found Our Hamster*). As we write, we focus on such things as the importance of choosing something that matters to write about, thinking about our audience and asking, "Will they find it fun to read?" We may decide which of the two sentences really says what we want to say. We try to capture our voices on paper by remembering exactly how the words came out of our mouths when we were telling our story.

7. I write a child's story on chart paper as he or she tells it. We think about the structure. "Are you finished?" We might ask, "Did you give us enough information at the beginning?"

FIGURE 3-6. Early First-Grade Experiences That Support Writing

My roles as storyteller and story listener are equally important. Because I really listen to what children say, I am able to respond to them in a natural way. If they tell about doing something naughty, I might say, "Should you have been doing that?" or "Did you get in trouble that time?"

Soon, they are involved in writing workshop, eagerly writing their stories down on paper. The early experiences (mini-lessons) I provide focus on things writers need to know to take their oral story to print (see Figure 3-6).

I believe that my writer-to-writer style helps my students realize that their ordinary life events can become special stories. My genuine sense of wonder, my laughing along with them as a writer, and my personal connections to their tale help them to know that they are writers who have stories that are valued.

Shelley Gilbert's Second Grade: Story Structure

We begin the year by telling personal narratives in a circle on the floor. We call our formation a story circle.

Second graders know what it means to tell and write about personal experiences. They have been supported to be storytellers and story writers from kindergarten on. I help them to build an even deeper understanding of the structure of personal narrative by reading many books that are written in first person from a child's perspective. Some of my favorites are *Alexander and the Terrible, Horrible, No Good, Very Bad Day* by Judith Viorst and *Tell Me Again About the Night I Was Born* by Jamie Lee Curtis. During or after reading I show how the books follow a structure. The moves are from the introduction, to what characters want, to mounting tension as the characters encounter obstacles that get in the way of them getting what they want, to the turning point where the character's desire is resolved, to closure. The schema we create on chart paper helps students to understand basic story structure (see Figure 3-7).

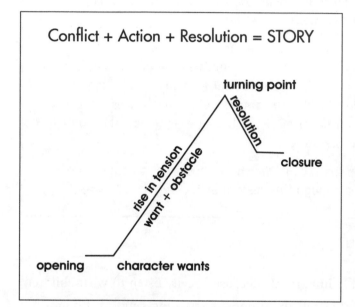

FIGURE 3-7. Story Structure

Some days, we add problems and obstacles based on the students' own life experiences. Sometimes, I even select books for guided reading that reinforce story structure. This reading/writing connection helps my children grow in their understanding of story structure. Using books as mentor texts enables me to easily teach that writing is just like "talking to a friend" as you "tell your story." The children enjoy analyzing how the authors used the personal narrative structure to create super stories!

The children and I continue reading and telling stories for two or three weeks. We compare our oral stories with the personal narrative schema. At times, we'll list on a T-chart what the characters want

Shelley Gilbert explains to her second graders that problems occur because characters want something.

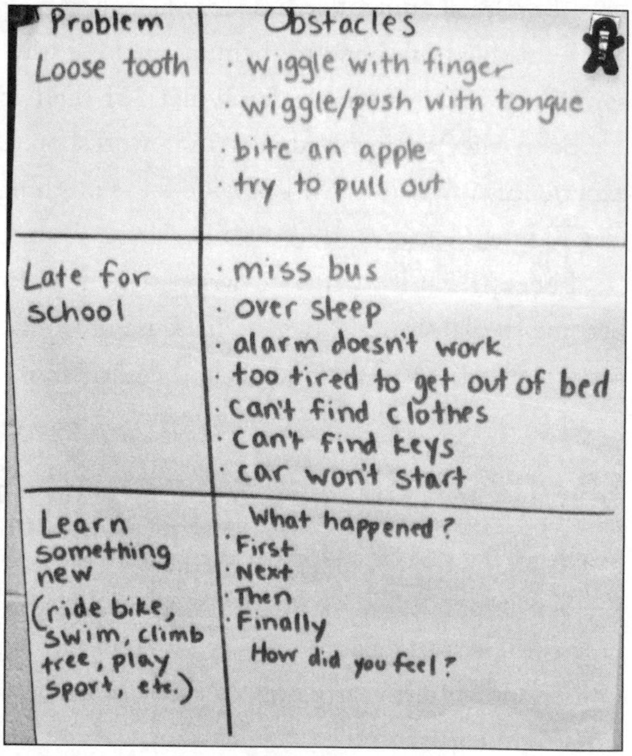

FIGURE 3-8. T-Chart of Problem and Obstacles

(problem) and the obstacles they encounter trying to get what they want (see Figure 3-8).

I want the children to have what they need to become knowledgeable writers. These clear criteria will help them to become meaning makers and problem solvers who can find problems, search for solutions, and check on themselves as they write (Clay, 2001). In other words, I am teaching for independence. For example, I might silently draw the story structure on chart paper as a child is telling their story and then talk about whether or not the story is complete. Sometimes children start with their problem regarding what their character wants with no introduction. Sometimes they stop when the problem has been resolved and have no ending. We then go on to talk about how the omission might be fixed.

As we tell our stories we create a number of charts that will help us to be better storytellers and writers. Our first chart is entitled "Story Starters." It helps us see the way writers sometimes begin their stories—the way they lead into their stories. We talk about phrases such as, "One day" or "When I was a baby." This language helps us get into the storytelling mode (see Figure 3-9).

We collect adjectives that help us to "see" what we say (see Figure 3-10). We also talk about different ways a writer can indicate exactly how a speaker sounded or felt by using such words as *cried*, *exclaimed*, or *whimpered* instead of *said* (see Figure 3-11).

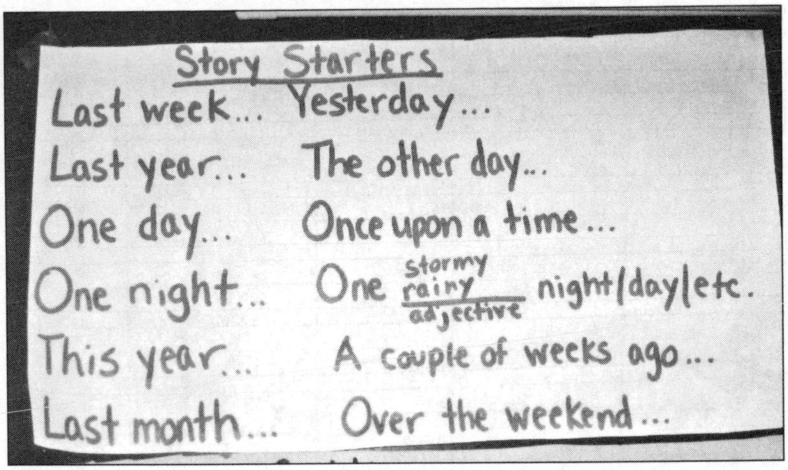

FIGURE 3-9. Story Starters Chart

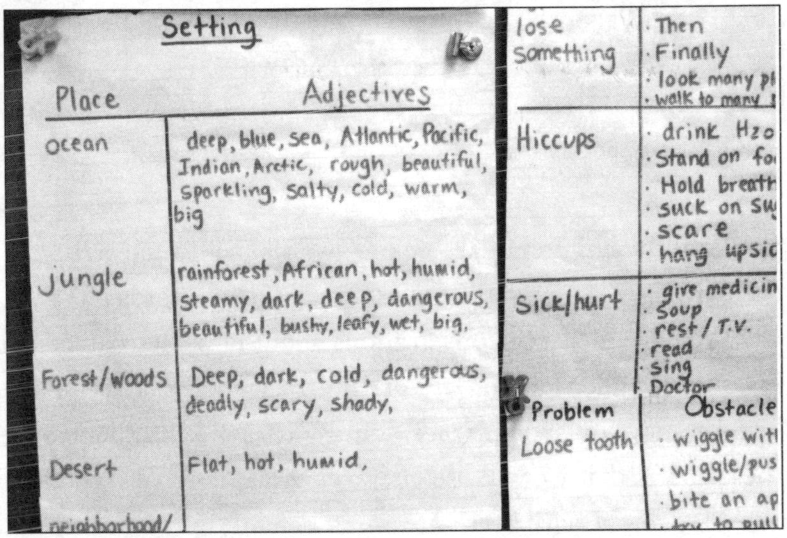

FIGURE 3-10. Adjectives Chart

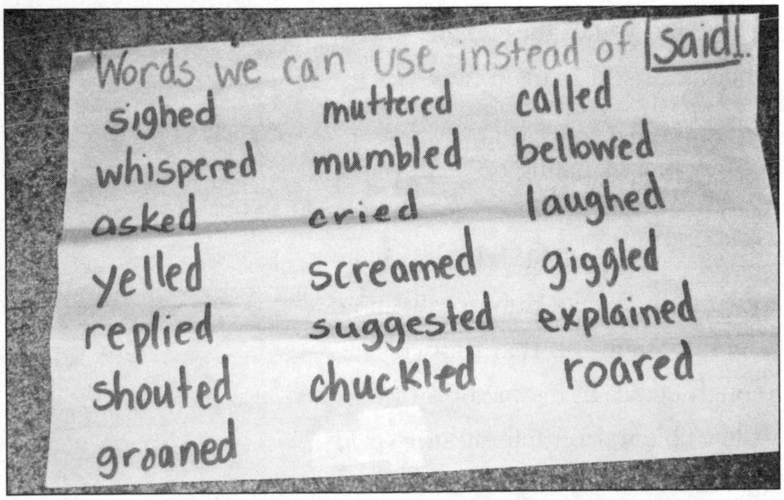

FIGURE 3-11. Alternatives to *Said* Chart

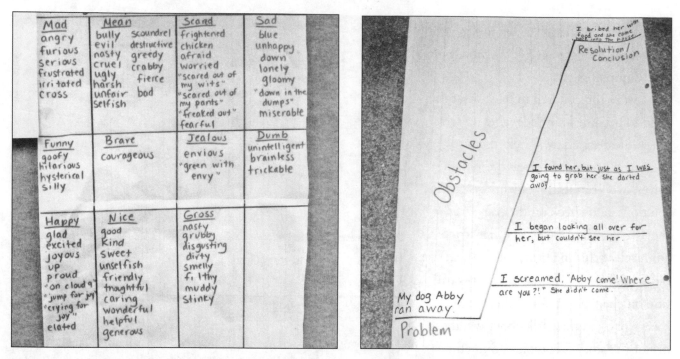

FIGURE 3-12. Synonym Chart

FIGURE 3-13. Story Structure Schema for Personal Narrative

I tell the children that "feeling" words make their writing more engaging. We have fun thinking and then charting synonyms for overly used feeling words like *glad*, *sad*, and *frustrated* (see Figure 3-12).

We have in-depth conversations about how the characters in our stories felt. My hope is that by having a deep understanding of not only what their characters did, but also how they felt, my students will begin to develop greater voice. During and after reading aloud, we brainstorm and continually add to these charts that we will use later as a visual reference when writing.

All along, I have been informing parents, in my weekly notes, about what we are learning in school, and I encourage the families to become engaged in oral storytelling/writing at home.

Now, we are ready to plan our first written story with the support of a storyboard. First, I share orally a story from my life. As I tell my story, I accompany my telling on chart paper by drawing a schema for personal narrative (see Figure 3-13). Next, I illustrate my story. As I draw, I talk about how important it is that I provide enough details in my pictures so that I will be able to later tell my story from the pictures. I add key words to the storyboard using the Story Starter and

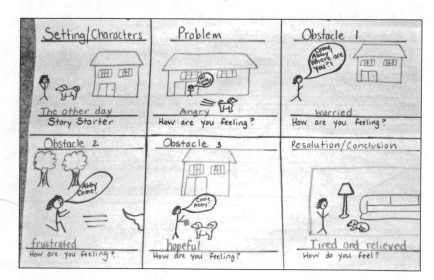

FIGURE 3-14. Teacher Storyboard

Guiding K-3 Writers to Independence

Feeling Words charts in the room. Then, I tell my story using the storyboard as a support (see Figure 3-14).

Now, the children begin their storyboards. They quickly sketch their stories, add starting phrases, and indicate the emotions their characters are feeling. A few students tell their story to the group using their completed storyboards. We ask them clarifying questions and support them, as needed. Some of them need help to think through what their character wants, for example. The whole class practices telling their stories to a partner and then to their families at home (see Figure 3-15).

After I model the writing of my story utilizing the storyboard (see Figure 3-16), the students begin to write and illustrate theirs (see Figure 3-17).

Later in the year, we fine-tune our stories. In November, we realized that many of the problems in our stories (or what the character wants) are related to the physical needs of their bodies—such as mending a broken arm or being rescued from the deep end of a swimming pool. At this time, I'll read a mentor text, such as *Sometimes I Feel Like a Mouse* by Jeanne Modesitt, that tells about characters' emotional desires rather than physical needs. Then, my students will begin writing

FIGURE 3-15. Student Storyboard

Abby Ran Away

The other day at my house the doorbell rang. The mailman was delivering a package. When I opened the door, my dog Abby ran outside. I yelled in an angry voice, "NO! Come back!" She just kept running. She ran so fast and so far, I couldn't see her. The more I looked, the more I worried. I kept screaming her name and then I saw her. I started running after her, but she ran the other way. Now I was frustrated! Finally, I remembered if I bribed her with food she would come. I got her favorite treat and waved it in the air. She came! I was tired and relieved!

FIGURE 3-16. Completed Teacher Writing Using a Storyboard

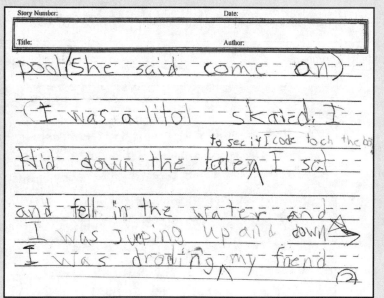

MY FRIEND'S POOL
Last month my friend knocked at my door. She asked if I would like to go swimming. I said, "Yes." I got my bathing suit on. My friend jumped in the

pool. (She said come on.)
I was a little scared. I slid down the ladder to see if I could I slipped and fell in the water and
I was jumping up and down
I was drowning. My friend

came and got me out of the water. I felt happy.
The end

FIGURE 3-17. Completed Student Writing Using a Storyboard

Guiding K-3 Writers to Independence

Going to Wyandot Lake

Written and Illustrated by Dana Talbott

Last year I went to Wyandot Lake. My uncle said, "I will go on the front of the boogey board if you will get on back." Instead, he pushed me down the slide. He made me mad! "You lied to me!" I yelled at him. I was scared and mad at him.

I landed in the pool. I screamed at him in the pool. We all laughed. We left because grandma was tired of us screaming!

FIGURE 3-18. Second-Grade Story With Emotions

about their emotional needs for such things as love and security (see Figure 3-18).

During the third quarter of the school year, I will help the children make the shift to fictional writing by simply changing the "I" in their stories to an animal or another character. I ask them to write about problems they have had (universal human issues) but to be open and creative when choosing obstacles (as long as they "make sense"). The charts we have created are still on the walls to support writing (see Figure 3-19).

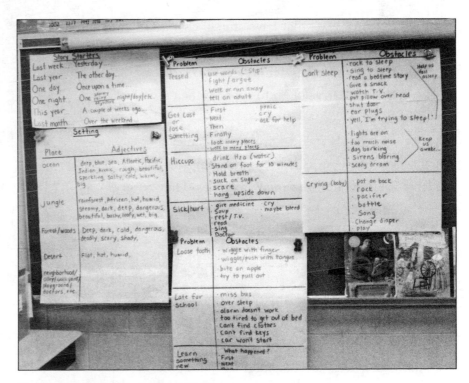

FIGURE 3-19. Charts to Support Writing

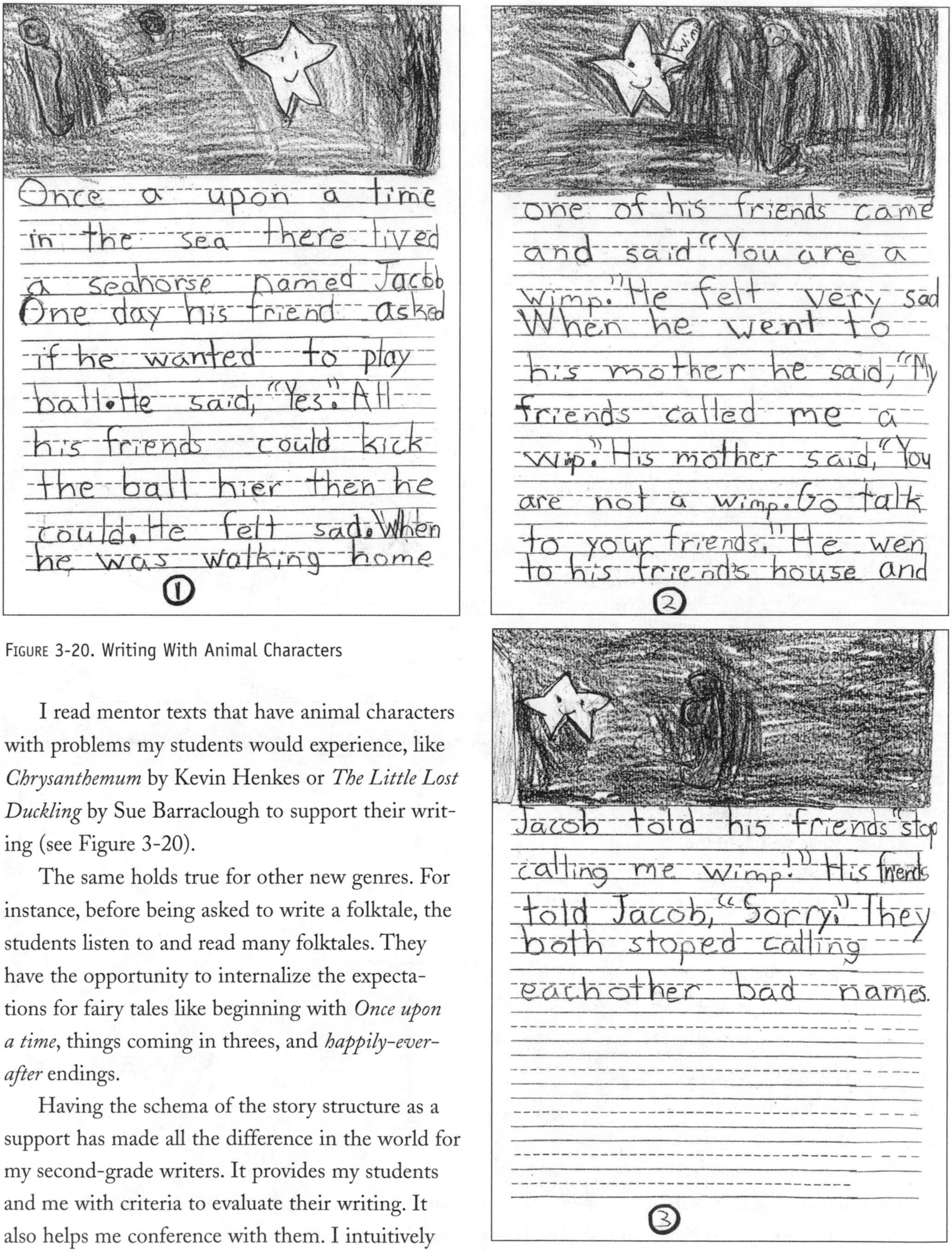

Once a upon a time
in the sea there lived
a seahorse named Jacob.
One day his friend asked
if he wanted to play
ball. He said, "Yes." All
his friends could kick
the ball hier then he
could. He felt sad. When
he was walking home

①

one of his friends came
and said "You are a
wimp." He felt very sad.
When he went to
his mother he said, "My
friends called me a
wimp." His mother said, "You
are not a wimp. Go talk
to your friends." He wen
to his friend's house and

②

Jacob told his friends "stop
calling me wimp!" His friends
told Jacob, "Sorry." They
both stoped calling
eachother bad names.

③

FIGURE 3-20. Writing With Animal Characters

I read mentor texts that have animal characters with problems my students would experience, like *Chrysanthemum* by Kevin Henkes or *The Little Lost Duckling* by Sue Barraclough to support their writing (see Figure 3-20).

The same holds true for other new genres. For instance, before being asked to write a folktale, the students listen to and read many folktales. They have the opportunity to internalize the expectations for fairy tales like beginning with *Once upon a time*, things coming in threes, and *happily-ever-after* endings.

Having the schema of the story structure as a support has made all the difference in the world for my second-grade writers. It provides my students and me with criteria to evaluate their writing. It also helps me conference with them. I intuitively know when a story is not finished, when a lead is weak, or when more tension needs to be added for engagement. My writers know this too, and by the end of the year they become quite good at proofreading and revising their own work. I have helped my students become better writers every time they write because they know what makes for good writing and they monitor their own work accordingly.

Storytelling Supporting Story Writing

Across emergent, early, and transitional writers there is power in writing personal stories from life. When writers have lived what they are writing, they can more easily fill in details and get deeper emotionally. This deep understanding of the topic helps writers write more effectively. Additionally, it is important for writers to know that storytelling supports story writing. As storytellers retell their stories, they edit and embellish their message in reaction to hearing their own words and their audience's responses, and by so doing their stories get better.

Andrea, Kate, and Shelley offer sound, practical advice. They have thought deeply about how to put theory into practice as they support young writers during writing workshop. They have emphasized:

- the importance of understanding what a story is
- the fact that we all have stories in our lives that can be talked about and written down
- that story has a structure that begins with an introduction and ends with a conclusion. In stories the characters overcome obstacles to get what they want.

It is their hope that what works for them will, with modification, work for others as classroom teachers take on the task of getting writing workshop off to a good start. They also hope that as the year progresses, classroom teachers will make decisions in writing workshop based on the stories that are being written by their students. Teachers' selection of mini-lessons, conference foci, and who shares will emerge when they ask themselves, "What will best help these writers to tell their stories?" For example, students are not taught how to add dialogue or when to paragraph simply because this is what some writers do. They are taught about the craft and conventions

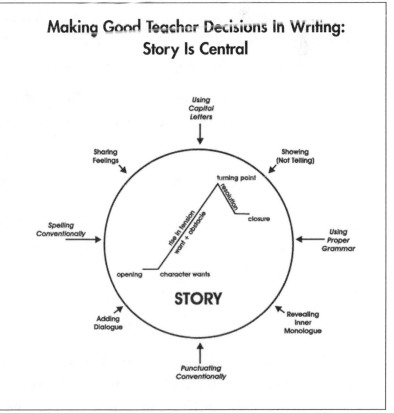

FIGURE 3-21. Story Is Central Chart

of writing because this is what they as writers might choose to do because it will help to make their story better. Story is central; craft and conventions are ways authors work the story. Decisions will not be made haphazardly. They will be focused and in tune with making the story better (see Figure 3-21).

Teachers are powerful decision-makers who can shift instruction so that it appropriately matches the needs of the children being taught. "The only good instruction is that which marches ahead of development and leads it" (Vygotsky, 1934, p. 188). This is what makes writing engaging and effective for Patti's students and others—instruction and materials that pull their development forward in their zone of learning.

Suggestions for Professional Development

Work with a group of your colleagues to explore the following activities.

1. Share children's literature books by asking everyone to bring a favorite narrative that they read aloud to their classes (e.g., *Shortcut* by Donald Crews, *Kitten's First Full Moon* by Kevin Henkes, or *Owl Babies* by Martin Waddell).

    Model by reading aloud the book you brought. As you read, stop briefly and talk about the story: for example, what the character wants and where problems that impede that goal are encountered. Show the rising tension as the character struggles with multiple obstacles; discover how the character overcomes or is defeated by them at the turning point; and discuss how the character resolves the issue and in so doing is changed in some way.

    Afterward, have the group discuss the following issues:

    • Would this make a good mentor text? Why or why not?
    • For what type of writer (emergent, early, or transitional) would this text work best? Why or why not?

    At the table level, have the teachers share the books they brought by giving a book talk. Discuss the pros and cons of using the text as a mentor text to help teach story structure.

2. Using writing samples from average kindergartners and first and second graders, identify the different elements of language that might be the focus of a mini-lesson or conference (adding dialogue, using voice, revealing inner dialogue, showing feelings, and so on). Using a collection of children's literature books, identify different books that could be used in a mini-lesson or conference to show a good example of an element of language.

3. Have each teacher bring recent samples of independent writing from three of his or her middle-progress writers. Have the teachers work in grade-level groups to examine the samples. Then, have the groups determine the children's current strengths and needs. Next, have each group determine some of the common needs at their grade level. For example, emergent writers may need to add words

to a drawing, learn how to say words slowly and listen for the sounds, put spaces between words, expand their work, or know how to go beyond "I like...." Have teachers pair up to plan a mini-lesson that would help these students. Use the following framework to organize the lesson:

WHAT: Talk about the learning principle.

WHY: Tell students why it is important.

HOW: Teach them how to do the task.

CHECK: Show students how to check on themselves.

Share your plans with the group. ✦

Section II

Building a Community of Writers

"Building a Community of Writers" begins with Gay Su Pinnell and Irene Fountas's discussion of the role of oral language in writing instruction, followed by the introduction of a new concept—Community Writing—by Andrea McCarrier in Chapter 5. Marsha Levering's chapter, "Becoming a Writer by Noticing the World," continues the discussion of how teachers can support young writers by helping them talk and write about their surroundings. The last chapter of this section reminds us that writing is more than getting down the first draft. In Chapter 7, Kecia Hicks encourages writers to celebrate the effort to look critically at our writing as well as at determining what's needed to make revisions that strengthen the quality of the message.

CHAPTER 4

Oral Language as a Foundation for Writing

by Gay Su Pinnell & Irene C. Fountas

Throughout our lives, oral language is our vehicle for communicating and constructing meaning. It pervades every human activity and is essential for creating a community. Through oral language, adults in a community pass on critical understandings to the young. Oral language is essential for human survival.

Oral language takes many forms. In some settings, language may be elaborate, for example, in storytelling or description. In other settings, language may be spare but include rich nonverbal elements and demonstrations. The gestures we make, for example, while nonverbal, are part of the oral communication system.

Oral language always adjusts itself to the purpose, the setting, and the speakers/listeners at any particular time. Think about how you talk differently with infants, elementary school children, and adults. Think about how your style, sentence structure, intonation patterns, and even vocabulary vary in different situations. You talk differently to an old friend on the phone than you do in a parent conference about a student. You talk differently in a university class than you do at a neighborhood barbeque. Yet, across all of its variations, oral language is the most powerful human tool. It is how we create our world and, in turn, it shapes us as thinkers and doers.

In this chapter, we briefly describe the enormous amount of language learning that children bring to the task of learning to write. They learn much about language before they even begin to connect it with written signs. We then examine how oral language is a critical learning support across different instructional contexts, all related to the language arts. Finally, we offer a description of the role of oral language in writing workshop.

Oral Language: The Child as a Constructive Language Learner

We hear a great deal about phonemic awareness these days, and it may be surprising to learn that what is really being talked about here is oral language. The phonological system is an identified component of the huge and complex system that we call language (Harris & Hodges, 1995). You can think of language as an integrated set of three systems—phonological, syntactic, and semantic.

A Phonological System

The phonological system is the *sound system* of a language. The *phoneme* is the smallest unit of sound that we can identify in a word. In fact, a single *phoneme* or sound may actually have a few different "shadings" of sound, but they are close enough to be categorized as a "sound." The phoneme is the smallest unit that makes a difference in meaning. For example, one phoneme distinguishes between *meat* and *neat* or *made* and *make*. Phonemes may be harder to hear (for example the sound of /n/ in *bend*), or they may be easier to hear (for example the sound of /t/ in *cat*). In any case, several sounds, in sequence within a word, have meaning to the speakers of a language. You may have had the experience of going into an elevator where a group of people are conversing in a language you do not know. The phonemes flow around you like so much "noise," and you pay little attention. If in the midst of it, you hear a term such as *New York*, then suddenly the phonemes are clear and meaningful. Recognition of meaningful strings of phonemes is something that every speaker of a language learns.

Phonemes are very important in the education of young writers. In fact, the process of learning to write has added value in that it sharpens children's listening powers. Chapter 5 describes teachers helping children say words slowly and prompting children to make the first connections between spoken words and letters (also see McCarrier, Pinnell, & Fountas, 2000). Teachers help children learn how to pronounce the words as accurately as possible. I do not advise teachers to constantly correct children's everyday pronunciation of words; everyone has casual ways of speaking and no one appreciates continual correction. But teachers can easily explain that writers often say words very carefully to help them spell the words correctly.

When young children say words slowly, they can hear the sequence of sounds and feel the position of tongue, lips, and teeth as they say them. This process then makes it easier to connect sounds to the letters that they can write. The process is complex, because children must not only hear the phonemes but think about how the letters look as well as about the directional movements needed to write them (see Chapter 16 about handwriting).

Young children acquire the phonology of the language they speak. Many learn the phonology of several languages when they are young and very flexible in the sounds that they can make. So, some fortunate individuals can speak two or more languages and sound almost like native speakers. Many of us learned languages such as Spanish or French as adults; in this case, it is very difficult to speak the second language without an accent. Why? Because we can only approximate the phonology.

A Syntactic System

As important as phonology is, we must examine the syntactic and semantic systems to understand the full power of oral language. The *syntactic* system (or syntax of language) refers to the way words are arranged according to *rules*. Here I do not mean "correct grammar rules," although there is a relationship between syntax and grammar. Rather, I mean that it is simply the case that language is very predictable. We do not have an infinite number of ways that words can be strung together in phrases and sentences and still make sense. *To the river* cannot be *river the to*. It can be *river to the* only when surrounded by a sentence, such as in *We went over the river to the island.*

All speakers learn these rules. If you think about your own learning of a new language, you realize that the hardest part was not just using your dictionary to find individual words. In fact, nouns were probably the easiest words to acquire. But putting words together in sentences with verbs and phrases—*that* was difficult! The interesting thing about your native language is that you learned the rules of syntax through interactions with other speakers; your knowledge is largely unconscious. Sometimes you cannot even say *why* a sentence should be organized in a certain way—you just know that it should be. This makes it very easy for you to understand and use the system. In oral language, you "parse" or process the sentence into meaningful units without effort.

Just as young children learn the sounds of language, they also learn the underlying rules of language. They rely on their knowledge of syntax as they read their first books; knowledge of language structure is clearly helpful. For example, a text may say something such as *I like peanut butter and jelly*. The first word, *I*, must be recognized by the reader, but she knows that the next word is likely to be a verb. She does not know *which* verb; it is still necessary to look at the letters and associate them with sounds. But the predictability is increased; the possibilities are narrowed. After reading *I like*, the readers know that there is a good chance that the next word is either a noun (or perhaps a verb made into a noun with *-ing*, such as *running*). Again, the possibilities are narrowed, so the reader's use of sound-to-letter analysis is more efficient. A young reader can think whether a sentence "sounds right," meaning that she can check her reading against her knowledge of the syntactic system of language.

Syntax is also important in writing. Here, children must compose messages, stories, and informational pieces by putting words together in sequence in rule-governed ways. Like reading, writing is much, much more than simply learning to spell some words. No amount of practice on isolated words can build a writer. The young writer must draw on everything she knows about oral language to compose a sentence that is meaningful and to hold it in memory while thinking about the individual words and how to write each of them. It helps the child to have some high-frequency words that she can write without effort. Young writers also need to learn to reread what they have written to recapture the syntax and meaning again.

As we think about the resource of a child's knowledge of the syntax of oral language, we realize how important it is to make opportunities for children to expand this knowledge. For a variety of reasons, children may come to school with somewhat limited knowledge of syntax. Sentences may be short and very immature; vocabulary may need development. Oral language is a system that expands through *use*, so we want to give students ample opportunity to engage in conversation; and there is no better way to expand the syntactic system than reading aloud to children and discussing books (see chapters 9 and 10).

A SEMANTIC SYSTEM

It is impossible to select the most important system of a language. All languages have phonological, syntactic, and semantic systems. All systems work together to convey meaning. But the semantic system refers directly to the *meanings* or ideas in our heads, which is the primary purpose of language. Speakers build meaning through experience and interaction. Writers have their ideas and they map them onto a page by composing messages with acceptable syntactic patterns. The meaning system of a speaker is comprised of everything she understands. For example, think again about the sentence *I like peanut butter and jelly*. A reader who has experienced peanut butter and jelly sandwiches will have less difficulty in predicting the words *and jelly* than one who has never heard of this food item.

SO, WHAT ABOUT WRITTEN LANGUAGE?

Written language represents oral language, so it reflects the same systems. But there are some differences between the syntax and vocabulary used in speech and those used in written language. Because written language is "frozen," it is easier to construct well organized and complex sentences such as, *"The lake is a frozen bowl of ice," Dad remarked as he entered the cabin door and shook the white flakes off of his jacket.* Words such as *remarked* are infrequent in oral language but more common in the specialized language of books that young children read and hear read aloud. Oral language has nonverbal gestures and tone of voice, but when we are reading, we have to infer these features. The punctuation helps, but attention to the meaning is also required. So, one of the ways young children start to expand their language systems is by building an awareness of the syntax and vocabulary of written language.

The Child as a Language Learner

It may seem to be an overwhelming task to learn thousands of sound sequences that make up words and to develop an unconscious awareness of all of the complexities of oral language. Yet, every child, all over the world, at about the same points in time, develops language with no apparent instruction. Many scientists argue that our brains are "hardwired" to develop language, and that is a very good thing.

Children interact with people around them. They acquire words and ways of putting them together to convey meaning. Their first attempts at sentences may sound quite primitive, for example, *Me go bye-bye* or *Me go Papa*. Similarly, 2-year-old Lauren calls out, "Oh Hi Ho" when she sees the Ohio State University's marching band on television. When her mom tells her to "hold my hand," she abruptly says, "Me do it!" And, she clasps her own two hands together. Her understanding of pronouns is not quite correct, but her meaning is clear!

Notice that even in these primitive sentences words are arranged in rule-governed ways. Adults around children understand these utterances and seldom correct them, although they may expand them in reply, for example:

- *Yes, it's time to go bye-bye. Say bye-bye.*
- *You want to go with Papa? Okay, you can go with Papa.*
- *I know you can hold your own hands, but right now you need to hold my hand!*

Gradually, over time, children expand and expand their oral language, always moving toward "following" the rules. Scientists hypothesize that almost every utterance represents a little experiment. The child knows she is understood when someone replies. She is part of a turn-taking, meaningful conversation, and that is inherently pleasurable. It is its own reward.

So what does this tell us about oral language? Below is summary of some important points that can guide our examination of the developing writer:

1. Oral language is a complex, integrated system with many subsystems—sound, language structure or syntax, and meaning.
2. Writers and readers use their knowledge of the sound system of language and link it with letters and letter clusters.
3. Writers and readers use their knowledge of the syntactic system of language to create and access meaning.
4. Writers and readers use their background knowledge of the world and language to create and understand texts.
5. Language is learned through use and is supported and expanded by interaction with more expert users.
6. Talking about texts is a way to expand oral language to take on the particular characteristics of written language.
7. School offers the opportunity for children to use oral language as a primary resource in becoming literate.

Oral language is even more important for English language learners than for the rest of the students we teach. In today's schools, we have a wonderfully diverse mixture of students from different cultures and language groups. All are in the process not only of becoming literate, but also of learning all aspects of English. Language is learned through *interaction*. In every setting described in the next section, we need to ensure that these English language learners have maximum opportunity to interact with the teacher and other students orally. They will listen and learn; but they will learn even more as they begin to produce language. Their growth will be scaffolded by the language of the people who talk with them. So, for every point in the following section of this chapter, double the effort and the explicitness for English language learners.

Oral Language Across Different Settings

This book contains many rich descriptions of how teachers can help children expand their writing abilities. The entire process is supported by the oral language that children use across many instructional contexts. The conversations that students have with you and each other set the tone for the learning. Talk creates a literate culture within the classroom. Through talk, concepts flow across whatever the particular activity might be. Let's look at four important instructional settings: interactive read-aloud, shared/performance reading, guided reading, and poetry workshop.

INTERACTIVE READ-ALOUD

When you read aloud to students, you are making language accessible in a very powerful way. Interactive read-aloud is an essential daily activity and it is all about conversation. In fact, the term *intentional conversation* can be used to describe the teacher's shaping of this language event (see Fountas & Pinnell, 2006).

Interactive read-aloud has great general benefits and also specifically supports high-quality writing (see Figure 4-1).

Through interactive read-aloud, you build a foundation that increases your students' pleasure and interest in books while at the same time helping children understand the inner structure of various genres. For example, listening to and discussing a range of books that represent personal narratives helps students become more expert in crafting their own stories. The books in Figure 4-2 are first-person, personal narratives by award-winning authors Patricia Polacco, Faith Ringgold, and Cynthia Rylant. (For additional titles of quality children's books, see Appendices A, C, and E.)

Using Oral Language in Interactive Read-Aloud

Interactive Read-Aloud	General Benefits to Learners	Specific Support for Writers
The teacher reads aloud to students. The teacher and students think about, talk about, and respond to the text—before, at intervals during, and after reading.	• Provides a model of fluent reading • Expands knowledge and control of written language structures • Builds a repertoire of known texts that can be connected to others • Enables students to engage in thinking activity—making inferences, interpreting the meaning, and synthesizing new ideas and understandings • Expands content knowledge and vocabulary • Builds understandings of the characteristics of genres • Provides models of well-crafted writing • Develops a shared vocabulary for talking about written texts	• Expands writing vocabulary by presenting students with interesting new words • Expands knowledge of written genres and their characteristics so that students can more easily learn how to produce them • Provides high-quality examples of writing that students can try out for themselves

FIGURE 4-1. Oral Language in Interactive Read-Aloud

Freed from decoding words, students have maximum opportunity to process and understand the language of texts. How do writers begin their stories? How do they use words to make them interesting? How do they show the passage of time? How do they create a good ending? How do they show how people feel? These and many other questions occur to writers; and they can be answered by examining high quality texts. Through interactive read-aloud, students expand their knowledge of vocabulary, especially words that do not occur very often in their oral language; and they develop a shared vocabulary for talking about written texts, for example, *beginning, ending, character, illustrations, table of contents*, and *index*. These terms apply not only to the texts children hear read aloud, but also to those that students produce. They are gradually acquired over time when students have the opportunity to participate in daily interactive read-aloud.

We use the term *interactive* to remind ourselves that the benefits of reading aloud are not realized unless the reading is surrounded by talk. From your opening remarks to your final comments, you can intentionally use language and invite students to respond. For example, Figure 4-3 shows some opening remarks of an interactive read-aloud session. The text was *Let Them Play* (Raven, 2005), the story of an African American Little League team that was excluded from competition in South Carolina in 1955 after every white team quit the league in protest. The boys never got a chance at the national championship, but they were invited to attend the event and won over the crowd with their spirited warm-up. The 5,000-person crowd shouted, "Let them play!"

Personal Narratives in Picture Books

Patricia Polacco
- *My Rotten Redheaded Older Brother*
- *My Ol' Man*
- *Meteor!*

Faith Ringgold
- *Aunt Harriet's Underground Railroad in the Sky*
- *Tar Beach*
- *Dinner at Aunt Connie's House*

Cynthia Rylant
- *When I Was Young in the Mountains*
- *The Relatives Came*

FIGURE 4-2. Personal Narratives in Picture Books

Opening Remarks: *Let Them Play*, by Margot Theis Raven

T: We've been reading some books about baseball. Do you remember Jackie Robinson?
Arouses prior knowledge.
BETH: He was the first African American baseball player in the big leagues.
KARL: He played for the Dodgers, but they were in Brooklyn then.
T: Yes, that was back in the 1950s. There was a lot of segregation then. Most teams were either all white or all black. This story is about that same time. Listen while I read the first sentence of *Let Them Play*, by Margot Theis Raven: "Most folks say it was Coach Ben Singleton who pulled the all-star dreams from the sky over Harmon Field and sprinkled them in the eyes of 14 boys the summer of 1955." What does that make you think about?
Provides important information about the setting.
Draws attention to language.

AVERY: It's going to be a championship game.
DUKE: It was so long ago that maybe they are trying to get them to let them play. And they can't because of segregation.
T: And what do you notice about the language?
XANDRA: I like where it said sprinkling dreams kind of.
KARL: He saying dreams are like stars.
T: It is about wanting to play and about a team having a dream. Sometimes people say you "have stars in your eyes," meaning that you are really happy or excited about something. You are going to hear about the Cannon Street Little League, the only black league in South Carolina, where no white team had ever played an African American team. So, as I read, be thinking about what the times were like in 1955, and also about how these boys felt about Jackie Robinson and about baseball.

FIGURE 4-3. Opening Discussion

The teacher stopped twice during the reading of *Let Them Play* to allow students to participate in "turn and talk," a routine that she had taught them. In this routine, students turn quickly to form pairs, or groups of three; and they talk for a very brief time (perhaps a minute) in response to the text. At the teacher's signal, they "turn back" and listen again or there may be a few spontaneous comments or questions. This activity stimulates oral language by allowing students to respond immediately to the story they are hearing. They can interpret events or characters' feelings and motivations; they can make predictions about what might happen next. These brief conversations are not long enough to interrupt the meaning of the text, and the teacher does no heavy-handed teaching. The purpose of the discussion is to make the process more interactive.

For example, the teacher stopped after reading page 25 of the book. The Cannon Street boys were allowed to take the field for a warm-up in the Little League World Series. With the white teams' boycott of the South Carolina league, they were the champions by default. The text is as follows:

LET THEM PLAY! It was a chant that told the 14 players they were on the ball field where they belonged. A chant that said you can't steal a boy's dream to succeed, like a Jackie Robinson slide into home. A chant that said they were *not* the team *nobody* would play (p. 25).

Students were able to predict whether or not the Cannon Street team would be allowed to play, a quick conversation that lead into the discussion after reading. By the end of the session, students were talking about some complex concepts, such as:

- The real dream was more than just to play baseball; it was a dream of living equally rather than separately with white people.
- The writer brought in *separate but equal* at the beginning and ended with the idea of living *equally—everywhere—not separate—anywhere.*
- "Let them play" could also mean more than baseball—for example, let them have their dream.
- The team went to the championships in a battered old blue bus and came home in it. They were sad because they didn't get to play, but glad that they had won over the crowd.
- Forty-seven years later, all fourteen team members went in a big new bus to the championship. The crowd cheered them and they remembered their dream.
- The coach, Ben Singleton, knew "the man you condemn today is the one you become tomorrow." That means he wanted them to have their chance and stay hopeful for the future. And he made that happen.

In using this text, the teacher was working for deep comprehension. The more students talk with each other, the richer their understanding can be.

Interactive read-aloud is especially important for English language learners. Here, they are engaged in processing large amounts of English texts. Using illustrated picture books is very helpful to them, as is rereading favorite texts to them (or providing an opportunity to hear the texts again through technology). Make sure that your English language learners can see and hear clearly during interactive read-aloud sessions. Engage in discussion to be sure they understand the concepts and language of the text.

SHARED AND PERFORMANCE READING

In order to participate in shared reading, choral reading, or readers' theater, students have to think deeply about the meaning of a text (see Figure 4-4). For very young students, shared reading provides a highly supportive situation in which they can "behave like readers." For older students, choral reading and readers' theater provide the opportunity to interpret texts with their voices. In all settings, students read the same language several times, thinking about how the reading *sounds*. They are looking at the print and many things are happening at once. They are building visual knowledge of words, which contributes to their reservoirs of known high-frequency words as well as to word analysis. They are using new vocabulary and language structures, which become familiar through rereading and in the process, increases the odds that students are internalizing them. The expansion of vocabulary, sight words, and language structure is of great benefit to children as they compose their own messages.

Using Oral Language in Shared and Performance Reading

Shared and Performance Reading	General Benefits to Learners	Specific Support for Writers
Students read aloud for their own pleasure and for listeners, with emphasis on interpreting the text using the voice. Includes: • *Shared Reading—reading in unison from a shared text* • *Choral Reading—reading in unison from a shared text or individual copies—may have "parts"* • *Readers' Theater—reading a script in parts (usually based on a longer story)*	• Provides a supportive context for students to notice and use the language of texts • Helps children take on and internalize new vocabulary and patterns of language syntax • Builds understanding of different types of texts, formats, and structures • Helps students to understand text features (headings, paragraphs, dialogue) • Promotes deeper discussion of the meaning of texts • Leads to an appreciation of the language of texts • Promotes fluency and expressive reading • Promotes word solving—letters, sounds, word parts, and high-frequency words	• Helps students expand their knowledge of the syntax of written language, making it easier for them to compose • Contributes to spelling ability • Contributes to knowledge of high-frequency words, which frees attention for composing • Helps students compose texts in different genres • Increases awareness of text features so that students can use them in their own writing • Draws attention to interesting vocabulary and language that can be used in composing texts

FIGURE 4-4. Shared and Performance Reading

GUIDED READING

In guided reading, you work with a small group of children whose reading levels are similar enough that you can introduce a suitable instructional level text for all members to read. Guided reading is *instructional*; its purpose is to help students read increasingly complex texts with comprehension, accuracy, and fluency. Guided reading has several components (see Figure 4-5). Across these components, oral language plays a major role.

When planning a guided reading session, select a text for a group with language in mind. Prior to the lesson, analyze the text in great detail, for example, looking carefully at the language syntax. You might plan to draw students' attention to particularly tricky phrases and even have the children say the words aloud. Through

Guided Reading

Selecting the Text	The teacher selects a text that is appropriate for the group. It is a text that they can process with high accuracy and that still provides new opportunities to learn.
Introducing the Text	The teacher engages the students in conversation about the text they are going to read. The introduction focuses on language structures that may be challenging, the meaning of the whole text, and words that might be difficult to solve (either meaning or decoding).
Reading the Text	Each member of the small group reads the whole text individually or a significant portion of it. The teacher listens and interacts briefly to support the reading.
Discussing and Revisiting the Text	Students enter into a discussion of the meaning of the text and may revisit parts of it.
Teaching for Processing Strategies	The teacher provides a brief, explicit teaching point to help students expand the systems of strategic actions that they use to process texts.
Working With Words (Optional)	The teacher guides students to work for one or two minutes on some aspect of word solving; the teacher demonstrates or students use magnetic letters or white boards.
Extending Understanding (Optional)	The teacher invites students to extend understanding through further talk, drawing, or writing about reading.

FIGURE 4-5. Guided Reading (Fountas & Pinnell, 1996)

conversation, you prompt students to begin thinking actively about the meaning even before they start to read the print. Thinking and talking about a text before reading deepens students' comprehension of it.

Quick interactions during the reading serve to direct the reader's attention without unduly interrupting the reading. Here, too, oral language is a powerful support in showing readers how to be more strategic in parsing language meaning. Oral language carries the discussion of the meaning, which adds to each reader's understanding. You can help students to notice text characteristics, such as sequence of time, figurative language, and organization of information. You can also help them understand actions writers take to make a story interesting, for example, the lead sentence and the use of dialogue, suspense, and humor. The more children become aware as readers, the more resources they have to bring to writing (see Figure 4-6).

Using Oral Language in Guided Reading

Guided Reading	General Benefits to Learners	Specific Support for Writers
The teacher selects and introduces a text to a small group of readers who are similar in their reading development. The teacher supports students' reading of the text in a way that helps them learn and expand a range of reading strategies.	• Helps students learn to read more difficult texts, and, in the process become better readers • Expands students' ability to comprehend texts • Increases known words • Promotes fluent and phrased reading • Provides the opportunity to extend meaning through talk, drawing, or writing • Helps readers think about what writers do • Expands understanding of the characteristics of different genres • Helps readers learn how words "work" by analyzing them in isolation and also taking them apart while reading continuous text	• Expands vocabulary • Offers experience with many different texts offering examples of ways to organize information • Increases repertoire of known words • Supports spelling because of many visual encounters with the same high-frequency words • Offers examples of punctuation use • Offers language that students can borrow when engaged in their own writing

FIGURE 4-6. Oral Language in Guided Reading

Guided reading is a setting within which you can do very explicit teaching of any aspect of the reading process. As you work across instructional contexts, you will find that you can make important links through conversation. For example, you can point out aspects of fiction and nonfiction texts that help the reader and suggest that students might want to use them in their own writing. Leaning on these texts that they have processed effectively, children can create their own stories that achieve the following:

- Show a clear sequence of action
- Reveal a character through description
- Use exciting vocabulary (*cried* or *shouted* for *said*)
- Use description words
- Add details
- Construct an interesting lead

Through discussion of high-quality texts, children can learn that authors write about things they know and care about and transfer this concept to their own work.

Using Oral Language in Poetry Workshop

Guided Reading	General Benefits to Learners	Specific Support for Writers
Children engage in listening to and reading poetry. They collect poems and illustrate them. They write poetry and write in response to poems.	• Exposes children to unique words and language structures • Demonstrates how meaning can be communicated in few words • Provides the opportunity to internalize new language syntax because poetry is meant to be read and reread • Familiarizes children with different kinds of poetry • Provides an authentic reason for oral reasoning	• Helps writers learn how to create visual images with words • Helps writers use words in new ways • Provides models for students to try out in their writing • Encourages writers to read their own work aloud and to think about how it "sounds"

FIGURE 4-7. Oral Language in Poetry Workshop

POETRY WORKSHOP

No classroom literacy program is complete without the inclusion of poetry. Poetry offers condensed language that is heavy with meaning. Many teachers have a "poetry workshop" each week or every other week, in which they read, collect, talk about, write about, and write poetry (see Figure 4-7).

In poetry workshop, students get acquainted with a wide variety of poems; they learn that poetry does not have to rhyme and that they can find poems that engage their interests—sports, nature, sensory images, memories, stories. A single short poem can be the foundation of a rich discussion. In poetry workshop:

1. The teacher reads poetry aloud and invites students to discuss it.
2. The teacher may show children something specific about a poem, such as figurative language or words that stand for sounds (*roared*).
3. Children explore poetry through reading and writing. In many classrooms, children collect poems that they like by copying them in a personal poetry anthology which they then illustrate. Children may write why they like the poem or what it makes them think about; and they may also write their own poems in the same style or on the same theme. They may listen to poems in a listening center, read poems in a shared way from charts, and illustrate individual poems.
4. Children end the workshop by sharing the poems that they have selected and illustrated or written.

This work is so successful that students' personal poetry anthologies become treasured items and a real resource for talking and writing. Students may visit their poetry anthologies for ideas just as they visit a writer's notebook. (See Chapter 6 for a description of the writer's notebook.)

Oral Language—Building a Bridge to Written Language

Finally, oral language plays a very important role in the teaching of writing. As is obvious in the previous section, writing workshop is embedded within a larger language and literacy framework. Each element supports students' writing by providing the opportunities that will build language resources and knowledge of texts. The chapters of this book contain specific descriptions of the components of writing workshop. In this chapter, we emphasize the role of talk.

The more students can "read like writers," the easier it will be for them to "write with readers in mind." We know that developing voice and a sense of audience are critical aspects of proficient writing (Fountas & Pinnell, 2007). So, when you plan the curriculum for writing workshop, you can also plan to use oral language as the major tool for learning (see Figure 4-8). Section I in this book describes the components of writing workshop:

1. **Mini-lesson:** The teacher provides a brief and explicit demonstration or description of any aspect of the writing process, often including a specific and concrete example.
2. **Independent writing and conferring:** Students work on their own pieces of writing while the teacher interacts with individuals to support the process.
3. **Sharing:** Students share their progress in writing and talk about what they have learned. Sometimes they read parts of their writing aloud. The teacher takes the opportunity to reinforce the mini-lesson principle.

Through writing workshop, you are working to create a *writing community* in which people talk with each other about their writing. In every way possible, students will be learning more than how to write in specific ways—they will be learning how to be writers.

AREAS OF WRITING COMPETENCY

Writing competency may be divided into four different areas: (1) genre, (2) craft, (3) conventions, and (4) process (Fountas & Pinnell, 2007).

Within this list, we would embed "writing about reading," which is a very specific way of expanding understanding of text through writing (see Chapter 8).

Genre

Genre may be divided into four types of texts:

*   **Narrative** texts, such as memoir and short fiction, that "tell a story"
*   **Informational** texts that report facts and ideas in an organized way
*   **Poetic** texts that communicate feelings and images in concise and vivid language
*   **Functional** texts that help people communicate with each other (e-mail, letters and notes, lists, directions)

Writing about reading may take the form of any of these genres.

Using Oral Language in Writing Workshop

	Mini-lesson The teacher . . .	Independent Writing and Conferring The teacher and an individual student . . .	Sharing Students . . .
Genre	• Presents examples that show the characteristics of narrative, informational, poetic, or functional writing • Often uses mentor texts that have previously been read and discussed by the class	• Talk about the genre of the piece • Discuss characteristics of the genre • May go back to a mentor text to get ideas	• Talk about the kinds of texts they are writing • Share parts of their writing with a partner, a small group, or the whole group
Craft	• Demonstrates aspects of craft, such as the way a writer organizes text or how ideas are supported by details • Points out interesting language and discusses what it means • Uses examples from texts that students know • Records language and interesting words on charts so that students can refer to them	• Talk about and improve the organization of a text • Generate details to support main ideas • Generate words and specific language to communicate the writer's meaning • Refer to resources such as charts and mentor texts	• Share language that they have produced • Comment on the language other writers have used • Talk about the way they have organized their ideas • Ask questions of other writers to elicit more details or explanations
Convention	• Teaches brief lessons on conventions such as spelling, capitalization, punctuation, and grammar • Explains why conventions are important in writing	• Work to apply what the student knows about conventions • Use resources to help in applying conventions • Co-edit when a piece is near completion	• Read their pieces aloud to notice use of conventions • Talk about how they figured out the spelling of words • Talk about punctuation and capitalization and how it helps the writer/reader
Process	• Teaches specific lessons on each component of the writing process • Provides information on authors students like, to show how they engage in the writing process • Helps students see themselves as writers	• Become aware of the components of the writing process and what they mean • Move through the writing process, engaging in the appropriate behaviors	• Report where they are in the process of writing a piece (planning, drafting, revising, editing, publishing) • Reflect on their best writing and say what they learned • Set goals for writing

FIGURE 4-8. Oral Language in Writing Workshop

Craft

The craft of writing involves elements such as the following:

- The way the text is *organized* (categories, temporal sequence, beginning and ending, presentation of ideas)
- The way the *ideas in the text are developed* (main and supporting points)
- The way the writer uses *language* (sensory images, variety, "showing rather than telling")
- The *words* the writer selects (precise meaning, memorable)
- The writer's *voice* or unique personal style and perspective

Conventions

The developing writer demonstrates an increasing control of the conventions that are necessary to make meaning clear, including aspects of writing such as text layout, grammar, capitalization, punctuation, spelling, and handwriting or word processing. Skilled use of conventions is necessary for proficient writing. We would not expect young children to produce perfect spelling or punctuation, because we want them to take risks; but we do expect that they will use everything they know about writing conventions at any specific point.

Writing Process

In order to become writers, children must engage in the process regularly. The writing process is *recursive*, which means that it is not strictly linear. For example, you might be writing a first draft and stop to revise a sentence. You might be in final publication, but still do some revising or draft a new section. In general, though, there are definitive components within the writing process, including the following:

- Writers do a great deal of *rehearsing and planning*. They think about purpose and audience. They try out their ideas in oral language. They often "gather seeds" by writing thoughts, sketching, making lists, or outlining ideas in a writer's notebook. They may engage in research or inquiry to gather information about a topic. They select an appropriate genre or form for their ideas (story, letter, and essay). Often they use other writers as mentors. When you read aloud to children or they read independently or in guided reading, they are encountering texts that they can use as models.
- Writers *draft and revise* their pieces. They get their ideas down quickly but then reread to add or delete information, reorganize it, or make changes.
- Writers *edit* their pieces, using everything they know about the conventions of writing.
- Writers produce a final draft or *publish* the piece and go on to other writing. The final draft or publication represents the writer's best work at this time.
- Writers *reflect* on their writing. Through self-evaluation and thinking about what they have learned, they bring more understanding to the next piece.

SUPPORTING LEARNERS THROUGH USING LANGUAGE IN WRITING WORKSHOP

The elements of a writing workshop are ideally suited to allow you to use oral language skillfully to help children develop as writers (see Figure 4-8).

Mini-lesson

Mini-lessons involve quite a bit of "teacher talk" because you are demonstrating something to students in very explicit ways. At the same time, you want to invite students to interact for three reasons:

- Their interactions and questions help you know what they understand from the mini-lesson.
- They will be more engaged if they enter into conversation about the lesson on genre, craft, conventions, or process.
- They will learn more if they interact with you and with each other.

The mini-lesson offers a wonderful way to capitalize on all of the learning you have accomplished through interactive read-aloud and the talk that surrounds it. If you keep a list of all the texts you have read aloud, you have a ready reference for selecting mentor texts (Fountas & Pinnell, 2001; 2006). Mini-lessons come alive when you bring out some of their favorite texts for a discussion of the writer's craft. You do not need to take the time to read the text because students already have it as part of their repertoire.

Independent Writing and Conferring

As students are engaged in independent writing of their own pieces, you can move around the room and talk quietly with individuals. These conferences may focus on any aspect of writing. A simple beginning, such as "How's it going?" can encourage the writer to talk about process, craft, or conventions (Anderson, 2000). The purpose of the conference is not to "fix" the particular piece of writing, although it may indeed lead to improvement. Instead, the teacher works collaboratively with the writer in a way that leads to expanding proficiency. The writer is not only producing a product. The writer is engaging in the process in a way that expands writing power.

Sharing

Sharing brings closure to the day's work. During sharing, students have an opportunity to talk with each other and with the teacher about what they have learned. You can remind them of the principle demonstrated in the mini-lesson or offer clarification. Often, teachers have students turn to a partner or work in threes or fours to share something about their writing. They may bring their drafts or the writer's notebooks to the class meeting for sharing. A great deal of conversation surrounds the work that they have just completed. Sharing does not take very long—perhaps five minutes—but it sets the expectation that something has been done during writing workshop that day and it allows students to recognize their progress.

Language as the Foundation

If we have to identify one foundation for literacy learning, it must be oral language. Children do not simply "practice" language; they engage in it. They use it to represent their experiences and themselves (Britton, 1973). Young children use language to take on the world and many use it to begin the process of becoming literate long before schooling. They respond to stories and even pretend to read. They play with words and poetry. When they enter school, oral language is an even more important tool in the process of learning to be a proficient reader and writer. Language is the wind that fills the sail and allows the learner to stay on course. As teachers, we recognize that our language has a powerful influence on students. It tells them what we think of them as learners. And when we invite them into conversation, they become active partners in their own learning. Examples of teachers and children talking about written texts and about what it means to be a writer populate this book. As you read, take the opportunity to talk with your colleagues about this powerful process.

Suggestions for Professional Development

The most powerful way to expand oral language in every area of the curriculum is to engage children in text-based talk around a work of children's literature. Work with colleagues to create collections that intentionally build language knowledge—you will be teaching comprehension at the same time! Gather a group of grade-level colleagues (or cross–grade-level groups) for the following activity to help teachers prepare for talking with children about books.

1. Plan a core curriculum for interactive read-aloud. Meeting before school starts for the year is helpful, as is having a budget to buy some new texts. With good planning, texts can be shared across three or four teachers. If you have a school librarian, that important person should be involved in the curriculum planning. Of course, the core curriculum does not need to include every book that you and your colleagues read aloud to children. Instead, set a goal of including 20 to 30 books for this first plan. Examine each text for its potential in terms of the following:

    *   Expanding knowledge of the syntax of written language
    *   Developing vocabulary
    *   Expanding content knowledge
    *   Developing oral language through discussion

    Place the texts in sequence or group them by genre, content, or style. (You may want to consider doing an author study, because that helps children notice how a particular writer uses language.) Make a brief (half-page) plan for using each text that includes an "opening" for each text (informal plan for the way you will introduce it to your class) and one or two points in the text where you will stop and ask children to "turn and talk" or make brief comments about what they have heard so far. Write one or two goals for post-reading discussion and plan some writing or drawing exercises to extend the meaning of some of the texts.

Organize teachers' schedules so that each teacher can use the group of texts for about a month in the classroom. (Of course, some texts might be so important that everyone will want to have them all year!) Hold a follow-up meeting toward the end of the year to discuss the interactive read-aloud program's results and to plan for next year. ✦

CHAPTER 5

Encouraging Children in a Writing Process Through Community Writing

by Andrea McCarrier

As writers work, they often seek the support of a community. Within that community, they can talk about their ideas, try out language, and give each other suggestions.

My OSU Literacy Collaborative colleagues and I have worked over the years in classrooms where young children's first experiences with writing take place within a unique setting—one that involves teachers and children working together as a group to produce a written text. They *share* the work. As we have studied this setting over the years, we have realized that these teachers and children were engaged in what we now call *community writing.* Through community writing, young children

- Learn to collaborate with others
- Talk about their ideas and build on the ideas of others
- Develop a sense of audience
- Become deeply engaged in the writing process

In this chapter, I present the concept and process of community writing as an instructional context in which teachers include children in the process of writing. Community writing takes place within a comprehensive literacy framework in which children have many different experiences as they engage with texts.

As collaborators in the process, students become a "writing community" with the support of skilled teaching, making decisions together as they move from ideas to oral language to messages they want to write. As a foundation for community writing, teachers often use "mentor texts" (high-quality books that engage children and become their favorites to hear read aloud). Close examination of mentor texts supports even very young children in becoming storytellers and story writers. In essence, the children "stand on the shoulders" of other writers.

An experience in Jennifer Beck's kindergarten classroom provides a good example of community writing. Jennifer used *Tacky in Trouble* (Lester, 2005) as a mentor text to expand her students' oral and written language through community writing. A summary of this exciting text is provided in Figure 5-1, and you can see from the photographs in Figures 5-2, 5-3, and 5-4 that the children have provided a sequenced, accurate, and interesting representation.

This engaging text provides children with many opportunities to notice a sequence of exciting events and many interesting details. The illustrations also provide opportunities for children to construct meaning.

A glance at this piece of art and community writing reveals that the children did indeed notice a great many details and were able to represent the story in sequence. In the next sections of this chapter, I examine the process in detail.

FIGURE 5-2. Tacky Beginning—Left Panel

FIGURE 5-3. Tacky Middle—Middle Panel

FIGURE 5-4. Tacky End—Right Panel

Summary of *Tacky in Trouble*
(Helen Lester, 1998; illus. Lynn Munsinger)

Tacky is an independent-thinking penguin who always finds himself at odds with his five penguin companions. In this story, Tacky decides to go surfing on a piece of ice instead of taking a nap with his five penguin companions. As he's surfing, a sudden wind springs up and fills his shirt so that it acts as a sail, and Tacky's afternoon surfing trip becomes a wild adventure to a tropical island. His predicament worsens when he mistakes Rocky, an elephant, for a big rock. The elephant thinks that Tacky is a bouquet of flowers because of the floral pattern in his shirt. He picks Tacky up, carries him home, and plops him in a vase. To get himself out of this predicament, Tacky has to prove that he is a penguin, not a bouquet of flowers. In his attempt to do this, he accidentally spills food on the elephant's drab tablecloth. Instead of being angry, the elephant is delighted to have a colorful tablecloth and tells Tacky that he and his floral-print shirt are free to go. Tacky then finds a floating log and sails back to his friends on the iceberg.

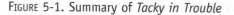

FIGURE 5-1. Summary of *Tacky in Trouble*

Guiding K-3 Writers to Independence

Community Writing Within a Comprehensive Language and Literacy Framework

In Jennifer's classroom, community writing is embedded in a comprehensive language and literacy framework for instruction that helps children make connections between reading and writing, and provides for varying levels of support. Over time, she has learned to use this integrated set of instructional contexts, which is shown in Figure 5-5.

Levels of Support in Instruction Contexts Within a Comprehensive Language and Literacy Framework		
	Reading	**Writing**
High Support	Interactive Read-Aloud—The teacher reads and discusses carefully chosen pieces of children's literature. Because these read-aloud events expand the children's knowledge of books and how they work, they become resources that children draw on as readers and writers.	Community Writing—The teacher engages children in a writing process in order to communicate a message to an audience. During the process, the teacher may decide to do all of the writing (shared writing) or decide to share the pen with the children (interactive writing).
	Shared Reading—The teacher uses an enlarged text to teach a strategic action that children need to know. These strategic actions range from problem-solving new words to learning how to infer what a character is thinking.	
	Guided Reading—The teacher groups her students according to their instructional needs as readers. Books are carefully selected from a gradient of text difficulty. The teacher releases more of the responsibility for reading the text to the student.	Writing Workshop—The children continue to develop a writing process by writing stories from their own lives—personal narratives. Children also can explore other genres of writing, such as retelling a story they have written in community writing or a nonfiction piece, such as directions for baiting a hook. Whatever the piece, the writing grows from the children's personal experience.
Low Support	Independent Reading—Children read books that they have read in guided reading or new books that are at an easier text level. During this time children not only experience the joy of reading but also develop a more effective processing system by practicing what they are learning in reading lessons.	Independent Writing—Children apply what they are learning as writers to pieces of writing of their choice. This writing usually occurs during managed independent learning.

FIGURE 5-5. Levels of Support

This integrated system of approaches has several advantages:

1. The framework provides for varying levels of support for student learning. Jennifer can move from demonstration to guided practice and then to independent work, in accordance with the theoretical concept that "What the child can do in co-operation today, he can do alone tomorrow" (Vygotsky, 1962, p. 164).

2. The framework also provides a strong emphasis on the reciprocity between reading and writing, a theoretical concept consistent with the work of Clay, who writes, "Writing contributes to the building of almost every kind of inner control of literacy learning that is needed by the successful reader" (1998, p. 150).

3. Instruction involves teaching for strategic cognitive actions rather than spending instructional time learning isolated "items" or pieces of information. Children learn about letters, sounds, and words, but they also apply this knowledge as they work with continuous text as readers and writers. The goal is to foster independence in children by teaching them how to develop self-extending systems for reading and writing (Clay, 1991).

4. The entire framework is embedded in a sea of talk such that learning is constructed through conversation. This last point is critical. Jennifer knows that for her students to become readers and writers, they will need to increase their competencies as speakers and listeners.

Interactive and shared writing (which we categorize as *community writing*), are key components of the framework, especially for younger students. Shared and interactive writing share many characteristics:

- The writing emerges from real talk and experiences
- The teacher and children compose a common text, which the teacher guides so that it will be readable (through shared reading) for the particular children in the group
- The text is often illustrated and is read many times

The major difference between shared and interactive writing is that in shared writing, the teacher acts as scribe, while in interactive writing, the teacher decides at particular points in the writing of the text to "share the pen" with a student. This intentional teaching move has high instructional value because it requires children to attend more closely to visual aspects of print. (For more information, see McCarrier, Pinnell, & Fountas, 2000, pp. 24–25.)

The entire process of community writing is infused with meaningful talk. The conversation is ongoing and involves the skills of both speaking and listening, as the teacher and class do the following:

- Engage in conversation about the topic
- Discuss the purpose of the writing
- Talk about composing the message and reach agreement on the particular language to use
- Talk about the conventions of written language—how to write what they want to say
- Comment on interesting features of words
- Make connections between the text and other texts

- Make personal connections between the text and their own experience (McCarrier, Pinnell, & Fountas, 2000, p. 11–12).

Community writing has eight components, each of which contributes to the learning experiences of children (see Figure 5-6).

Essential Elements of Interactive Writing

1. Provide a Base of Active Learning Experiences	May be either a story the children will retell or innovate upon or a hands-on activity, such as a field trip or recording the results of an experiment.
2. Talk to Establish Purpose	The group decides: • What message they want to communicate • Why the message is important • The audience for whom the message is intended
3. Compose the Text	The group works within the hierarchy of written language to decide: • The genre or format that will communicate their message most effectively • The structure of the text: will the story be paragraphs or be a series of speech bubbles? • Sentences that communicate the message using just the right words
4. Construct the Text	Putting the message on paper. Children are learning the conventions of written language and why these conventions make it easier for the reader to read the message. These conventions include: • Formation of letters • Use of capital letters • Use of punctuation marks
5. Revise and Edit	The group of writers may decide to change or revise their text to add clarity or improve cohesion. For instance, they might edit their text by inserting a set of quotation marks they discovered were missing.
6. Revisit for Word Solving	The teacher uses a word the children worked on during the construction of the message to reteach the word-solving principle involved.
7. Summarize the Learning	At the end of the community writing lesson the teacher chooses two teaching points. In the first, the teacher reminds the children of what they learned about the craft of writing. The second focuses on a convention that writers use to make their text readable.
8. Extend the Learning	Children may extend the learning in multiple ways, from dramatizing the piece they have written to writing their own piece at the writing center.

FIGURE 5-6. Essential Elements of Interactive Writing (adapted from McCarrier, Pinnell, & Fountas, 2000)

Community writing is based on active learning that is embedded in talk. Conversations between students and between students and the teacher are critical to learning as students compose and construct the text. Once created, the text can serve as a shared reading text and can be revisited during mini-lessons. Children may also revisit a text produced in community writing and use it as a mentor text as they write their own stories.

Planning for Community Writing

As you implement community writing, remember that in this setting, you can accomplish many instructional goals simultaneously. Through listening to and discussing texts and extending understanding through art and writing, children are expanding language, acquiring new vocabulary, learning about the structure of stories, and developing a sense of the conventions and craft of written language. As you develop a long-range plan for a unit of study, you can address many goals within a single community writing project, making your teaching effective and efficient.

PLANNING WITH STANDARDS IN MIND

Like many other teachers, Jennifer is responsible for teaching specific academic content standards, and she took these standards into account when planning the activities in which children would participate. She knew that as a kindergarten teacher, she is expected to teach her students

- How to retell a story
- That stories have a beginning, a middle, and an end
- How to write a simple story using conventions of written language, such as spacing between words, accurately spelling high-frequency words, and hearing and recording sounds in words

Jennifer's tentative plan for teaching the academic content standards appears in Figure 5-7.

ESTABLISHING GOALS FOR COMMUNITY WRITING

Jennifer finds community writing to be an effective way to address academic content standards as well as other goals. Her specific lesson goals are presented in Figure 5-8 and discussed below.

Jennifer knew that she could use *Tacky in Trouble*, or another piece of quality children's literature, to help children understand that stories have a beginning, a middle, and an end. She planned to develop the mural in three parts in order to more explicitly demonstrate the concept of a story having a beginning, a middle, and an end.

Her plan included teaching the children how storytellers and writers make decisions about what information they need to include if they want people to understand their story. The process was designed to expand students' oral language skills by asking them to recall or narrate the story, either by looking at the illustrations in the book or by using the artwork on their own three-part mural. Jennifer's goal was to increase children's linguistic skills as users of both natural, everyday language and literary or book language.

Levels of Support in Instruction Contexts Within a Comprehensive Language and Literacy Framework

WHAT TO TEACH Academic Content Standards	HOW TO TEACH Activity	WHERE TO TEACH Instructional Context
Retell Story	• Listen to and talk about stories to build a repertoire of stories • Retell stories using illustrations in storybooks • Dramatize stories • Write a retelling of a favorite story • Narrate a story illustrated on a mural • Write their own retelling of a story	• Interactive read-aloud • Independent reading • Drama play center • Community writing • Read around the room • Writing workshop or managed independent learning

Beginning—Middle—End	• Discuss how a story can be divided into parts as children listen to stories
	• Dramatize each part of a story
	• Divide the mural into three panels in order to highlight the three parts of a story
	  — Illustrate each panel
	  — Write text for each panel
	  — Label each panel
		• Interactive read-aloud
		
		• Drama play center
		
		• Art center
		• Community writing
		• Community writing

Writing Process & Conventions of Written Language	• Plan illustrations by writing a list of items to illustrate for each panel • Write speech bubbles for each panel	• Community writing • Community writing

FIGURE 5-7. Teaching Plan

She wanted the children to develop a deliberate memory for parts of the text, especially for some of the songs and dialogue that appeared in the book. So, she would incorporate the language of the book in her talk. For example, she might say, "Tacky was an 'odd bird' wasn't he?" Additionally, she could introduce dialogue into the children's retelling by asking them what a character said or thought. For example, when one student, Steven, said that Tacky hopped on Rocky the elephant's back, she asked, "And what did

Teaching Goals to Help Children

• Understand the structure of stories

• Learn how writers make decisions

• Expand their oral-language skills

• Develop the ability to remember parts of a text

• Engage in thoughtful planning

• Understand dialogue in stories

FIGURE 5-8. Teaching Goals

Tacky sing when he danced on Rocky's back?" The children responded with Tacky's favorite jingle. Asking the children to repeat the jingle meant that Jennifer expected that her children had developed deliberate memory (Bodrova & Leong, 1995).

Her lesson structure also supported thoughtful planning on the part of her students. Jennifer realized that for emergent readers, a great deal of information is carried in the illustrations. By thinking about the details and sequence of their own pictures, they could enter into the process of text construction. So, she adjusted the independent work period to include enough time at the art center for the children to complete their illustrations.

Her use of speech bubbles had several advantages. Some of her higher-progress readers were beginning to read simple texts with one, two, or three lines of print. Jennifer could draw on the reciprocity of reading and writing by connecting the "talk" in the speech bubbles with the dialogue children were encountering in these easy texts. Further, she could demonstrate how the speech bubbles could blend story retelling with "real" reading in order to achieve a cohesive retelling of the story. She believed that the combination of oral storytelling and reading print would increase their oral-language skills.

SUPPORTING COMMUNITY WRITING ACROSS LEARNING CONTEXTS

Jennifer's next step was to co-construct the curriculum with her children. In this way, she was able to meet content requirements while using dynamic methods of instruction to engage her students' interest.

Figure 5-9 shows how Jennifer connected community writing across several components of the framework. Jennifer used interactive read-aloud and independent work—including independent reading and "read around the room," independent writing, dramatic play, and art—to support ongoing work with one piece of community writing.

INTERACTIVE READ-ALOUD

Writers need to know some stories well enough to use them as mentor texts. Before expecting children to retell stories in dramatic play or use them as a foundation for community writing, Jennifer knew she needed to read aloud several of the books in the Tacky series. Conversation enriched these interactive read-aloud experiences. Children talked about the plot, explaining what might happen and why. They enjoyed repeating language from the text that had captured their attention. They expanded their knowledge of words. They fell in love with the character, and when Jennifer asked them

FIGURE 5-9. Connecting Community Writing Across Learning Contexts

which book was their favorite, they immediately responded, "*Tacky in Trouble!*" So, it became the mentor text for their community writing lessons.

Independent Work

As the children became familiar with the stories, Jennifer provided additional opportunities for them to rehearse stories during their independent work. Jennifer has taught the children specific routines for working independently while she teaches reading in small groups. (See Fountas & Pinnell, 1996, pp. 53–72 for additional information about managed independent learning.)

Independent Reading. Even though most of the children were only beginning to read and could not read *Tacky in Trouble* independently, Jennifer was able to provide for two kinds of independent engagement with texts during the independent work period: (1) rehearsing the language and sequence of the story as the children looked at the picture books, and (2) reading "around the room" the written material they had already produced.

Whenever Jennifer finished reading a story aloud, she placed the book in a basket. Children were invited to look through the book's illustrations and tell the story in their own words. Sometimes two or three children would tell the story together. After Jennifer had read the story several times and the children were quite familiar with the plot and language of the book, she often invited a child to sit in her chair and retell the story to the class as she or he paged through the illustrations. When the storyteller needed support, the audience chimed in.

Also during independent work time, children read the print on the classroom walls, including the name chart, the word wall, and displayed pieces of community writing. Even if a community writing project was only partly completed, it became part of the activity as children read texts around the room. Jennifer intentionally designed the panels of *Tacky in Trouble* to have a limited amount of text. That allowed the community writers to embed the speech bubbles into the mural narration, which required them to remember the story and draw on their own linguistic resources as storytellers—not just story readers.

Independent Writing. Sometimes, the children were so excited about the piece that the community of writers was producing, they wanted to write and illustrate their own version. This writing usually happened during managed independent learning. At other times, children wrote their own stories at home and brought them to school to share with their fellow writers.

Dramatic Play. Dramatic reenactment of story books helped Jennifer's students understand the story's sequence, characters, and plot. The students used simple paper-plate masks to act out the story, using language that would later help them to develop voice as writers. This activity also helped them develop a sense of audience, and they were able to revise their play in response to audience reaction. All of these opportunities to hear and reenact the story helped them internalize the story's sequence, plot, and storybook language.

Art. Working on the illustrations for the mural provided another opportunity for children to revisit the mentor text. Sometimes the children thought about how they could capture the author's meaning through their artwork. If we look at their art, we can see how the illustrations in the book influenced their work (see Figure 5-10).

The children's deeper knowledge of the book became a resource that they used as they rewrote and illustrated their story in community writing.

The time line for integrating these instructional contexts is shown in Figure 5-11.

Description of the Three-Panel Mural

There are strong parallels between the children's artwork on the first panel of the mural and the illustrations in the first page of the mentor text. In both, Tacky's companions are gathered on an iceberg.	In the middle panel, the children borrowed from the book again. Their entire island scene, which includes Tacky standing on Rocky's back and the trees, looks very similar to the scene in the book. One difference is that the students chose to show the passage of time through their artwork but not in printed text.	This panel is less closely tied to the illustrations in the book. In fact, the children did not have Tacky wearing his shirt when he sailed home on a log. Jennifer wondered whether the children would notice that it was missing. They never did!

FIGURE 5-10. Description of the Three-Panel Mural

Moving From Planning to Writing

After the text had been revisited several times in different ways, it was time to begin composing the community writing piece. Jennifer wanted to use art as the way to begin, and she understood that the mural would require planning.

RETELLING THE STORY

Before the children illustrated each of the three parts of the story mural, the group revisited that part of the story in the book. As the children talked, they suggested items that needed to be illustrated, and Jennifer acted as scribe so that they could brainstorm. Let's look at a transcript from some of the conversations as the children decide on a list of illustrations for the middle part of the story, which has several episodes. The children needed to decide how they were going to use the artwork to convey the complexity of the story.

The children were gathered on the carpet, listening to Terrence retell the first part of the story. Terrence was sitting next to the illustrations for the first part of the mural, which the group had finished the day before. Notice how Terrence blended book language into his retelling. For example, he used the word *companions*, which would be unusual in a kindergartner's oral vocabulary, because he remembered specific language the characters used.

Time Line for Integrating the Language Arts

	Interactive Read-Aloud	Managed Independent Learning	Community Writing
Weeks 1&2 Days 1–10	• Read books from Tacky series	**Independent Reading Center** • Retell stories using picture books that the teacher has read aloud **Dramatic Play Center** • Use puppets to reenact the story	
Week 3 Day 11	• Read aloud stories from Tacky series	**Dramatic Play Center** • Dramatize *Tacky in Trouble*	• The children choose *Tacky in Trouble* for their retelling
Day 12	• Read aloud stories from Tacky series	**Art Center** • Begin painting illustrations	• Create a planning sheet of artwork for the first panel of the mural
Day 13	• Reread *Tacky in Trouble*, especially the first part	**Dramatic Play Center** • Dramatize *Tacky in Trouble* **Art Center** • Finish the illustrations on the first panel	• Compose and write speech bubbles for the first panel of the mural
Day 14	• Reread the first part of *Tacky in Trouble* • Retell the rest of the story using illustrations	**Dramatic Play Center** • Rehearse the story through a puppet show **Independent Reading Center** • Retell the story using the book **Read Around the Room** • Use the mural to retell the first part of the story • Read the first speech bubble	• Add a second speech bubble • Compose and write the second speech bubble on the first panel
Day 15	• Retell *Tacky in Trouble* using illustrations • Reread parts of the middle of the book as students talk about illustrations	**Dramatic Play Center** • Dramatize *Tacky in Trouble* **Read Around the Room** • Retell the first part of the story using the first panel of the mural; incorporate the speech bubbles into the retelling **Art Center** • Begin painting illustrations on the middle panel	• Write a planning sheet of artwork for the second panel of the mural
Week 4 Days 16–20	• Reread *Tacky in Trouble*	**Dramatic Play Center** • Dramatize *Tacky in Trouble* **Read Around the Room** • Retell the first part of the story using the first panel of the mural; incorporate the speech bubbles into the retelling **Art Center** • Finish painting illustrations on the middle panel	• Decide to add Tacky's song to the second panel • Continue until project is complete

FIGURE 5-11. Time Line for Integrating the Language Arts

TERRENCE: Tacky is sleeping on the iceberg.

JENNIFER: And what else?

TERRENCE: Tacky went surfing and then he woke up. And he went surfing. And they said, "Go away."

Earlier, Jennifer had clarified that "they" referred to Tacky's companions. A storyteller must be sure that if he uses a pronoun, his audience understands to whom or what it refers.

JENNIFER: Terrence, you said, "They said, 'Go away.'" I'm not real sure who told him to go away. Could you tell us who told Tacky to go away?

TERRENCE: The companions told him.

JENNIFER: OH! The companions told him to go away. They really did not like being bothered by Tacky, did they?

TERRENCE: No.

JENNIFER: What were the companions doing when he was going surfing?

TERRENCE: They were sleeping, but they didn't feel they were in charge without Tacky.

In the next part of the transcript, Jennifer wanted Terrence to retell what happened next without referring back to the pictures in the book, a competency that children needed to develop according to her state's standards. At the same time, she was activating prior knowledge for the entire class.

JENNIFER: So, for the next part of our story, what do we need to do?

TERRENCE: Draw another picture of the story.

JENNIFER: What picture will we draw for the next part?

TERRENCE: They said, "Do it quietly." And the wind caught his shirt like a sail.

JENNIFER: What was Tacky doing?

TERRENCE: Surfing.

JENNIFER: Tacky was surfing and the wind caught his shirt and made his shirt into a sail. Now, how are you going to draw that? How will we show the wind is in his shirt and makes his shirt a sail?

TERRENCE: (motioning with his hands) Lines coming down.

JENNIFER: (opening the book) How did they show it in the book? How did they show that the wind was getting into his shirt?

The illustrations in the text show the water painted with strokes that might be described as "lines coming down." In order to direct the group's attention to the illustrator's technique, Jennifer opened the book to the page where the wind caught Tacky's shirt.

JENNIFER: Look at his shirt. What does it look like?

TERRENCE: It has flowers.

As teachers, we often wonder why children say what they do. It is good that we wonder about this, because children are always acting in a way that indicates how they are trying to make sense of their

Guiding K-3 Writers to Independence

world (Wells, 1986). Jennifer had said, "What does it look like?" but Terrence had forgotten the topic of the conversation—the effect of the wind on Tacky's shirt. His response shows that he remembered the importance of the floral pattern on the shirt to the story. (In the story, when Rocky, the elephant, sees the flowers on Tacky's shirt, she thinks that Tacky is a bouquet of flowers that she can use to brighten up her table setting.) Because of Terrence's response, Jennifer flipped back a few pages to show Tacky's shirt before it was filled with air. She drew the children's attention to the way the shirt looked.

> JENNIFER: Yes. And let's look back here. Here is his shirt. Look at his shirt. He's just wearing his shirt. But look at how his shirt looks on this page. What happens to it when the wind fills up his shirt?
> CHILDREN: It blows.
> JENNIFER: Yes. The wind blows. When it blows, it stretched his shirt out and made it big, didn't it?
> CHILDREN: Yeah!
> JENNIFER: So what do we need to think about when we're drawing this part about Tacky? We'll have to make his shirt like that (as she points to his shirt billowing in the wind) so we know he is surfing because of the wind. The wind is what takes him over to where Rocky is.

MAKING A PLANNING LIST

After the text refresher, the children and Jennifer began to make a list of illustrations for the middle part of the story.

> JENNIFER: Let's think about the next part of our story and what we're going to add to it. What was happening in the next part of the story?

Jennifer flipped to a blank piece of paper so that she was ready to record their ideas. If we look back to the chart on the essential elements of a writing process in interactive writing, Jennifer moved from the first element, providing a base of active learning experiences, to the third and fourth, composing and constructing the text. She "skipped" the second element, the purpose of the writing, because it already had been established.

> JOSEPH: He went to the island; the jungle.
> JENNIFER: But *before* he met Rocky and the birds, what happened?

The setting of the story moves from the iceberg to the ocean to the jungle and back again. Jennifer hoped that her comment would prompt the children to think and talk about Tacky's decision to take a piece of ice and go surfing in the ocean, but the language she used did not provide enough support to enable them to do this. Because she was teaching the children the importance of chronological order in retelling, Jennifer wanted the children's list to begin with *surfing* rather than *jungle*.

> JENNIFER: Yes. But before he did that, what happened?
> JASMINE: He met Rocky.

ISAAC: He met the bird.

ARTURO: He went to the jungle.

Jennifer's lower-level prompt, using the word "before," did not seem to provide enough support. She was concerned that the conversation might be becoming a guessing game. She immediately adjusted the level of support by drawing the children back into the story. She flipped through the first part of the story retelling it for them. As she retold it, she emphasized the sequence of events.

JENNIFER: He did. But look at the first part of the story. We had all of the penguins. Tacky is the odd bird. He's not doing what his companions are doing. Then they decide to take a nap. And what does Tacky do?

MIA: Surf!

JENNIFER: So do we need to put Tacky surfing in the next part?

MIA: Yeah!

Jennifer began the list of illustrations by writing "Tacky surfing" on the board. As she wrote, she said the word *surfing* slowly, demonstrating the strategic action of hearing and recording sounds in words. Next, she prompted the children to make a link from a known word to an unknown word.

JENNIFER: Tacky surfing. Whose name starts like *surfing*?

JASMINE: Sonia.

JENNIFER: Sonia. *Surfing* and *Sonia* both start with an *s*. Let's read what we've written.

CHILDREN & JENNIFER: (as Jennifer points) Tacky surfing.

The children added the following items to their list: island, rocky, birds, stars, and moon. There was a lot of talk about the importance of each item, especially the stars and moon. The children observed that if Tacky surfed when the stars and moon were out, that meant he was surfing at night—which meant he had been surfing for a really long time. Note that the children's idea to illustrate the stars and moon came from the book's language rather than its illustrations, indicating their memory of the text: Tacky sailed, ". . . on and on, through starry nights and sunlit days." Understanding and representing the passage of time is a challenge for young children, but this group would later manage to capture the passage of time through art.

REVIEWING THE TEXT TO ADD IDEAS

When the children seemed to have run out of ideas, Jennifer asked one of the students to retell the story as she paged through the book. During this review, Jennifer asked the children to incorporate the language of the book, such as the song that Tacky chanted when he hopped around on the elephant's back. Within the series of community writing lessons, Jennifer moved back and forth from developing an active base for learning by reviewing the story to composing and constructing the message. After the review, the children decided to add three more items to their list: sun, clouds, and wind.

Using Talk to Understand Concepts

In the next piece of transcript, the children use talk to problem-solve how to show the wind. The wind is essential to the story. The wind is blowing and when it fills Tacky's shirt, Tacky's shirt acts like a sail. The wind blows him from his home on an iceberg to an island in the tropics.

During her interactive read-aloud and in Terrence's retelling earlier that day, Jennifer had drawn the children's attention to the illustrations of Tacky's shirt. Perhaps Darrell's memory of those conversations triggered his suggestion to add *wind* to their list of illustrations.

> JENNIFER: Darrell, you said we would need wind, and we do because when Tacky was surfing he needed wind. That was smart thinking. Now, how are you going to draw the wind? What does it look like?
>
> DARELL: A circle.
>
> AARON: We'll have to draw a white swirl.

The children may have been referring to the illustrator's technique of using sweeping brush strokes to show the movement of the waves in the ocean. Jennifer accepted their suggestion and then asked them to think of other ways to show that the wind was blowing.

> JENNIFER: Okay. Draw some white swirls to look sort of like wind? What else can we do to show that there is wind?

Jennifer paused, but no one responded, so she elaborated.

> JENNIFER: When Tacky is surfing, what else can we draw to show that there is wind?
>
> ISAAC: His shirt blowing.
>
> JENNIFER: And how are we going to do that? What is his shirt going to look like when it's blowing?
>
> ISAAC: Draw it blowing. Puffing.
>
> JENNIFER: Show his shirt poking out like they did in the book to show wind? All right. Some of you said we need an island and trees. How can we draw the trees to show the wind is blowing?

The children move side to side, imitating the trees swaying.

> JENNIFER: Will the trees be leaning or standing up straight?
>
> ARTURO: Leaning over.
>
> JENNIFER: The trees are leaning this way and that. Leaning over. Will that show the wind is blowing?
>
> ARTURO: Yes.

After the children finished the list of illustrations for the middle part of the story, Jennifer took the list to the art center. The children working at the art center used the list as a guide for painting the setting on the middle panel. The decision-making process in the art center is discussed in the next section.

Artwork and Community Writing

As teachers of emergent writers, we know that initially, most children will tell their stories by drawing pictures, not by writing. We also know that in the first simple books children read, the story's meaning is enriched by illustrations. Jennifer wanted to strengthen the reciprocity between reading and writing by helping the children understand how to use art and text together to create their message.

DECISION MAKING AT THE ART CENTER

The following are some examples of the kinds of decisions that the children made as they illustrated the middle part of the story. In these examples we can see how the children drew on their conversations about the illustrations during interactive read-aloud and community writing as they illustrated this part of the story.

Showing the Wind in an Interpretive Way

Even though the class had looked at and talked about how Tacky's shirt billowed in the wind, the group of children who painted Tacky's shirt decided to portray this differently than had been originally decided. The children working at the art center decided not to paint Tacky's shirt billowing in the wind—the choice that the illustrator of the book made and the choice that Jennifer had thought they would make. Instead, they painted a normal-size shirt and glued only the top of it to the figure of Tacky. This ingenious arrangement allowed them to blow at the shirt, causing it to "flap in the wind" as they retold the story. They had successfully moved their illustration beyond the two dimensions used by the illustrator.

Showing Faraway Companions (Perspective)

Aaron decided that Tacky's companions should be on the mural, so he added five small black dots of paint to the iceberg he was making. He made them so small because they were so far away from Tacky, providing evidence that Aaron was beginning to understand perspective in art.

Showing the Passage of Time

To help carry the plot, the kindergartners used a few speech bubbles and communicated other events through the illustrations they painted on the mural. The mural filled in some of the information gaps. One such gap was in the passage of time, a plot point that the author conveyed in the book with the phrase ". . . through sunny days and starlit nights." The list of illustrations for the middle of the story included stars and moon and sun. At the time the children came up with those items, Jennifer commented, "Yes, the story says he sailed through sunny days and starlit nights."

The next day, the children at the art center began illustrating the middle part of the story. Aaron was in charge of painting the stars and moon. He began to paint and then stopped.

"There is a problem," he said. "We need a sun and the moon and stars." Some of the children who were painting with him at the art center pointed to the mural of the *Three Billy Goats Gruff* hanging on the wall behind them.

"We only have one sun there," several children commented.

"But Tacky sailed through sunny days and starlit nights!" said Aaron.

The group at the art center continued to grapple with the dilemma—how to illustrate sunny days and starlit nights on the same panel. They were problem-solving how to show the passage of time. They continued to talk together to problem solve the passage of time.

"I have an idea." said Aaron. "We can make part of the sky night and part of it day."

They divided the sky in the middle panel of the mural into two parts, one painted blue and one painted black, representing day and night. They painted the sun on the blue half and the moon and stars on the black half.

At about that time, Jennifer came over to find out what they were talking about. After hearing Aaron's idea, she asked all of the children to stop what they were doing and listen to the suggestion of the illustrators at the art center. Jennifer believed that children would lose a feeling of ownership if the entire community of authors and illustrators were not involved in the decision. When the illustrators shared their thinking, the rest of the class agreed with the change. The art group went back to work and divided the sky in half. They captured in art what the author had described in words.

Creating Borders

When Jennifer had read *The Mitten*, by Jan Brett (1989), as part of a collection of winter stories, the children were captivated by the borders Brett had drawn on each page. The children were particularly fascinated by the way the pictures foreshadowed something that was going to happen in the story. When the class was almost finished illustrating and writing their story about Tacky, they asked whether they could make borders for each part of their mural. The group decided that each person could have a turn at adding to the border when his or her group was at the art center. Jennifer decided to let the children design the borders without any whole-group planning. Looking at Figures 5-2, 5-3, and 5-4 on page 68, you can see that the children used objects and characters from the story.

Drawing on another book and using it as a mentor text for adding more detail to their panels suggests that the children understood that they had taken on the roles of author, illustrator, and decision maker. These children have had the opportunity to:

- Learn techniques that other writers use to tell their stories
- Try those techniques with teacher support
- Try them independently in a supportive context like community writing

Through this process, Jennifer helped her kindergarten students become storytellers and story writers.

Community Writing: Composing and Constructing the Text for the Mural

Early in the process, Jennifer had made an instructional decision not to rewrite the entire story, but rather to combine oral storytelling with speech bubbles that present language close to talk so the children could capture the rise and fall of tension in the story line. This text would be simpler for emergent writers to compose and ultimately to read because they could focus on the characters and what they might say or think.

Jennifer used community writing for the text but varied her approach to use both shared and interactive writing. She was being highly selective about which approach she used for specific purposes. At times, she chose to share the pen interactively because she wanted the children to attend to the conventions of written language in a more deliberate way than they might if she were doing all the writing (shared writing). At other times, she used shared writing because she wanted to get their ideas down quickly and move the lesson along. Figure 5-12 shows what Jennifer and the children composed and constructed on each panel of the mural.

USING POETIC LANGUAGE FROM THE TEXT

During the interactive read-aloud, the children loved to chant the song that Tacky sang as he hopped on Rocky's back; they never failed to chime in. When it was time to create the middle panel of the mural, they were emphatic about including Tacky's song. The song is quite long in comparison to the text in the other speech bubbles. Jennifer tried to dissuade them for two reasons.

First, Jennifer used shared writing when the group brainstormed their list of illustrations, and she was the scribe. This time, however, she wanted to have the children help her write the message, so they would have hands-on experience with the process of going from idea to spoken structure to printed message (Clay, 1998). She also wanted to teach the children how to hear and record sounds in words.

	Text	Type of Writing
First Panel	Beginning Sunrise on the iceberg. What's happening?	Interactive Writing Interactive Writing Interactive Writing
Second Panel	Middle I don't need shoes, And I don't need socks, Just my mellow yellow feet for hopping on the rocks. Something is tickling my back. HEY!	Interactive Writing Shared Writing Interactive Writing Interactive Writing
Third Panel	End What have you done to my Tablecloth? Uh-oh! We miss Tacky	Interactive Writing Interactive Writing Interactive Writing Interactive Writing

FIGURE 5-12. Composition and Construction of the Text Using Shared and Interactive Writing

Second, she was concerned that in reading the piece in a shared or independent way, the children might rely on their memory of Tacky's song and give little attention to the print, especially when presented with such a large amount of it. Jennifer worried that some children might assume that reading is reciting from memory rather than matching oral language to print.

Ultimately, however, Jennifer followed the children's lead as the composers of the piece and switched from an interactive writing lesson to shared writing to make this particular speech bubble. In the process, she took the opportunity to show children how to use a known word to write an unknown word.

JENNIFER: *Just* starts with the letter *j*, just like my name. Listen: *Jennifer. Just.* It starts with a *j*.

USING A DIRECT QUOTE FROM THE TEXT

The children chose another direct quote from the book, Rocky's reaction to Tacky's dancing on his back, as the text for the second speech bubble, "Something is tickling my back." Because the sentence was much shorter than the previous composition, Jennifer shifted back to interactive writing and had the children help her construct the message. She asked Ernesto to write the *s* in *because* and the *m* in *something* to help him learn more about hearing and recording sounds in words. She asked Daniel to write the word *is* and Andrew to write *my* to reinforce a known word for each of them.

Finally, the children were ready to present their mural through oral storytelling and story reading. Pairs of children told the story to the class as part of their interactive read-aloud time, pointing to the text where needed. They told the story of *Tacky in Trouble*, but they read the print in the speech bubbles verbatim. Jennifer was glad to note their close attention to print as they read Tacky's song, pointing to each word.

Extending Community Writing Through Writing Workshop

Jennifer's students were so proud of their work as authors and illustrators that they wanted to write their own stories of "Tacky in Trouble." Typically, in Jennifer's writing workshop, students work on personal narratives, but occasionally Jennifer varies the task. In response to the class's enthusiasm, she decided to suspend other writing for a short time and use writing workshop as a time to support them as they each wrote their own Tacky story. This process provided a valuable opportunity for Jennifer to assess students' learning in the following ways:

- Retell a story using oral language, written language, and illustrations
- Write stories with a beginning, a middle, and an end
- Move from oral to written language
- Control the conventions of written language, such as:
  — forming messages using sentences
  — inserting spacing between words
  — hearing and recording sounds in words

Each child's writing provided ample evidence that the child had internalized some of the precise understandings required to meet the academic standards of the state and that he or she was beginning to understand the function of print and the deep structure of stories. Just look at the example in Figure 5-13.

FIGURE 5-13. Steven's Independent Writing

Guiding K-3 Writers to Independence

Conclusion

Several weeks after the class's experience with retelling Tacky's story, Jennifer and I reflected on her unit of study using community writing and a mentor text. She had met her instructional goals. Over a four-week period, these young children had accomplished the following:

- Retold a story using oral language, written language, and illustrations
- Written and illustrated a story with a beginning, a middle, and an end
- Moved from oral to written language
- Gained control over hearing and identifying sounds in words and then representing them with letters
- Used the conventions of written language such as:
  — forming messages using sentences
  — using punctuation
  — inserting space between words
  — demonstrating control over the strategic action of hearing and recording sounds in words

The children had engaged with a mentor text with deep understanding and used it as a foundation for the construction of their own text. Through art, they had expanded their control of the text as well as their ability to take on and use some of its language. Jennifer's knowledge of a continuum of learning is guiding her efforts, and she always takes into account her students' prior knowledge and experience. For these children, talk was the vehicle for learning. Through sharing language, they could expand their repertoires. Finally, Jennifer's unit of study emphasizes the reciprocity of reading and writing. And, all of this learning is facilitated by the integration of community writing with other literacy activities. This was not the only writing experience these young children will need, but it was an excellent beginning.

As Jennifer continues to work with her young literacy learners, they will have many more opportunities to use mentor texts as a basis for community writing. In the process, they will not only learn more about what it means to compose and produce printed texts, but also how it feels to be part of a community of literacy learners. And finally, they will learn about themselves as readers and writers.

Special thanks go to Jennifer Beck, an extraordinary classroom teacher, and Sharon Frost, her literacy coordinator at Mineral Springs Elementary School, for their essential contributions to this chapter.

Suggestions for Professional Development

Share the results of the following activities with your colleagues.

1. Choose a folktale from the bibliography in Appendix E to read to your class. After the children have heard the story several times, have the class illustrate the setting. Next, ask them to retell the story using the illustrations to help sequence the story. Finally, design a series of community writing lessons in which the children write the folktale in their own words. With your colleagues, discuss what the children have learned as writers and what you learned about using community writing to teach for a writing process.

2. Make an audio recording or a videotape of a community writing lesson with your students. Listen to or watch the tape to find two or three examples of instructional conversations in which you used explicit language to clarify a concept or to teach for a strategic action or skill. Share your examples with your colleagues and discuss the importance of clear, explicit language in teaching writers.

3. Incorporate community writing into your social studies or science lessons. For example, you could write down a hypothesis for an experiment, develop a time line, or write a brief biography. Share what your class has done with your colleagues and reflect on the value of incorporating community writing into content area teaching. For example, how does community writing help to teach children about writing in a variety of genres? Why? ✦

CHAPTER 6

Becoming a Writer by Noticing the World

by Marsha Levering

When thinking about ways to support young writers, consider what is important and interesting to them in their daily lives. All students have unique experiences that impact their view of the world and serve as great writing material. But in order to become writers about that world, students need guidance in choosing ideas and topics. They wonder and talk about events that happen, and they sometimes engage in activities related to their surroundings, but often they do not know how to write in response to those events.

How can teachers tap into what students are noticing around them in order to support early writing? How can teachers create opportunities that encourage students to broaden their views, and to notice and record what they observe? How do teachers engage students in talk about their writing that expands what students document and understand?

In this chapter, I discuss how teachers can be models for young writers. I also discuss how we can help young writers become more aware of events around them and learn to talk about and document what they see, hear, and think. As students move through the primary grades and into intermediate grades, increasing opportunities for them to observe, note, and orally share will encourage their exploration into even the simplest events and will support their progress as writers.

Writing as an Adult

When we look into the writing lives of authors, we find that many of them use notebooks for writing and sketching. Writers carry these notebooks with them everywhere, using the notebooks to record things they want to remember or refer to in the future. These collected descriptions of events, details, and ideas often form the basis for stories or poems. James Howe (*Pinky and Rex and the School Play*, 1998) describes how he uses walking as an excuse to daydream (Fountas & Pinnell, 2001). As he walks, he carries a notebook with him in which to jot down thoughts and ideas that might someday turn into a story. Eve Bunting (*Butterfly House*, 1999) also carries a notebook with her wherever she goes, and often writes stories out in it before "writing" them in a more formal sense (Fountas & Pinnell, 2001). Some authors sketch and draw as a way to record their observations and thoughts. They have all discovered that writing comes from objects, places, or events found close by in their everyday lives or in the world at large. Their experiences often form a basis for more extensive writing.

Teachers of writers are most effective when they share genuine experiences and learning with students, and use their personal writing as a model. Teachers who develop a habit of recording ideas, thoughts, or questions in a notebook can share those clear examples with students. They also can demonstrate various ways to record observations, which allows students to be flexible in their own documentation. Verbally sharing what is recorded, and then listening to responses, helps teachers and students think critically about their work. In fact, those responses often influence what that writer does next.

Through the teacher's modeling, students begin to look more closely at their surroundings and convey to others what they notice, wonder, and think about. Teachers often talk about what they see happening in the nearby world, and show students how to be observant. When teachers place a high value on their own recordings, sketches, and thoughts, the teacher can be a writer in the minds of students. In turn, when students see their teachers as writers, they may become interested in the process. And when they are encouraged to use their surroundings as writing material, they become free to notice, explore, and record what occurs around them.

Noticing Our Surroundings

Let's look at how we help students become aware of the world. When we first begin to look closely at what is around us, it is common to focus on those things that are remarkable, interesting, or unusual in some way. As we gather more ways to view our world, we find meaning in previously unnoticed situations. What appears to be a small detail or event suddenly takes on new meaning when we realize how deeply it affects us. A bit of conversation overheard on the sidewalk may trigger a memory so strong we actually relive that moment in our lives. At other times, a nagging question may demand our attention and involve us in research. These incidents are actually writing opportunities.

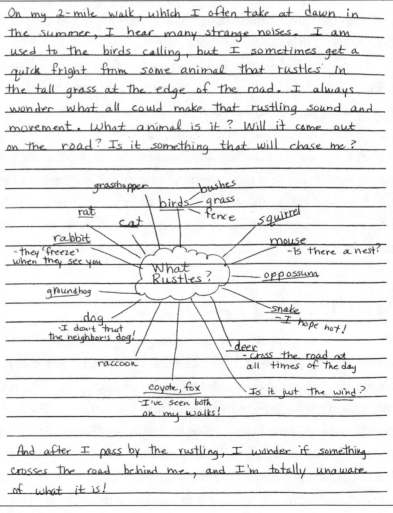

FIGURE 6-1. Example of a Web

When we think of ourselves as writers, we are compelled to get that question, memory, or detail down on paper, then let it guide us toward purposeful work.

This is where a writer's notebook is invaluable, because it can be used to record those things that are important to us. The notebook is a special writing tool that allows us to jot notes, sketch, create webs (see Figure 6-1 for an example of a web), ask questions, and otherwise document our thinking. The following examples from my own writer's notebook are used to model ways of recording events in my environment.

When I jotted Figure 6-1, I was wondering what kinds of animals might startle me as I walked along an overgrown country road. As seen in the web, several possibilities existed, and each label represents actual animals/insects that I saw or crossed paths with at some time during my walks. As a writer, I think about each of the labels, because I am connected to them either through events that have already taken place on my walks or by questions that I want to have answered. At any time, I can choose one of those labels from the web (for instance, the neighbor's dog), place the single word or phrase on another page of the notebook, and begin to write about it, communicating my thoughts, my past experiences, or my questions about it to a reader. I might write a poem, a personal narrative, or even a persuasive letter to a neighbor, asking him to keep the dog on his own property.

In another notebook entry (Figure 6-2), I wrote about releasing a newly emerged monarch butterfly while a class of third graders looks on. I described what it feels like to be there in that moment, experiencing a rare interaction with nature. The image raised all sorts of questions that I could investigate at some time in a nonfiction writing project. How do the butterflies know where and when to migrate in order to avoid a killing winter? How can their frail bodies and wings support a flight of three-thousand miles? What genetic code enables them to return the following spring to a place close to where they hatched? These questions and many others guided my thinking for writing at a later time.

Sharing such examples with students helps

FIGURE 6-2. Butterfly Notebook Entry

them begin to record their own ideas. Giving them a chance to discuss those ideas allows them to expand and clarify their thinking even more. Speaking and listening are crucial for rehearsing our lives as writers. Notes, lists, stories, poems, webs, menus, interviews, and a host of other recordings are perfectly suited for discussion. Successfully explaining to another person why an event is noticed and documented requires clear and concise thinking and language, and talking about what is written can help us see the importance of the recording through more focused attention.

For example, during writing share time a student read about the main events of his baseball game which had been played on the previous day. Although there was nothing unusual about the event, the students who were listening asked a few questions. One of the questions was about which family members were there to watch the boy's game. The student suddenly became quite animated and quickly shared that his grandfather, who rarely got to attend his games, was there to see him hit a double. Afterward, the grandfather took him to get ice cream, and they talked about the game in detail. With the teacher's input, the student was able to see that the game's events were only superficially important; it was the grandfather's presence and attention that were clearly more significant. If the student had not had an opportunity in which to talk with others, he might have missed the chance to deepen and expand the meaning behind what he wrote.

For some students, recording thoughts by sketching is a precursor to writing. More hesitant writers may find it easier to begin writing if they have sketches to use for recollection and inspiration. A sketch does not need to be elaborate; it needs to provide only enough detail to help reconnect it to a significant event or memory. A sketch provides an opportunity for students to represent an image or idea and to talk with others about what it means. Such talk may prompt writers to add another segment to the sketch or to extend certain details to broaden the writer's or listeners' understanding of the drawing. Students build up to the process of actual writing through the prewriting actions of drawing, talking, and revising their thoughts; once these action are taken, students are then prepared to put words to paper that more closely convey the message they want to communicate to others.

How do we support young writers so that when they reach third grade, they are prepared to develop their writing by observing the world and by using a writer's notebook? Let's begin in the primary grades and see what kinds of support are needed.

What Happens in Kindergarten and First Grade?

Young children are quite curious about what happens around them—just think of the questions they ask adults! Natural, everyday activities tap the curiosity of kindergartners and first graders, and give them much to talk about. Even a simple event such as recess gives them an opportunity to interact with the people and things around them. Take young students on nature walks, do simple experiments with them, and provide them with trips to the pumpkin farm and petting zoo. These activities give students experiences to notice and discuss. Talk with students about what they see, hear, smell, taste, and feel. Encourage them to make connections between what is happening now and something they have experienced before. Help them to hear and comment on what classmates have to say. The talk that surrounds what young children do and observe provides them with oral language structure, which lays the foundation for written language structure. The more they engage in discussion, the easier the transition into creating messages in writing.

Sketching and labeling also play important roles in helping students develop into young writers. When students draw or sketch what they observe, they recapture a moment. Associated with that moment are unique feelings, questions, and emotions that students can then start to notice. Thus, sketching helps students begin a process of thinking and talking about what happens in their lives. Labeling the event through recording letter sounds in words, short phrases, or sentences helps students formulate their thinking in written style.

What Happens in Second Grade?

Second graders continue to notice, talk, sketch, and write in response to what is happening around them, but with expanding sophistication. Their thinking is deeper and more complex. They have greater writing fluency, which allows them to be flexible in the ways they respond and more thorough in conveying a message. Supported by demonstrations and encouragement, they behave as writers, especially when there is a relaxed atmosphere that fosters genuine curiosity and interaction with one's surroundings.

In a visit to a second-grade classroom, I asked students to sketch or draw a favorite room in their houses. They shared their work in small groups, often adding to their drawings as other students suggested ideas through questions and comments. Then, I shared a mentor text to help students engage more deeply in thinking about their homes. Students listened to *Let's Go Home: The Wonderful Things About a House* (Rylant, 2002) in which the author (Cynthia Rylant) and illustrator (Wendy Anderson Halperin) combined their talents to identify the significant features of our homes. The book's rich text and meaningful illustrations established a strong sense of the importance of home life. After listening to this story, students added details to their sketches based on the book's text and pictures and then shared their revised sketches with other students.

When the students shared their pictures with the class, they talked about their reasons for adding to their sketches, which included being prompted by the language and illustrations in the mentor text, as well as by classmates' questions and comments about their sketch. They also gained ideas from listening to other students explaining their drawings; this sometimes caused them to recall something important they wanted to add to their own sketches. (See Jackie's finished

FIGURE 6-3. Jackie's Finished Sketch

sketch in Figure 6-3.) One student, Jackie, made a first drawing that included her bed, drawers, beanbag chair, basket, and closet. As she talked and listened to other students, she went back and added a rug and a hamper, as well as adding items to the drawers. Her thinking and representation of her room were expanded as she interacted with her peers. Jackie and the other students were also able to tell stories about the items in their room—where they came from and what was special about them. This drawing and oral sharing can be the foundation for later writing; the sketches and drawings might also be compiled into a class book, arranged on a bulletin board, or shared with parents.

On another day, I helped second graders examine several types of seeds. Using another mentor text, *Seeds* (Robbins, 2005), I set the stage for observation and inquiry by first asking students to listen as I read the book and to study the photographs of the different seeds. We discussed characteristics of seeds— their size, shape, color, and texture. Next, I gave each student two types of seeds: milkweed and burr (stick-tights). The students examined the seeds and recorded observations and questions about them. Finally, we discussed various modes of transportation of seeds. Based on their previous experiences, the new ideas gained from the mentor text, and their own observations, students recorded descriptions and their own questions about these seeds.

In Figure 6-4, a student named Ryann clearly noted characteristics of a seed such as pointy, oval-shaped, sticky, prickly, brown or black, and little. She told how the seed might be transported—by machine, people, wind, or sticking to animals. She also wondered how the seed grew, how it stuck to a place where it could grow, and what part of the world it was first found in. With this information, Ryann was prepared to write a factual piece, a fictional tale, or even a poem about the seed. And, her questions could lead to further investigation about seeds and plants.

What occurred with Ryann also occurred with other second graders (see Figure 6-5 for an additional second-grade example). As students discussed their observations with classmates, new understandings surfaced and additional questions appeared. The students began to connect facts they already knew about seeds and to wonder more deeply about them. These second graders were anxious to share

FIGURE 6-4. Ryann's Notes

Guiding K-3 Writers to Independence

their discoveries with parents and planned to look for more seeds in places near their homes. Thus, they grew interested in the natural world because of a simple, unhurried opportunity to explore it. With further teacher support, students might find and write answers to their questions; compare and contrast new seeds; look more deeply into how seeds are transported; or discuss how seeds influence our lives. Any of these activities would further catch the attention of young minds as they figure out the world they live in. These processes give students a chance to behave as budding scientists and to respond in writing to something that has become significant to them.

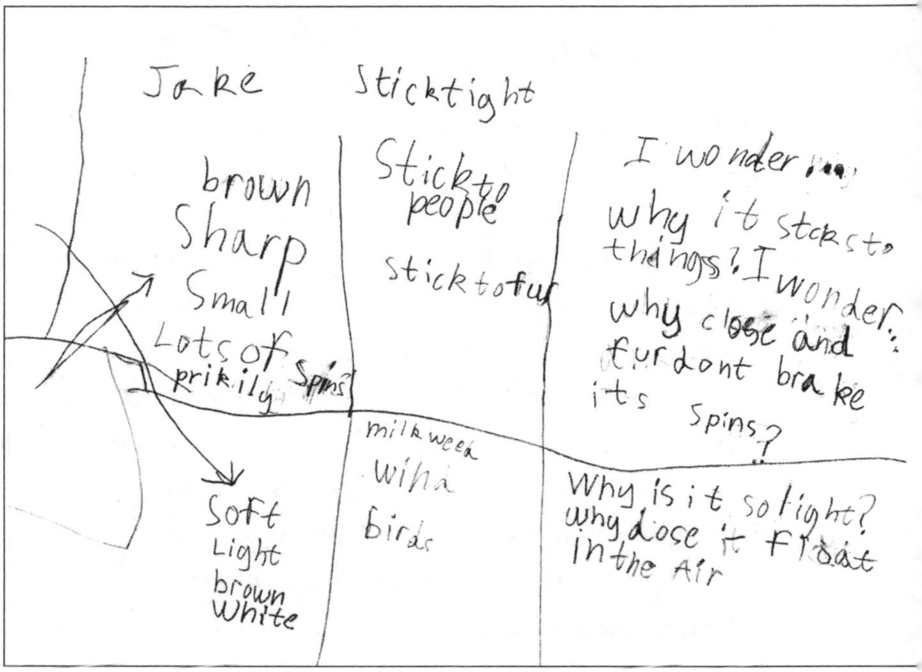

FIGURE 6-5. Additional Second-Grade Example

Extensions in Primary Grades

What makes these shared classroom events and recordings more meaningful? As mentioned earlier, teachers might collect students' observations, sketches, questions, and ideas for classroom sharing into a class book; these items might also be kept in student portfolios. (In either form, the students can revisit and revise the work over time.) These items also can be shared with other classmates and parents at suitable times, and can become a basis for written pieces when students are given a choice of writing topics. Class books contain work that students revisit over time. Displays of students' work invite passersby to comment and ask questions that can be recorded on a special board by the display and then shared with the class. Students also could begin at-home collections of items that interest them; such collections allow students to categorize, sort, and organize the items in them.

Second graders also enjoy using a Think Book (Fountas & Pinnell, 2001). A Think Book is a spiral notebook used at specified times throughout the school day for recording such things as charts and observations about experiments, responses to read-alouds, lists, sketches, ideas for future writing pieces, or informational notes from content areas. This book is a special item that should be used only when teachers want students to record something in written form. The Think Book helps second graders organize their thinking through writing and helps them become familiar with the use of notebooks and journals. It also prepares them for a writing tool that will be introduced to them in third grade: a writer's notebook.

Transitioning Into Third Grade: Using a Writer's Notebook

For students in third through sixth grades, a writer's notebook is useful for storing thoughts and ideas (called "seeds") for future writing projects. Seeds come from all aspects of our lives, at any time and from any setting. Stored seeds are writing possibilities: They can take the form of charts and observations, questions and wonderings, memories, lists, drawings, special words and phrases, webs, interests, and feelings. They can be artifacts, such as photographs, invitations, bulletins, notes, and ticket stubs. Natural artifacts might be leaves, seeds, plants, flowers, grasses, feathers, insect shells, abandoned nests, and so on. These seeds are found not only in special events, but in everyday occurrences, when we are aware of the world around us.

For third graders and beyond, the writer's notebook becomes a collection place for observations, writing, and sketching. If students create lists or webs, it is helpful to have them extend the entry through a "short write"—a few sentences or even a paragraph that extends the initial single idea. For example, in Figure 6-1, I created a web of possible creatures that might make a rustling sound in the grass along the road. I would create a short write by lifting one of the ideas from my web, such as the coyote, and writing about that animal:

> "He is sneaky, slinky, and oh-so-silent! Once, I heard a faint rustle in that tall grass, not down toward the ground, but higher, more at waist level. I didn't even turn my head and look. It felt safer to pick up my pace and get far ahead of that spot. When I finally dared to turn around, there he was, trotting across the road behind me like he owned it. I wonder why he is living so close to my house. I wonder what would happen if we met face to face."

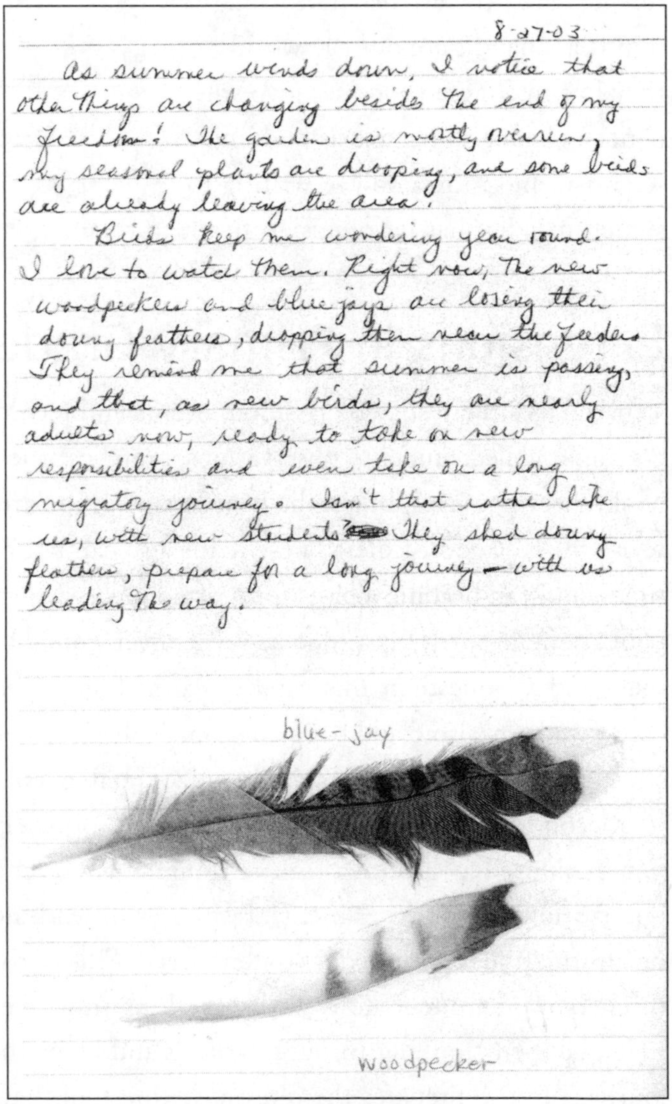

A short write simply holds and records the main points or thoughts the author is considering at that moment. It might become a more complex writing project and could fit a number of writing genres such as personal narrative, nonfiction, investigation, poetry, or persuasive writing.

Similarly, if an entry includes an artifact, observation, or sketch, students might document the reason for the entry and add a few descriptive phrases or details. Figure 6-6 shows actual feathers

FIGURE 6-6. Notebook Page With Feathers

taped onto a notebook page and the author's thinking at that time. When such seeds and artifacts are placed in a writer's notebook and surrounded by bits of text, they may later trigger memories, sketches, poetry, questions, and research. Completing a bit of writing around an entry allows the writer to return to it at a later date, reconnect to the original motivation behind it, and delve more deeply into the entry as a writing project.

Samantha was beginning third grade when she used her writer's notebook to sketch and label ways she could help someone who is sick (Figure 6-7). Later in the year, that page prompted Samantha to produce this narrative about what her mother means to her (Figure 6-8). It is obvious from the piece that Samantha is communicating a message to an audience: the importance of her mother in her life, and the warmth and compassion the mother exhibits toward her daughter. Through the recording of ideas and thoughts in her notebook, Samantha had at her fingertips a seed that expanded into a writing project. Her notebook proved to be a useful tool in influencing her decisions for the written piece.

Over time, a writer's notebook becomes a treasured collection of writing possibilities—a collection that is revisited for writing projects, and that is replenished frequently by the events of our lives. When third graders are given earlier support as writers through talking, listening, and recording their ideas and observations, they are quite successful in building up a notebook that generates further writing. Accumulating meaningful entries in the notebook ensures choice, interest, and motivation for writing.

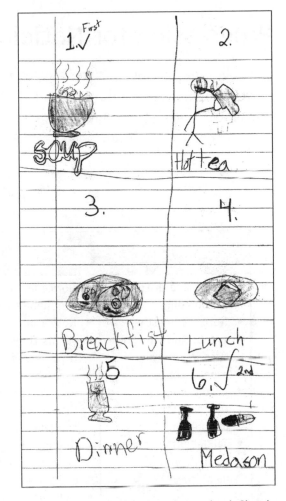

FIGURE 6-7. Samantha's Writer's Notebook Sketch

> My mom always helps me when I'm sick. She makes me tea and lets me lay in her bed. It's so soft I fall asleep.
>
> If I'm sick a day and the class learned something new my mom would help me understand. When the class learned times five my mom helped me understand.
>
> When I'm at school she sleeps alot. She watches tv for one or two minutes but the next she's asleep. She tells my dad that she's going to take a short nap but she sleeps for two hours.
>
> My mom will always love me no matter what because I love her. How I know she loves me is she helps me when I'm sick and helps me understand. Another way I know she loves me is she hugs me with both arms and makes me feel safe.

FIGURE 6-8. Samantha's Narrative

Progression for Noticing and Writing About the World

The following chart summarizes the progression for noticing and writing about the world as students move from kindergarten through grade 3. At all grade levels, discussion and oral sharing are necessary elements in preparing for future writing.

Writing About the World K–3

Kindergarten	First Grade	Second Grade	Third Grade
• Notice and discuss surroundings • Notice interesting events through short trips, recess, and experiments • Record ideas and thoughts through pictures and labels • Talk about events and what they have recorded	• Notice and discuss surroundings • Notice interesting events through short trips, recess, and experiments • Record ideas and thoughts in pictures and labels, and through short phrases or sentences that explain and describe • Talk about events and what students have recorded; begin to make changes based on read-alouds, peer comments, and teacher scaffolding of self-reflection	• Notice and discuss surroundings • Observe nature and experiments, attend field trips • Use a Think Book to record observations, words and phrases, lists, notes and questions from content, responses to read-alouds, sketches, charts, or experiments • Orally share recordings; make changes/additions based on interactions with others, and on deeper reflection of what is written	• Notice and discuss surroundings • Observe nature, objects, experiments, and events close at hand; visit parks, museums, and other places of interest; discover what interests you • Use a writer's notebook to record ideas, memories, feelings, interests, and questions in many forms: webs, lists, sketches, facts, wonderings, interviews, how-tos, poetry, narratives, descriptions, comparisons, etc. • Include writings about artifacts, such as special objects and photographs • Orally share recordings; make changes/additions based on interactions with others, and on deeper reflection of what is written

FIGURE 6-9. K–3 Progression Chart

What Teachers Can Do

We have seen the importance of supporting early writers in their attempts to describe what happens in the world around them. Through listening, speaking, writing, and drawing, primary students revise and expand upon those early attempts. Introducing second graders to a Think Book offers students a more formal way to compose and record their thoughts. Through modeling, third-grade students are made aware of writing possibilities that stem from a writer's notebook. Teach them to use the notebook outside of school time, for documenting happenings inside and outside, at home and in the greater community and world. Once students create a special place for documenting, questioning, and exploring events in their lives, they learn to lift pieces out to develop into writing projects. All of these things happen because teachers take action with a specific purpose in mind—to link students to the world around them and provide valuable writing opportunities.

If you are committed to being an effective teacher of writers, keep these few suggestions in mind:

- Become a writer yourself!
- Demonstrate enthusiasm for using Think Books and writer's notebooks
- Create an environment that fosters the natural curiosity of students—bring the world to their attention through observation and experiences
- Help them look below an unremarkable surface to see what is truly significant
- Find the gems that spark imagination and then demonstrate and encourage authentic expression through writing

Teachers of writers give students chances to explore, record, and respond to happenings around them. They value what students say and write, then enjoy watching them turn into authors. The writing world is open and waiting!

Suggestions for Professional Development

1. Acquire a writer's notebook by purchasing a notebook, or using a notebook you already have. For two weeks, make daily, dated entries about events you observe, overhear, or participate in, in your everyday life. Challenge yourself to use a variety of entry forms: webs, narrative, poetry, charts, sketches, and so on. After two weeks, review your notebook. Are there entries with similar topics/thoughts? These may indicate a natural area of interest. Are you strongly attracted to one or more entries? If so, they might be significant to you in some way. Is there something you want to investigate further? If so, jot some questions about that topic.

   Share with colleagues your thoughts on using the writer's notebook. Discuss how you decided what events to record, what the entries reveal about you as a person and a potential writer, and what you might consider turning into a writing project. Talk about how the use of a writer's notebook initiates the writing process for students.

2. Working with several teachers, ask them to make a sketch of their respective neighborhoods. Then, have the teachers pair up to share their sketches and make individual lists of the memories that surfaced during the sketching and sharing. Have teachers draw stars by three of the ideas that could easily be written about and choose one of them to expand into a short write. Share your idea and writing with your partner. Discuss potential writing projects that could stem from the memories (narrative, persuasive piece, letter, poetry, research, and so on.). As a whole group, discuss writing process insights gained from this experience. Talk about whether this activity could be used in the classroom. (K–1 teachers might expect students to share orally or label their sketches rather than complete short writes.)

3. Choose one of the activities presented in the chapter (appropriate to your grade level) and complete it with students. If suitable, expand the activity to a writing project. Share some interesting highlights, results, and thoughts with colleagues. Reflect on what this activity tells you about students and the writing process.

CHAPTER 7

"Revising" Our Approach to Writing Workshop

by Kecia Hicks

Chances are that writing instruction for your kindergarten and first-, second-, and third-grade students looks nothing like the writing instruction you received when you were in those grades as a student. When I was a student in elementary school during the seventies, writing instruction consisted of handwriting lessons, isolated worksheets on grammar and punctuation, and a weekly spelling test. Never, to my recollection, was I able to put these skills to use in a meaningful context, to express my own thoughts and ideas, or share stories and anecdotes from my life through writing. Today, in contrast, many students are fortunate to be members of a community of writers within their classroom. Daily writing workshops are being facilitated by these classroom teachers who are encouraging students to share experiences from their lives and express their thoughts on the world through the written word. It is within this instructional context that students are able to orchestrate all of the traditional item knowledge of writing, such as spelling, punctuation, and grammar, as they share meaningful experiences from their lives.

It is exciting that such a paradigm shift has occurred in the field of writing instruction, as it certainly makes sense to us now that we learn to write by actually writing continuous, meaningful text. Those who have incorporated the writing workshop format into their classroom are seeing children write more than they ever have done in previous years. They are hearing students' writing voices emerge in their pieces as they write about things that matter to them. The students are supported in their efforts through daily mini-lessons, individual conferring, and community sharing.

Learning to Think as a Writer

Just having the structure of a writing workshop in place, however, is not enough to develop writers. Yes, students are writing more in terms of quantity. Yes, students enjoy participating in a writing workshop. But, teachers have to take a critical look at the instruction that is taking place within the writing workshop and determine whether or not it is truly meeting the needs of the writer. The key question we as need to ask is, "How are we teaching our students to think as writers?" Teachers with writing workshops in their classrooms need to determine whether or not students are growing as writers and independently taking on the multitude of decisions writers must make when composing a piece. Alternatively, are we as teachers doing all of the thinking by suggesting how students might fix their pieces and consequently the students are just going through the motions and follow what Calkins and Bleichman (2003) have called "our marching orders"?

A few years ago, I found myself struggling to plan a mini-lesson that would help my students grow as writers. My implementation of the writing workshop seemed to be faltering. I was teaching my students everything I had learned about good writing but providing the information as isolated pieces. One day we would work on crafting inviting leads; on another we might think about using exciting words. But—being brutally honest with myself—I began to wonder whether my students thought of these mini-lessons as the "hoop of the day." They would "perform" and do what I suggested, but were not taking on this thinking on their own. They were reliant upon my prompting, and many never incorporated this thinking across writing pieces. I talked with other teachers who were experiencing the same difficulties. Though my students enjoyed writing workshop, I was not enjoying it much because I was the one running around the room composing and fixing 25 pieces at once. A shift was needed. I knew that I needed to teach the writer, not be the one who was fixing their writing (Calkins, 1994). I was not ready to abandon the writing workshop; I knew that within that setting there was a way to help students accept the responsibility of using what they know about what makes great writing and instill in them the drive to diligently work to accomplish this feat.

I came across important insights about this common struggle of writing workshop implementation by accident. I found myself with the task of writing a KEEP BOOK, a little paperback book for young readers published by the Ohio State University. This project was good for me because it required me to sit down and actually write my story, *Garden Giant* (Hicks, 2006), as seen in Figure 7-1. As I wrote and reread my writing, a question occurred and kept reoccurring in my mind throughout the process: "How can I make this piece of writing even better for my readers?" As I tried to revise my work, I realized that this is really what writers do. They are continually asking themselves this very question and spending significant time on a mission to "re-see" what it is that they wrote and to think about how they can change it to better communicate their message to their reading audience.

FIGURE 7-1. Fact & Fiction KEEP BOOKS, *Garden Giant* and *A Sunflower Plant Life Cycle*

It dawned on me during my own writing experience that I needed to teach students how to engage in this pursuit of clarity for their readers in their own writing. I would need to help students realize that writing is hard work, that writers are never satisfied with the first thing they write on paper, and that they search for ways to improve their writing. Until my epiphany, I knew revision was a step in the writing process, but I did not realize that it must be the centerpiece of my instruction within the writing workshop. It needed to be given more weight instructionally than anything else within the writing workshop. I realized that I needed to begin to notice if, when, and in what ways my students were engaging in the self-questioning of "What can I do to my writing to make it better?" Furthermore, if some students were not working toward changes in their writing or drafting, or if they were relying on me to do it for them, then I knew I needed to teach them how. Revising is the heart of the writing process. If students are moving through the process without asking, "What can I do to make my writing better?" then our instruction is doing them a disservice. Effective teaching of writing workshop means teaching for revising.

What Is Revision?

When writers engage in revision, they make minor or significant changes—adding or deleting material, changing the order of the material, adding details for greater clarity or sensory appeal. Writers revise to make meaning clearer to the audience. Revision is a continuous part of the writing process. It occurs when a writer pauses a moment and rereads his or her piece; as a result of this rereading, changes may be made to the writing to improve it.

Revisions are done not for the sake of making changes, but in service to meaning-making for the reader. Editing also involves changes that a writer makes to his or her writing, such as fixing spelling errors, checking for grammar and punctuation, or making changes to enhance clarity.

Teaching Our Writers to Reread and "Re-See" Their Writing

To help our young students learn to revise their writing, we can ask a very simple question—what would make this writing better for the reader? The first step is to encourage students to reread their work frequently. Rereading can take place during the process of writing a draft as well as after it is finished. Rereading a piece multiple times helps young writers "re-see" their work or explore different ways of stating their ideas. When writers reread their work, they are taking on the role of the reader, which is who they are writing for in the first place. It is often the simple act of rereading that prompts students to make changes to their writing on their own.

Pam Warren teaches her third-grade students that once they go back and reread their writing, they probably will find ways to alter it to make it better. Below, Pam shows in a mini-lesson that rereading often results in a writer adding to, taking away from, and/or changing the order of the way something was written.

PAM: During yesterday's writing workshop it was really exciting to see all of the stories from your lives that you are choosing to write and share with your readers. Your readers are going to be so interested to read these. Today, a lot of you may get to the end of the story you are telling and will feel that you are done with your writing piece. However, it is very important to know that writers are never satisfied with the very first draft of their story. They know there are ways they can make some changes to their writing to make it better. They know this because they reread their piece and find places in their writing where they can add new ideas, or take away some things that just don't fit. Let me show you what I mean by this.

Pam conferring with Dustin.

(Pam shares a first draft she has written about her recent trip to Italy.)

PAM: I finished writing this piece last night about my recent trip to Italy. However, I know that as a writer I shouldn't just quit here. There are probably some things I can do, some revisions I can do to make my writing even better. I'm going to reread to find out.

(Pam models rereading her piece aloud to her students. As she rereads, she thinks aloud about ways that she can change her writing to make it better.)

PAM: Oh, look here. I'm talking about the pizza I had at lunch. This seems like it doesn't really go with the rest of the story I'm telling about the tour of the Coliseum. I'm going to take out the pizza part. Maybe I can use it for a different piece of writing later . . . and here, at this spot where I'm telling about the guard outside the Coliseum, I'm going to add more detail because that's what I really want to get across to my reader, the very interesting people I met in Rome. Maybe I could add, "He wore black armor and a helmet. His cape was bright red and could easily be seen from across the street. He definitely caught my attention."

(Pam reinforces the mini-lesson with the chart in Figure 7-2 for students to refer to: Writers are not satisfied with their first draft because they know they could make changes to it to make it better for their readers. They do this by rereading their piece and finding places where they can add details, take away information that's not important to their story, or change the order that something is written.)

> Writers are not satisfied with their first draft, because they know they could make changes to it to make it better for their readers. They do this by rereading their piece and finding places where they can add details, take away information that's not important to their story, or change the order that something is written.

FIGURE 7-2. Pam's Mini-lesson Chart

Guiding K-3 Writers to Independence

PAM: Today, writers, when you finish your first draft, I want you to realize that your work is not yet done. You will need to reread your writing to see what changes you can make that will make your writing better.

(Students from Pam's class then get the opportunity to apply what Pam has taught them. As Pam sits down to conference with Dustin, Pam is mindful that she is teaching the writer, not the writing.)

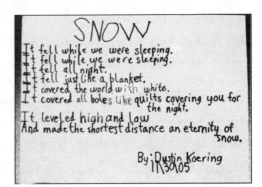

FIGURE 7-3. Dustin's Writing of *Snow*

PAM: Hi, Dustin. What are you doing as a writer today?

DUSTIN: I'm writing a poem about the snow that fell last week.

PAM: Wow! Lots of writers choose to write about nature. That's going to be an interesting poem for your reader. Why did you choose to write about that?

DUSTIN: Because the snow was pretty.

PAM: It was pretty; I agree. It looks like you are about finished with your first draft, so why don't you reread your piece aloud and see whether there are any ways to make your poem even better.

(Dustin begins rereading his poem in Figure 7-3. When he finishes rereading it, Dustin pauses and then rereads the poem again.)

PAM: I noticed that you reread your poem twice. What are you thinking right now?

DUSTIN: I don't think the last two lines match the rest of the poem.

PAM: Tell me more . . . .

DUSTIN: Well, the rest of the poem is like . . . soft, and the last two lines are fun. They could almost be another poem. I think I'm going to cross them out.

PAM: I really like how rereading your writing helped you to re-see your piece with readers' eyes. You made a good revision choice by taking away information from your writing. You wanted your readers to feel a particular way when they read your poem and the last two lines didn't fit. Keep reading through your piece and see if there are any other changes you want to make. Maybe you could share some of your decisions as a writer with the rest of the class during sharing.

DUSTIN: Okay.

Pam praised Dustin for his rereading and reinforced Dustin's move to revision. As a result, Dustin learned that writers reread their writing, which is something he can take on across the pieces that he will write in the future. Dustin learned that writers sometimes will take away unnecessary information as a result of their rereading in an attempt to make their writing better. Pam provides us with a clear example of how we can teach, prompt, and praise for the decision making of writers, not the product.

At the conclusion of that day's writing workshop, Pam reemphasizes her mini-lesson by having students share what changes they made to their writing as a result of rereading their pieces.

PAM: As I was walking around and talking with some writers today, I noticed a lot of rereading going on. And, because of that rereading, a lot of writers were making some changes to their writing. Who would like to share a change they made today to their writing to make it better?

As students shared, Pam emphasized that rereading helped to initiate the changes. She reinforced that writers may want to add to, omit from, or rearrange the sequence of their writing as a result of their rereading. She praised their changes, because she needs the students to understand that writers are not satisfied with the first thing they write and that they always make an attempt to envision and try out new possibilities to make their writing better. This is why it is so important that children select what they write about. We want them to be passionate about their topic and willing to spend the energy necessary to make their writing the best that they can. If the topic is selected by the student, the topic becomes meaningful and relevant to that student.

This example shows how Pam initiated revising within her writing workshop. She is teaching the students to expect and celebrate change in their writing, and that writers rarely, if ever, are satisfied with the first thing they write. Once Pam finds that her students are taking on the act of revision, she will begin to give students various and more sophisticated ways to think about revision.

Teaching Specific Ways to Revise a Piece

Let's look at another example, again from grade 3, but with a more experienced group of students. Through careful observation, teacher Karen Green knows that her third-grade class is already comfortable with the notion of drafting and making changes to their writing, as she taught lessons similar to those that Pam did earlier in the year. Karen knows that revision is the heart of the writing process and that her students are beginning to ask themselves independently "How can I make it better?" She realizes that it is her responsibility as a facilitator of the writing workshop to expose her students to the crafting moves writers make to help improve their writing. She needs to help her students recognize when and why a writer chooses to make a particular change to their writing.

For the past week, Karen has been helping her students become aware of how writers slow down and speed up time in their writing, and when it is effective to incorporate such a "writerly" move. In previous days, she has shown this to her students by sharing examples from children's literature and her own writing. She has found that by staying with a particular idea over consecutive days, students are more apt to internalize when and why a writer might incorporate the move in their writing.

Karen teaching a mini-lesson during her class's writing workshop.

Guiding K-3 Writers to Independence

The following is a mini-lesson that Karen taught during one of her class's writing workshop:

KAREN: This week we have been talking about how writers use the element of time to make their stories more interesting. For example, in *Sister Anne's Hands* (1998), Marybeth Lorbiecki slows down her story at the point where someone throws a paper airplane. Why do you think she did that?

SAM: She wanted us to know how the students were feeling and how Sister Anne felt when she read the note.

SUZANNE: Yeah, she wanted us to wonder if the students would be in trouble.

KAREN: So, by slowing down the story, Marybeth Lorbiecki got you to really stop and think about what was important.

TOMMY: I tried that when I first wrote my story about our camping trip I just wrote a little bit about how the raccoon took the food off of the picnic table. When I reread it, I thought the reader would think it was kind of boring. So I went back and wrote more about that part.

KAREN: How did you slow the story down?

TOMMY: I wrote more about the raccoon. Like how you could see the little black hand come up and over the picnic table. How it snatched the bag of marshmallows and ran up the tree and ate the marshmallows right in front of us.

KAREN: Just like Marybeth Lorbiecki did, you slowed that part down because it was so important to your story. She slowed down the time on the most significant day. She even slowed it down at a specific time of the day, during lunch. She wrote four pages on lunch, yet the rest of the year took only two sentences. Why would a writer make a decision to speed up a story?

SUZANNE: Maybe to skip through the parts that are not as important. Like in my story about when we moved here from Florida. The reader didn't need to know about loading the truck or the move. I just wanted them to know how hard it was to leave my friends on the base, and that even though I was scared I made new friends.

KAREN: So, what we have discovered is that, whether it is to get the reader to stop and think about something important or to add tension, writers use time intentionally.

Karen's instructional aim with this mini-lesson, and all of her other mini-lessons on revision, is to add to the students' repertoire, or "toolbox" (Heard, 2002). She encourages students to try speeding up or slowing down their stories when it makes sense for them to do this and when they feel it will help them with their goal of making their writing clear for their reader. She does not present this as something they must do or incorporate in their writing that very day, because she understands that this remains a decision of the writer, and that all craft moves do not necessarily fit all writing pieces.

A single mini-lesson cannot fit the needs of all 25 pieces being composed at any given time during the writing workshop. Karen can teach for revision only by showing the students how to do something and reminding them that these writerly moves exist. She understands that if she insists that students make specific changes to their pieces, students likely will become passive about their writing and allow her to do all of the thinking and decision-making. Her role, instead, is to expose students to a variety of writing actions and encourage students to become critical of their writing and help them determine ways to best state their message.

The stance Karen takes in her writing workshop helps develop writers as thinkers—the ultimate goal of instruction. Karen knows that some of her students' decisions might not actually make the specific piece of writing better; but she values the process. It is the act of revision across many pieces of writing that will help build her students' expertise as writers.

When to Start Teaching for Revising? As Soon as They Start Writing

Though both teaching examples in this chapter are from third-grade classrooms, the concept of revision also has a place within kindergarten, first-, and second-grade classrooms. Once students learn to construct a simple message, even one sentence, they should be taught to go back and reread their message. That rereading may encourage a related thought, and the student might add another sentence or two to the existing message, especially if such behavior is being modeled in the supportive instructional contexts of shared writing and interactive writing. Furthermore, the act of rereading in the earlier grades helps students sustain their writing across days.

Many teachers of emergent writers (kindergarten or early grade 1, like Peggy Kvam) encourage rereading and revision by giving their students one sheet of blank copy paper to construct a meaningful message of their choice. Peggy then collects the papers at the end of writing workshop and returns them to the students the next day, along with an additional sheet of blank paper if the student chooses to reread and add to or elaborate on the previous day's message (see Figure 7-4). This process might continue for several days. Choosing to reread and add to existing writing is a writerly move, albeit one in its infancy, and teachers of young children can praise such a decision. These early writers are experiencing the power of rereading and are adding detail to make their writing better for their reading audiences.

Another popular way to promote revision, regardless of grade level, is the use of "spider legs," strips of paper with written additions that can be attached to any part of the draft, wherever the writer feels that more information or detail is needed. Students are encouraged to make such revisions by the presence of the spider legs. Though simple, this exercise promotes the act of rereading and adding to a piece.

Teachers of young writers can teach for the rereading of text during the instructional contexts of shared and interactive writing. Questions such as "What might be another way we could say this?" or "Is there anything we'd like to change?" help students naturally internalize this thinking for when they independently write. How powerful it would be for teachers to revisit a piece of community writing and ask, "How might we change this to make it better?"

Understanding that revising is the heart of the writing process is important for teachers and students. As teachers, we must help our students develop the willingness and intrinsic desire to make changes to their

Guiding K-3 Writers to Independence

writing in an effort to make it better for their reading audience. We can use the structure of the writing workshop to teach for, prompt, and celebrate the decisions our students make when they change their writing. We must monitor ourselves to make certain that we are not getting bogged down in making a student's written piece perfect, by telling a student how to change his or her piece. As we interact with students, we are mindful that it is the process of the writer's decision-making, more than the final product, that truly develops a writer. This has been, and shall always be, our goal in writing workshop.

FIGURE 7-4. Student Story From Peggy Kvam's Class, Written in Consecutive Writing Workshops

Suggestions for Professional Development

1. With a group of teachers, examine a class set of discovery drafts. As a group, select one "revision idea" (such as crafting strong leads, narrowing, word choice, and so on) that the majority of students might benefit from. Then, develop a minimum of three mini-lessons that could be used to help students take on the art of revision. These mini-lessons could support a specific unit of study on revision.

2. With a partner, examine a student's discovery draft. Take turns role-playing a teacher having an individual conference with a student. Note language that promotes helping students attempt to make their writing better, keeping in mind "process over product." ✦

Section III

Connecting Reading and Writing

"Connecting Reading and Writing" is the focus of this third section. Gay Su Pinnell and Irene Fountas begin this section by describing the range of opportunities students have to write about what they are reading in ways that support their growing abilities as writers. In Chapter 9, Patricia Scharer turns the lens to picture books by exploring how teachers and students can analyze these texts to learn about a writer's craft. The next chapter, by Justina Henry, explores how learning the story structures found in the personal narratives children hear and read can help young writers tell their own stories. This section concludes with a description of a school-home project involving KEEP BOOKS®, inexpensive "little books" designed by educators at the Ohio State University, that children can read in school and take home to keep. In this chapter, John McCarrier and Gay Su Pinnell team to discuss how John's work as a KEEP BOOKS author serves as a model for teachers to share their own writing.

CHAPTER 8

Writing About Reading

by Gay Su Pinnell & Irene C. Fountas

Carole Ross and a small group of first graders were reading the series book *Baby Bear's Present* (Randell, 1994). In this text, a bear family goes shopping to buy a present for Baby Bear. Father Bear *really* wants to get the train (because he actually wants to play with it himself). But Mother Bear convinces him that they should buy what Baby Bear wants—the car that he can drive himself.

Carole introduced the book and then listened as each child read the text with teacher support. Children were each reading aloud softly to themselves, but not in unison and not in turn (as in "round-robin reading"). They read simultaneously, with Carole listening alternately to each. After everyone finished reading *Baby Bear's Present*, she invited discussion.

CAROLE: What did you think about that story?

JOHN: It was funny, really funny.

CAROLE: You thought it was funny. Did anyone else think that?

BRIAN: It was funny because of Father Bear.

JOHN: Yeah, he, he...

CAROLE: He didn't want to get the car and Baby Bear wanted it.

BRIAN: I liked the car. He could drive it.

CAROLE: So, I wonder why Father Bear was acting that way.

BRIAN: He just liked the train.

CAROLE: I guess he thought Baby Bear would like the train just like he did. And it was funny how he just wouldn't even look at anything else.

CAROLE: But I noticed that he changed his mind at the end.

BRIAN: He changed because Mother Bear made him do it.

CAROLE: Maybe he changed because he knew it was Baby Bear's present, not his.

After a little more discussion, the children took out their reading journals to write a short summary of the book. They practiced aloud what they wanted to say—something important about *Baby Bear's Present*. Brian's summary statement is shown in Figure 8-1. John's summary statement is shown in Figure 8-2.

Both children were able to discuss their thinking about *Baby Bear's Present* and then to capture their thoughts in brief statements. In rich classroom environments, talk is always present. Teachers engage students in meaningful talk across many different instructional contexts. The conversation is natural, with the kind of give and take that you would hear among any group of people who enjoy talking together about interesting topics and, of course, about books. But this conversation is *intentional* on the part of the teacher, because he or she is always seeking to help children extend their thinking.

Intentional Conversations

As you engage children in "intentional conversation," you expand their ideas and help them to put their thinking into words. Children learn through talk. Clay (1991) has described oral language as an example of a "self-extending system," that is, one that expands itself as children use it. She writes that literacy should be a natural "follow-on from what they have already learned to do well" (p. 26). Extensive use of oral language is a critical feature in supporting the writing process (Calkins, 1983; 1986). All forms of writing work best within a broader context in which meaningful talk surrounds both direct experiences and engagement with texts (McCarrier, Pinnell, & Fountas, 2000).

FIGURE 8-1. Brian's Summary Statement

FIGURE 8-2. John's Summary Statement

And, extended talk supports children's writing—the higher the quality of talk, the higher the quality of writing. Many of us have had the experience of being "blocked" while creating a piece of writing. But if we discuss our topic with a friend, the ideas seem to flow again. Through intentional talk, you can increase your students' productivity and creativity in writing.

In a rich classroom environment, children have massive engagement with texts in a variety of ways.

- They hear books read aloud and they talk about them. During what we call *interactive read-aloud*, you have many opportunities to engage children in intentional conversation. They can extend their understanding of the literal meaning of the text, but also expand their ability to think beyond the text, bringing background knowledge to further their understanding, making connections to their own lives, and making inferences.

- They read books independently and have opportunity to talk about them with others. Younger children read from "browsing boxes" that the teacher has created. These boxes contain books that children have read during small-group instruction and discussed with others. Each time children reread these beginning books, they extend their understanding of the texts and the ways they are written. As children move into second grade, they begin to independently choose books for reading and often bring them to the "sharing" at the end of reading workshop to talk about them with their classmates.
- They participate in guided reading—small-group instruction that brings together children who can read at approximately the same level. The teacher selects the book and introduces it, and then the children read it. The reading is always followed by discussion and some specific teaching. A great deal of intentional conversation takes place during guided reading, which also gives you the option of supporting students in their writing about reading.

So, children talk and they talk about texts, a situation that can lead naturally to writing about what they are reading. Writing about reading helps children compose, using the kind of precise language they need to express their thinking. Through teaching, you can help them think in different ways about texts and then reconsider their thinking as they engage in writing. In this chapter, we explore "writing about reading," or "writing in response to reading," as a way to help children put their thinking into written form and, in the process, expand their ability to understand some important things about texts. For example, students learn how:

- To select the important information from a text
- To remember information in summary form
- Writers organize information in texts (sequence of events, compare/contrast, description, cause/effect, problem/solution, and others)
- Writers create characters that are memorable because of their attributes

Thinking and Writing About Texts

We begin by describing several ways of thinking about texts and then provide examples of how writing about reading can help young learners express their thinking while it provides evidence of comprehending. There are many genres for writing about reading. In this chapter we focus on three: (1) summarizing; (2) the structure of text (including compare and contrast); and (3) dialogue about texts.

SUMMARIZING

The first examples show young children's attempts at summarizing information from a text that they had read for themselves. Summarizing is deceptively simple; in fact, it involves complex cognitive operations. To summarize, the reader (or listener) must select important information from the text, an operation that involves *evaluation*. The individual must reorganize the information in a statement that reflects something important from the text in a concise manner that encompasses much of the meaning and includes all of the essential ideas but few of the secondary ideas.

After discussion of a later book in the bear series, Brian provided this summary (see Figure 8-3):

In this book, the bear family prepare for being snowed in for the winter. Father Bear brings home an appropriate gift to entertain Baby Bear—the train that he wanted in the previous book!

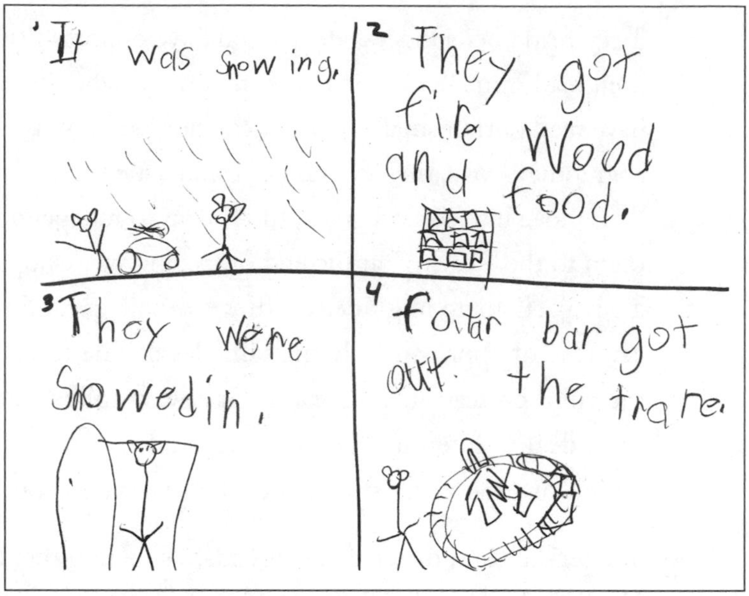

FIGURE 8-3. Summary of *Father Bear's Surprise*

Guided by the teacher, Christian described four important details from the text. It is important to note that the teacher and children first composed this summary as shared writing. That means that they discussed and composed the summary together while the teacher wrote it on a chart. Then, the children wrote their own summaries; they could use the shared piece as a basis for these, but were also free to innovate. Christian also provided this one-sentence summary of *The Pot of Gold* (n.a., 1971) and added a statement expressing his own opinion of that elf (see Figure 8-4).

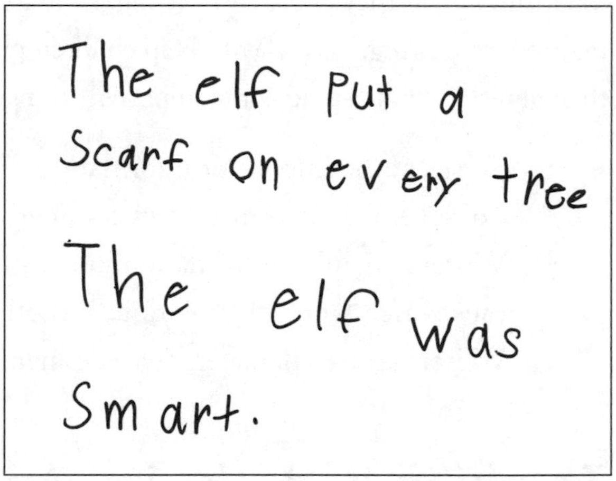
The elf put a Scarf on every tree

The elf was Smart.

FIGURE 8-4. Christian's Opinion Statement

In thinking about another text, Carrie summarized the events in *The Tent in the Yard* (Rollins, 1971), in which two boys decide to camp out in the yard and make a tent. Unfortunately, rain causes a problem, so the boys transfer the tent to the porch. Here is Carrie's summary statement of that story (see Figure 8-5).

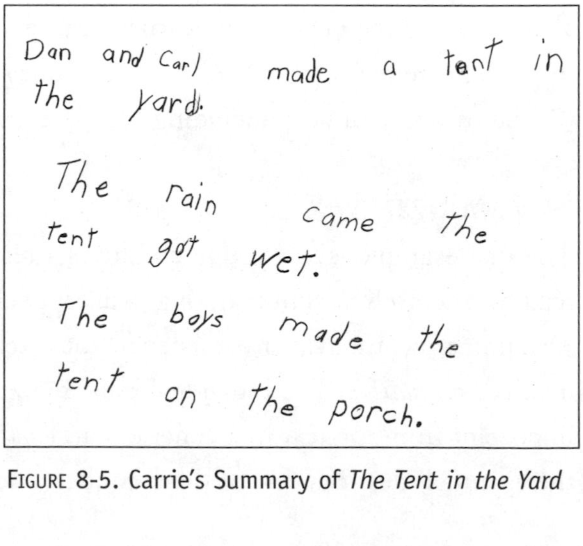
Dan and Carl made a tent in the yard.

The rain came the tent got wet.

The boys made the tent on the porch.

FIGURE 8-5. Carrie's Summary of *The Tent in the Yard*

Her text provides evidence that this young reader is learning to condense a text into a few statements that capture the essence—a skill that will help her to do the following:

- Understand the important ideas in a text (as opposed to trying to remember every single detail)
- Remember and recapture the text to make connections to other texts in the future
- Express or put into writing the important ideas in a text

It may seem that these brief pieces of writing are very simple; and, certainly, they take only a few minutes of a guided reading lesson. But when children use this kind of writing often, they develop the habit of remembering what is important about the material they read.

Does this kind of writing take the place of the extended time that children spend in writing workshop composing pieces from their own experiences? Not at all. You still need a time during the day dedicated exclusively to writing. For the young child, however, the use of reading and writing are not as separated as we teachers may believe. If you take on the goal of helping children write about their reading, you can

- Bring quick writing into instructional contexts such as guided and independent reading
- Use mentor texts (usually those you read aloud to children or read in a shared way) into writing workshop as examples

TEXT STRUCTURE

The structure of a text refers to its organizational patterns. For example, the structure of a story involves a beginning, the description of a problem, events occurring in sequence, resolution of the problem, and an ending.

Texts are organized in many ways. Text *structure* is a serious factor in comprehension. Every genre of text has its own structure. Understanding the structure of each genre helps the reader comprehend. Bomer (1994; also see Bomer & Bomer, 2001) describes structure as a "road map." For example, mysteries have a problem (often a crime, such as a theft or a murder), a description of characters, a series of events, and a solution (crime solving). Informational texts usually present information in categories, and writers often use underlying structures such as:

- **Temporal sequence.** The text is organized in time, beginning with the first event and progressing from there. Most narrative (story) texts and biographies are organized in temporal sequence.
- **Compare/contrast.** Two kinds of information are presented, along with information about how they are similar and different.
- **Problem/solution.** A problem is presented and explained, along with the solution.
- **Cause/effect.** The cause of a problem is described and a solution is proposed.
- **Description.** Details are provided to help the reader understand the text.

Readers who understand these important underlying structures have better comprehension. Teachers can help children accomplish this learning through talking and writing about reading.

Sometimes the structure of a text can be seen more clearly when information is placed in a diagram. This genre of writing about reading is often called a "graphic organizer." Graphic organizers are simply forms or diagrams that help readers/writers organize information from a text. The real value of these organizers is in the talk that surrounds their construction, so you will want to use them carefully—and the simpler the better. In the example below, a group of kindergarten children read *The Hungry Giant*

(Cowley, 1980), a story about an angry giant who threatens to hit people with his bommy-knocker. This delightful text can be used for shared or unison reading; in this case, children were reading it independently. After their second reading of the story, they discussed the giant as a character. Indeed, the giant certainly merits discussion, because he is a thoroughly disagreeable character. The group really got into it, and then they created their own webs to describe the giant with the teacher's drawing of the giant in the center (see Figure 8-6).

Children can think about the characters in the stories and compare what they do. Below you can see two examples of children who wrote about their understandings (see Figures 8-7 and 8-8).

In the text *The Clever Penguins* (Randell, 1994), Mother Penguin lays the eggs, but then Father Penguin sits on them while Mother Penguin goes out to sea and eats fish. Mother and Father Penguin have two distinctive roles.

In her comparison diagram, Sierra wrote about Mother Penguin's exciting escape from a seal. Kevin wrote that Mother Penguin ate a lot of fish. Both statements reflect important information from the

FIGURE 8-6. Character Web of the Giant

FIGURE 8-7. Sierra's Writing

text, and both can be compared with Father Penguin's actions. Both students wrote that Father Penguin sat on the eggs.

For this simple task, the teacher wrote the words *Mother Penguin* and *Father Penguin* at the top of two columns, respectively. Children could select any information they wished to record

FIGURE 8-8. Kevin's Writing

below each heading, but they had to relate the right facts to the specific character. As children created this chart, they were simultaneously:

- Remembering and recording important information
- Relating specific information (behavior, characteristics, etc.) to a character
- Comparing two characters
- Learning important content from an informational text

Even young children can learn to think analytically about texts and can do so without the use of technical terms, such as "temporal sequence" or "compare and contrast." Instead, you can encourage children to talk about what happened next in the story as they illustrate their favorite plots. The important thing is that the children are developing ways of looking more carefully at the way texts are organized.

CONTRIBUTIONS TO TEST TAKING

Through regularly talking together and then thinking about how they would write their understandings, children develop their ability to analyze texts. Writing adds the "edge" to this process because it requires children to put their understandings into concise language that can be written. Summarizing and comparing are the kinds of thinking that are valued on the tests that children take in schools (Fountas & Pinnell, 2001). During these tests, children often must provide short answers that require analysis of texts. We cannot depend on test-taking instructional programs that demonstrate ways to succeed on tests to help children learn how to execute this analysis. Children need to experience this kind of analysis over and over, reading text after text. One of the ways you can help your students become proficient at this process is to involve them every day in complex thinking across a range of instructional contexts, such as interactive read-aloud, shared writing, interactive writing, or guided reading.

If children write about their reading several times each week from kindergarten throughout the grades, then they should be well prepared to supply the kinds of responses that are expected on high-stakes texts. Test preparation does not begin at third or fourth grade; rather, it begins at the early levels. We cannot expect students to focus on decoding at the early levels and then begin analytic thinking at higher levels. The complex thinking must be there from the beginning, and talking about writing in response to reading and then making it happen can help.

Students' written responses to reading provide evidence of their thinking. The purpose is not to "prove" that the student has read the text, so you aren't looking for a piece of writing that shows "the more the better." In fact, you do not really want students to try to reproduce every detail of a text as in the old "book report" style. Writing about reading, as well as drawing, are vehicles for exploring and communicating the readers' thinking.

DIALOGUE ABOUT TEXTS

As children become more sophisticated readers, they benefit even more from dialogue with their teachers about texts. One of the most powerful tools for the teacher is the reader's notebook, which children typically begin to use at the beginning of grade 2 (Fountas & Pinnell, 2001). In their notebooks, children write letters to the teacher about the texts that they have chosen to read independently. The Reader's Notebook is an essential component of the reading workshop. The structure of the reading workshop is as follows:

- **Mini-lesson and book talks.** The teacher presents several books that students might like to read. She talks abut them for one or two minutes to engage students' interest. In her selection, she had considered the range of reading levels in her class. Typically, several students add the "book talk" selections to their own reading lists.
- **Independent reading and conferring.** Children read silently and independently the books they have chosen with teacher guidance. At regular intervals, the teacher confers individually with children, talking about their thinking.
- **Writing in a readers' notebook.** Once each week, children are expected to write one thoughtful letter in their notebooks. The letter is addressed to the teacher and is focused on their thinking about any text—one they have read independently, one that they have heard read aloud, or one that they have discussed with other children.
- **Sharing.** Students come to a community meeting and discuss texts. Often, they share what they have written about texts.

In the example that follows, we can see Danielle's letter about her reading and her teacher's answer. This letter shows so clearly how easy Danielle communicates with her teacher and how enthusiastic she is about books.

Figure 8-9 contains two letters from Danielle, a true fan of the Lemony Snicket series. Like many avid readers, Danielle is working her way through the series. Her comments in the first letter are about *The Hostile Hospital* (Snicket, 2001). In the first part of the letter, she devotes some space simply to retelling events of the story. Her report of details provides evidence that she is following and understanding the story. But her teacher wants her to do more—to express her thinking. Toward the end of the first letter, we find this evidence. She ventures an opinion about the bravery of the kids and wonders whether the stories are really true (it is doubtful she really thinks this) or if Lemony Snicket just makes it sound as if they are. Her last comments, about the author and her favorites in the series, provide evidence that Danielle is a reader.

The second letter shows that Danielle is continuing to gobble up the series. Many voracious readers become immersed in series books early in their reading careers. Each time the reader takes on a new book in the series, she has more background knowledge to bring to the processing. And, the appeal to the reader is huge.

- The characters become friends that you can visit again and again
- You learn about the setting as if it is a place and time you know
- The writer's style is familiar and easy to process
- Particular vocabulary terms become familiar

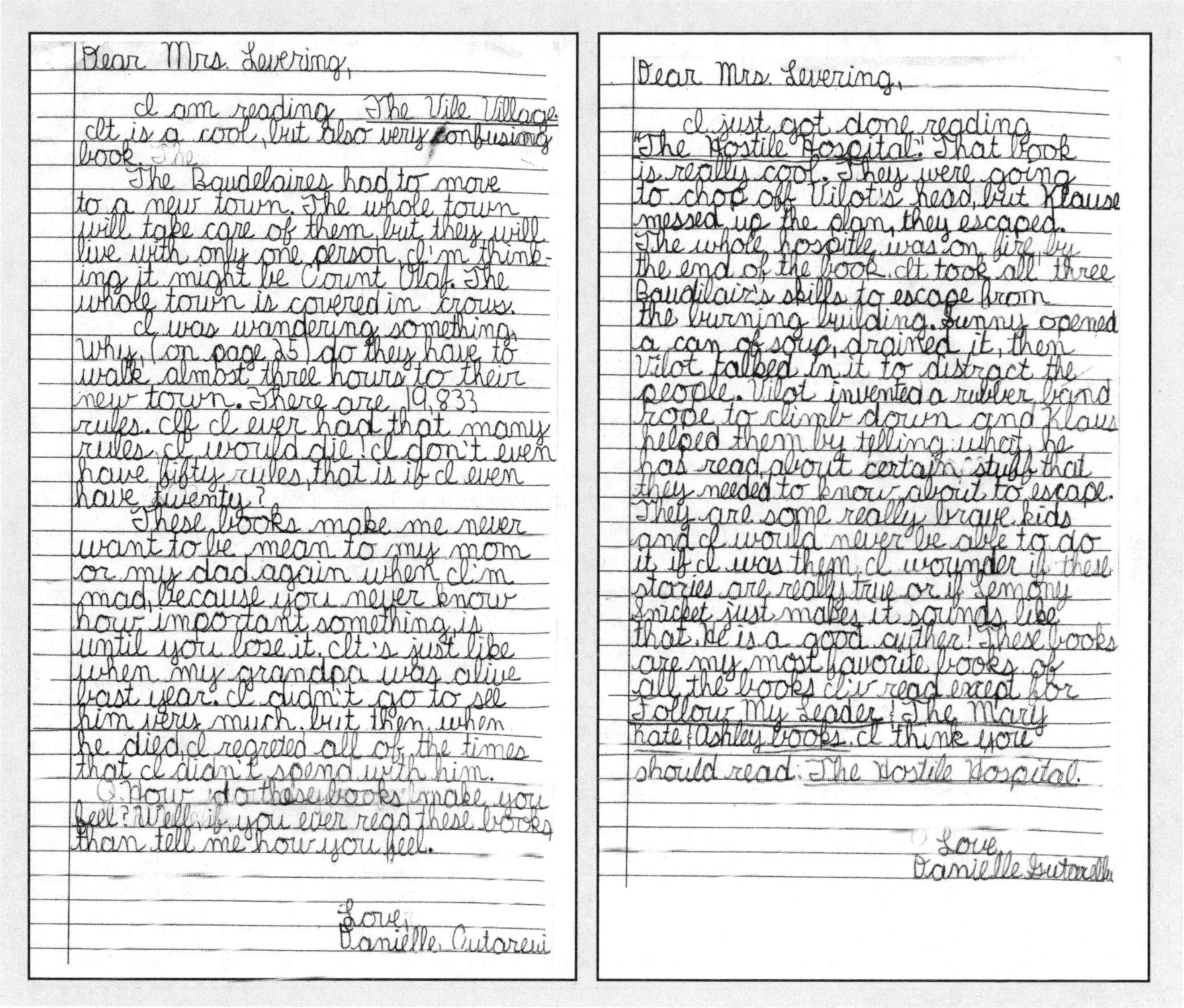

Dear Mrs. Levering,

I am reading The Vile Village. It is a cool, but also very confusing book. ~~The~~

The Baudelaires had to move to a new town. The whole town will take care of them, but they will live with only one person. I'm thinking it might be Count Olaf. The whole town is covered in crows.

I was wandering something. Why, (on page 25) do they have to walk almost three hours to their new town. There are 19,833 rules. If I ever had that many rules I would die! I don't even have fifty rules, that is if I even have twenty?

These books make me never want to be mean to my mom or my dad again when I'm mad, because you never know how important something is until you lose it. It's just like when my grandpa was alive last year. I didn't go to see him very much. but then when he died, I regreted all of the times that I didn't spend with him.

Q. How do these books make you feel? Well, if you ever read these books than tell me how you feel.

Love,
Danielle Cutarelli

Dear Mrs. Levering,

I just got done reading "The Hostile Hospital." That book is really cool. They were going to chop off Vilot's head, but Klause messed up the plan, they escaped. The whole hospitle was on fire by the end of the book. It took all three Baudilair's skills to escape from the burning building. Sunny opened a can of soup, drained it, then Vilot talked in it to distract the people. Vilot invented a rubber band rope to climb down and Klaus helped them by telling what he has read about certain stuff that they needed to know about to escape. They are some really brave kids and I would never be able to do it if I was them. I wounder if these stories are really true or if Lemony Snicket just makes it sounds like that. He is a good auther! These books are my most favorite books of all the books I've read exept for Follow My Leader! The Mary Kate & Ashley books. I think you should read The Hostile Hospital.

Love,
Danielle Cutarelli

FIGURE 8-9. Two Letters From Danielle

Of course, we would not want our students to concentrate only on this kind of book, but a well-written and interesting series can give readers the experience of effortless processing of a large amount of text. That is certainly true of Danielle, who is reading at least one of these books each week in addition to all the other texts she encounters at school. She introduces and questions the text, and then she makes some spontaneous comments about something in the text that amazes her—the 19,000+ rules the Baudelaires encounter in that small town. At the end of the second letter, she makes a thoughtful connection to her own life.

The weekly letters that students write to their teachers during reading workshop offer an open-ended way for children to comment on nearly any aspect of texts. The children's task is simple—to communicate their thinking. You can find much more detail about how to get started using a reader's notebook in Fountas and Pinnell (2000; 2006). You will also find many examples of students' letters there.

The Value of Writing About Reading

In the discussion of writing about reading, we should not forget that the process is often facilitated by *drawing*. We have found that many students write better and more organized pieces if they have the opportunity to produce illustrations for them. Even older children can benefit from the chance to collect

Ideas for Writing and Drawing About Reading

Notes and Sketches	Students can record words or phrases to help them recall connections, feelings, or confusions as they engage in later discussion of a text. They can make quick sketches to share in the discussion.
Short Writes	Students can learn to produce a few sentences or a paragraph very quickly in response to a book, including reacting to the writer's style, making predictions, revealing thoughts about the big ideas, and analyzing a character.
Graphic Organizers	Students can use writing and sketching in an organized way to help them think analytically about the characters, the setting, the timeline of events, or the underlying structure (such as compare/contrast, temporal sequence, cause/effect, problem/solution).
Written Dialogue	Using a reader's notebook or a simple journal, the student can write letters on any aspect of reading.
Letters to an Author	Students enjoy writing to an author; their letters can include their responses to texts or what they notice about a writer's style.
Response to the Language of a Text	Students can select a good quote or the teacher can preselect one. They place the quote in the first column and then write about it in the next column, to include what they notice about the language, what they think the writer meant, or how the language makes them feel.
Comparing Elements of a Text	The teacher uses an open-ended table or grid (often on a piece of large chart paper) that provides a framework for analyzing and comparing elements of a text, revealing interrelationships among characters, connecting and comparing one text to another, etc. After students have learned the process, they can begin to make their own grids.
Summary	Students write a sentence or a few sentences that summarize the plot or important aspects of a text.
Recommendation	Students can create a poster, bookmark, or brief advertisement that helps others understand what a book is about. This activity helps them develop the ability to critically review texts.
Cartoons	Students may develop a sequence of cartoons that reflect an exciting part of the text, a scene, or the whole text.
Readers' Theater	The teacher and students together can select language from a text in order to perform as a readers' theater.

FIGURE 8-10. Ideas for Writing and Drawing About Reading Chart

and form their thoughts while drawing. On the other hand, writers often enjoy producing a drawing after writing; in the process, they think about the "fit" between text and pictures and their additional information they may be providing to enhance the meaning.

We have mentioned only a few of the many ways children can use writing, often accompanied by drawing, to extend the meaning of texts. There are many more. Figure 8-10 summarizes several ways to write/draw about reading.

All of the activities included in Figure 8-10 require students to examine the text and think about it in different ways. The learning is not so much in the product; it takes place during the thinking and talking students do as they engage in the process.

Writing about reading can be used at almost any time during the student's day. It can be an independent assignment after a guided-reading group, or students may write about the books they are reading during independent work time. They may also respond to audio recordings of books that they hear at a listening center. During interactive read-aloud, you can stop at a strategic point to let them quickly write or sketch in a reader's notebook or on a clipboard. Or, after listening to an entire text, they can write before engaging in oral discussion.

The key to effective use of this teaching approach is to keep activities involving writing about reading integral to the oral discussion. It is usually a brief activity and should not take the form of tedious assignments. After all, if you know that you have to write about every single text you read, it could undermine your motivation to read! If you examine your schedule, you will find that it doesn't take much time to include writing about reading that can support talking and thinking in powerful ways.

Suggestions for Professional Development

Try this activity to help your students engage in writing about reading. Afterward, share your ideas with colleagues in your study group or in-service session.

- Select a book you have read aloud to students at least twice; it should be a memorable text that is one of their favorites.
- Using a large piece of chart paper, write a letter to your students that expresses your own thinking about this text.
- Make your letter age appropriate; write a very simple one to younger students and a more complex letter for older students.
- Then, have your students write their own letters about a favorite book.

If you are working with kindergarten students, you might want to use interactive writing of a letter to another class about a favorite read-aloud book. Send the letter to the classroom next door and wait for a reply. Classes can exchange several letters about good books. In this way, children can learn to express their thinking even before they can write letters for themselves.

If you are working with first graders, use the same process as that described for kindergartners. Then, after children have experienced the construction of several letters through interactive writing, invite them to write a letter to you about a favorite book.

If you are working with second graders, demonstrate letter writing before inviting students to write a letter to you about a favorite book. Take the letters home and write a response to each student. Have the letters on students' desks when they begin class the next day. Students can read their letters and then read them to partners. Ask the students to bring their letters to a class meeting and read some of their best thinking aloud to the group. Then, ask them to write another letter about a favorite book by the end of the week.

Schedule a follow-up session with other teachers so that you can share the student letters and discuss the process. Discuss the following:

- What is the evidence of thinking in student letters?
- How can student letters be improved?
- To what degree are students taking on the task of letter writing?
- What evidence of thinking did you discover in the oral language they used during the process?
- To what degree are students taking on the conventions of letter writing?

CHAPTER 9

Talking About Books to Learn the Writer's Craft

by Patricia L. Scharer

Collecting books for this chapter gave me a chance to revisit old favorites and study new ones while thinking about how quality children's literature supports young writers. As I reread and enjoyed Judy Sierra's *Wild About Books* (2004), I realized that Sierra's picture book already contains the essence of this chapter's subject.

Dedicated to the memory of Dr. Seuss, *Wild About Books* begins with a wrong turn of the bookmobile—and, suddenly, librarian Molly McGrew is setting up shop in the zoo. At first, the animals are shy and keep their distance, but as Molly begins reading from "the good Dr. Seuss," the animals soon are "stampeding to learn all about this new something called *reading*." They are quickly hooked and begin to select books for themselves. The pandas, of course, want books in Chinese, and the otter loves to swim while reading about Harry Potter. The animals read by themselves and they "read in bunches and llamas read dramas while eating their lunches." Even the "Tasmanian devils found books so exciting, that soon they had given up fighting for writing." As the new writers share their stories with the other animals, interest grows until all of the animals are writing— adventure stories, poetry, and novels. A high point, of course, is the hippo's award of the "Zoolitzer Prize." It is not too hard to link the plot and theme of this book to classrooms—when teachers (or librarians) read wonderful books to children (or zoo animals), the stories read inspire stories written by the children (or zoo animals).

So, there you have it—the essence of this chapter: quality children's literature offers much for young writers. Classrooms filled with quality books and opportunities to explore those books foster writers in the primary grades. This chapter focuses on the relationship between children's literature and the writing process and is organized into four parts. In the first section, I provide a rationale for the use of children's literature in writing instruction by describing the contribution of hearing, reading, and studying quality literature to children's writing abilities. Next, I focus on the instructional contexts where quality children's books and writing instruction intersect. Here, we will be thinking about the specific ways that young writers experience the texts of other authors to learn more about books, stories, and the writing process. The next section explores how studying illustrations as they relate to texts can support young writers as they create their own stories. I conclude with a proposal for a range of instructional practices that links quality children's books to students' understandings about themselves as writers.

The Contribution of Quality Books to Children's Writing

One way to think about how children's literature contributes to children becoming writers is to draw parallels between that process and how children learn about music. While listening to quality music of various types, children become acquainted with the rich variety of musical scores and their purposes. They may respond to some pieces with movement or emotions—sometimes happy, other times sad or lonely. The more music children hear, the greater their repertoire of understanding and appreciation. They begin to identify the differences among folk songs, opera, rock and roll, and lullabies, and to develop a preference for one or more types of music.

Reading aloud to children has the same effect on young writers, bathing them in the sounds of language found in quality books. These listening experiences with music and books provide a rich background of knowledge to help young musicians (or writers) begin to create music (or writing) on their own. The three-year-old who is learning to sing "Old MacDonald" because she has heard it over and over on a CD played in the car, similarly will begin to write her own messages inspired by the favorite books she has heard many times.

When young musicians focus on a particular instrument, however, they need a new kind of instruction so that they can learn the specifics of playing the piano, trumpet or string bass. Similarly, young writers need to know the specifics of writing a personal narrative, a letter, or a response to a text. They need instruction to show them how to write a story about what happened over the weekend or a thank-you note to the zookeeper or their thoughts about a favorite book. This is a time to not only learn about how musical notes (or words) work, but also how they work together to create a unified sound (or written composition).

Musicians learn in many contexts—band or orchestra settings, ensembles, and private lessons. Similarly, young writers can learn about their craft in a variety of contexts, each of which contributes in a slightly different way:

- Whole-group settings (interactive read-aloud, shared reading, interactive writing, shared writing, and mini-lessons)
- Smaller, guided-writing groups
- Individual lessons (writing conferences)

These learning contexts, for music or writing, are not in a particular order or mutually exclusive; they are not arranged in levels of importance. Each context builds on the others to help young musicians (or writers) deepen their knowledge of the craft and develop an appreciation for a particular genre.

Performance—important for both musicians and writers—engenders a feeling of satisfaction and rewards children's efforts. Musicians may play or even compose for an appreciative family member, peers, or a larger audience, while writers may complete a piece and share it with their teachers, classmates, and family, but they also may publish a polished piece intended for a wider audience. For both musicians and writers, however, the process itself can be satisfying. This chapter turns its lens on the learning contexts where quality children's books can support children as writers.

Instructional Contexts Where Quality Children's Books and Writing Instruction Intersect

Children's literature provides a constant flow of "wonderful words" for children to experience that can support them as writers. Authors of all ages "lean" on what they have read to select just the right word, phrase, or rhythm to fit their purpose and genre. For example, Mem Fox's award-winning *Possum Magic* (1990) begins, "Once upon a time but not very long ago deep in the Australian bush there lived two possums. Their names were Hush and Grandma Poss." Years later, in her autobiography, *Dear Mem Fox, I Have Read All Your Books Even the Pathetic Ones: And Other Incidents in the Life of a Children's Book Author* (1992), Fox reflects on her struggle to write those first few words and the 22 attempts she made in just one afternoon before finding the right words and rhythm. She writes that long after *Possum Magic* became the best-selling book in Australia's history, she realized that "the pauses, the phrasing, and the when, the where, and the who in the first paragraph of *Possum Magic* mirrored exactly the opening verse of the Biblical story of Ruth, which I'd learned by heart at drama school 17 years before: *Now it came to pass, in the days when the judges ruled, that there was a famine in the land. And a certain man of Bethlehem, Judah, went to sojourn in the country of Moab, he, and his wife, and his two sons, . . ."* (pp. 137–138).

Born of missionary parents, Mem Fox lived much of her early life in Africa, surrounded by oral readings of the Bible. She attributes much of her success as a writer to her study of both the scriptures and of Shakespeare, which serves as an example of the long-lasting influence of quality literature on writers. We could say that Fox's experiences provided her with a massive amount of information that she could draw on for the rest of her life; think about data being entered into a computer to form a giant searchable data base. Surrounding children with quality writing during read-aloud, shared reading, and independent reading provides a rich "input" of word combinations, writing styles, and interesting ways to communicate with writing that certainly affect their "output."

CRAFT LEARNING THROUGH INTERACTIVE READ-ALOUD

It seems fitting that Sierra's *Wild About Books* won the E. B. White Read Aloud Award for being a "terrific" book (as Charlotte, the spider, would write) because reading aloud is the foundation for talking about and learning about the writer's craft. It is the perfect setting for young writers to soak up the stories, messages, characters, themes, and craft of the excellent writers for children today. Listening to a new book or hearing again an old favorite enables children not only to enjoy the essence of the story or poem, but it also provides a context in which they can step back to look more closely at the writer's accomplishments.

- How did the first page grab the listeners and make them want more?
- How did we learn about the characters?
- How did the writer leave you on the edge of understanding, inviting you to predict what will happen next?
- How did the marriage of the author's words and illustrator's art lead to a new understanding of the book?

All these questions can be part of the authentic wondering and discussing that happens during an interactive read-aloud led by a teacher who enjoys sharing quality books and knows how to inspire the kinds of conversations that deepen the understanding of listeners. This skillful immersion in enjoyable texts, followed by thinking about the writing, enables children to use these texts as "mentors" that will help them in their own writing. The idea of using mentor texts is not to have children simply imitate specific writers (although all writers may "borrow" a bit from writing that they admire), so much as it is to help them internalize how skilled writers use words in so many ways. Mentor texts are typically introduced during interactive read-aloud. Through discussion, you can guide children to notice aspects of the text that will help them in their own writing. Later, these same mentor texts or others can be referred to in mini-lessons for additional, very explicit instruction. (See Appendix A for suggestions of mentor texts and discussion questions.)

Let's look at some examples of how mentor texts can work during interactive read-aloud and literature discussion. An interactive read-aloud of *Wild About Books* might begin with an invitation to explore the endpapers, which are covered with blue line drawings on yellow paper of many, many monkeys—each of whom is reading a book. Children may want to talk about why the artist, Marc Brown, designed such endpapers while thinking about the animals and title on the cover as well. Children also may wonder about the title page, which features a bookmobile just about to turn into the zoo, and talk about what kind of story this might be, with a title like *Wild About Books*. They might notice right away that the story is written in verse and even hop into the reading by predicting the rhymes of each stanza.

> Gently, Molly taught lessons in treating books right,
> For the boa constrictor squeezed *Crictor* too _____ ,
> Baby bunnies mucked up *Goodnight Moon* with their paws,
> Giant termites devoured *The Wizard of* _____ .

After enjoying several readings of *Wild About Books*, the children might talk about what they learned about Molly, the librarian, and discuss how author Sierra and illustrator Brown each contributed to her character. The conversation might continue as listeners are invited to talk about their favorite words, phrases, or rhythms, such as "they howled and they hissed till their funny bones ached" or "thin books and fat books and *Cat in the Hat* books," perhaps generating a large chart of "Favorite Words From *Wild About Books*." Each of these conversations offers important learning opportunities for young readers and writers to experience the following:

- Be an active listener, deeply thinking about the book
- Experience a deeper understanding of the book
- Express their ideas orally, knowing they will be appreciated
- Notice the ways authors and illustrators work
- Talk about word selection and how authors use words in particular ways
- Experience the rhyme and rhythm of a text
- Learn new vocabulary

CRAFT LEARNING DURING SHARED READING

Enlarged texts of quality books or chart poems are often used in primary classrooms during a shared reading time so that everyone can participate in reading and enjoying the text. These lessons are particularly important times for young readers to learn early concepts of print, such as left-to-right directionality, the concepts of a word or letter, or one-to-one matching. Many of these texts, however, may serve as early mentor texts, especially those with predictable story lines and language patterns that may inspire students to write their own similar versions independently or with the teacher using shared or interactive writing.

This writing would be heavily influenced by the big book or poem, but would have the stamp of children's composition as well. For example, Laura Joffe Numeroff's series of cause-and-effect books, including *If You Give a Mouse a Cookie* (1985) and *If You Give a Moose a Muffin* (1991), repeat a pattern through each book that has endless opportunities for variation. "If you give a mouse a cookie, he's going to ask for a glass of milk" could be rewritten as "If you give a kid a carrot, he's going to want some dip" or "If you give a Mom a kiss, she's going to want a hug" or any other variation of the pattern. Within this very supportive structure, writers have to think carefully about exactly which word to use for the cause and effect to make sense. Working through such word choices is important for writers of all ages.

In the author's note at the beginning of the big-book version of *No, David!* (1998), David Shannon describes the inspiration for this book—a book his mother sent to him that he had made when he was a little boy that was illustrated with all the things he wasn't allowed to do. Shared reading with this book might be filled with conversations about all the things children are not allowed to do and why. Thus, the idea of writing about naughtiness can come from this book, but the pattern is not necessarily the focus. One child may write an opposite book—things he can and cannot do. Another child may write about a particular time when he got in trouble (probably because of an older brother or sister. . .). In this case, the support from the mentor text is not a pattern of writing, but a more general topic that can inspire fascinating stories. As a follow up, Shannon's sequels, *David Goes to School* and *David Gets in Trouble*, could be models for students to write three-part chapter books, similar to those found in the Frog and Toad series by Arnold Lobel; Denys Cazet's books about her "udderly likable" characters, Minnie and Moo; or Cynthia Rylant's series about Mr. Putter and Tabby or Henry and Mudge.

CRAFT LEARNING THROUGH POETRY

Interactive reading and shared reading also are excellent contexts for sharing poetry in K–3 classrooms. Poems might first be introduced by having the teacher read from a collection, such as the award-winning *A Jar of Tiny Stars: Poems by NCTE Award-Winning Poets* (Cullinan, 1996), which features children's favorite poems from ten winners of the National Council of Teachers of English Award for Poetry for Children. During multiple expressive readings by the teacher, children can enjoy the "heavy" words used by Barbara Juster Esbensen in her poem about the elephant or Valerie Worth's description of a lawnmower, which begins:

The lawnmower
Grinds its teeth
Over the grass,
Spitting out a thick
Green spray;

Such poems provide exciting opportunities to talk about word choices within a concise text by discussing how the poet selected just the right word to express a meaning larger than the poem itself. Word selection also can be discussed relative to the mood created by the poem. The light, rhythmic calypso beat of *No Hickory, No Dickory, No Dock: Caribbean Nursery Rhymes* (1995) by John Agard and Grade Nichols may be contrasted with the slow, deliberate pace of some of the animal poems by Esbensen in *Words with Wrinkled Knees* (1986). Readers of Esbensen's poems about the elephant or the dinosaur will need to take a plodding, weighty tone quite different from the Caribbean rhythms.

The range of writing styles and formats found in children's poetry can also be discussed and compared. *A Jar of Tiny Stars*, for example, contains poems by five award-winning poets. Some collections have similar formats, such as Valerie Worth's "small poems." Eve Merriam's poetry ranges from step-by-step directions in her poem "How to Eat a Poem" to the rhythmic style of her "Skip Rope Rhyme for Our Time" or the fascinating layout of "Windshield Wiper," which is reminiscent of looking through a car window in the rain and noting the rhythm of the wipers, back and forth across the window:

fog smog	fog smog
tissue paper	tissue paper
clear the blear	clear the smear
fog more	for more
splat splat	downpour

Poems such as this one help young writers to think about word placement as well as word selection to convey their intended meaning.

Some poetry collections offer themes for listeners to explore. These books are particularly valuable as a starting point to discuss how writers convey meaning using different formats and word choices within the same topic. Sibling rivalry is explored in *No Boys Allowed: Poems About Brothers and Sisters* (2006), a compilation by Jon Micklos Jr. From the simple, partially repetitive format of Mary Ann Hoberman's "Half-Whole-Step" ("I have a half-sister / I have a whole-sister / I have a step-sister / That adds up to three.") to the dialogue and drama of "Who Ate the Last Five Cookies?" by David L. Harrison, the poems provide listeners with the opportunity to study the craft of many authors, each writing a poem or so about the same topic. Other poetry collections offer ideas about how to write personal narratives using poetic formats. Nikki Grimes' collection, *It's Raining Laughter* (1997), for example, is a collection of poems, mostly written in first person, and illustrated with photographs of elementary children. As children listen to several of Grimes' poems, they will notice the interesting ways that they begin—"I am melody. / I've a symphony in me" or "I remember that time / I stood on stage" or "When I run, / I don't have to think /about home or school." Talking about the ways the poet begins may inspire listeners to compose their own personal narratives and try out a free-style, rhyming, or other poetic device.

As children experience multiple readings of their favorite poems, you may want to write their favorites on chart paper and share the poems as shared reading. Seeing their favorites in print ensures successful readings and a new opportunity to study the writer's craft. As they see the poems, readers may want to talk about what they notice about the patterns, rhythms, rhymes, word choices, or format. Each conversation moves children ahead in their understanding of the writer's craft in ways that support their own poetic writing.

CRAFT MINI-LESSONS IN WRITING WORKSHOP

As quality children's books and poems are shared through interactive read-aloud or shared reading, they become part of the pool of resources the class can draw upon to think more deeply about the writer's craft. Planning mini-lessons begins with your ongoing examination of student writing to identify the needs of the class. The next step is to match those needs with the characteristics of well-loved books that can be used as mentor texts. Leaning on books your class has already heard multiple times is an efficient way to teach explicitly about the writer's craft, because the mentor texts have already been read and discussed, often numerous times. Students delight in returning to a favorite book and bring a rich background of experiences to the discussion. Mini-lessons that require the reading of an unfamiliar book may become too long and leave little room for discussion about the specifics of the text. It's much more efficient to revisit favorite books that students are already familiar with so that they bring a strong knowledge of the book to the discussion of the author's craft.

Writing Strong Leading Sentences

Teachers who review student writing folders and decide that students are ready to learn about how to start a story with a strong leading sentence could revisit books such as *Just Add One Chinese Sister: An Adoption Story* (2005) by Patricia McMahon and Conor Clarke McCarthy or *The Hickory Chair* (2001) by Lisa Rowe Fraustino. McMahon and McCarthy's first sentence reads, "Hey, big girl, would you like to help me?" while Fraustino's reads, "Sundays when I was small, that Gran of mine was good at hiding." These sentences invite readers into the stories in a way that encourages them to wonder about how the big girl is going to help her mom and be curious about Gran and what she hid. Similarly, the first page of *Tomás and the Library Lady* (Mora, 1997) establishes the setting, the feelings of the main character, and a hint of the plot within just a few brief sentences: "It was midnight. The light of the full moon followed the tired old car. Thomás was tired and hot too. Hot and tired. He missed his own bed, in his own house in Texas." Looking again at such favorite books to study the author's craft gives children an opportunity to see the book with a new lens—in this case, to study how writers begin stories in ways that capture readers' attention.

Using Dialogue to Tell Your Story

Mini-lessons about using dialogue could focus, for instance, on the ways that dialogue between Olivia and her mother move the story line along in Ian Falconer's *Olivia Forms a Band* (2006). Olivia is convinced that she has the capacity to single-handedly be the band for the picnic and fireworks one evening. Olivia's mother tries valiantly to convince her daughter that a single person cannot be a band, but Olivia has the final word with her reply, "This morning you told me I sounded like five people!" Revisiting Thierry Robberecht's *Sam Is Never Scared* (2006) provides students with an opportunity to explore how the author moves back and forth between first-person narrative ("I am Sam. And I'm not scared of anything") and periods of extended dialogue between Sam and his father ("Everyone is scared of something," he said. "Even you?" I asked. "Even me," said Dad). Each time students look more closely at dialogue, they learn another subtle difference about the ways authors use dialogue, and they deepen their understanding about how to use dialogue effectively to tell a story.

Writing Your Own Story

Young writers are often encouraged to write personal narratives—stories based on their own life experiences—so they can draw on events, thoughts, and experiences close to them as they write about meaningful topics they have selected. Looking at stories written in first person and stepping back to think about how authors write such stories can support beginning writers by helping them to develop their own writing style and to learn to write in ways that fully engage the audience.

Journals are a tool that young writers can use to note important events in their lives that may become a topic for their writing. As a mentor text, *Are We There Yet?* (2005) by Alison Lester provides students with a way to learn more about how to write about a trip or an extended experience. Told in the voice of 8-year-old Grace, this book documents three months of family travel throughout Australia in Poppa's old camper trailer. Events are organized using such headings as "Starting Out" and "On the Road at Last," and specific places are organized using such headings as "The Outback" or "The Far North." Each two-page spread combines sequential narrative, multiple small illustrations, and captions on select illustrations, all contributing to the overall story. Periodic maps track the family's journey; Grace's drawings and labels add a personal touch.

Personal narratives are typically told with the voice and from the perspective of a single narrator. *Baby Radar* (2003) by Naomi Shihab Nye is a particularly strong example of the author's use of perspective as readers are taken on a stroller ride narrated by a very young child. The text and illustrations are influenced by the low-to-the-ground visibility of the stroller rider. Readers see cars from the stroller seat through text such as "I love to see /the eyes of cars /their giant teeth /the red lights /on their behinds" and see shoes described as "Tennis shoes daddy shoes sleepy slippers fat shoes /crazy shoes high-up heels fancy-dancy shiny shoes /I stretch my legs /to show my shoes."

Mentor texts also can help children learn how to tell a story using the first-person perspective of the writer. Ed Young's *My Mei Mei* (2006) begins with an introduction of the writer: "I am named Antonia after Nonna, my grandma Antonia." Antonia continues her story of wanting a little sister, a real Mei Mei, and the trip to China to adopt the new baby. Her consequent disappointment in the new sister is emphasized through repetitive text: "She couldn't walk. She couldn't talk. She couldn't play. She took all the attention away from me. I felt left out." Happily, the relationship between the two sisters improves as Mei Mei grows older, culminating in the girls posing the following question to their parents: "Can we have another Mei Mei?" Young writers can think about how this story was organized—beginning with an introduction of characters, continuing with a problem, and finishing with a solution and plot twist. In doing so, they can better understand ways to organize the information and to write about their life experiences.

Caldecott Honor book *The Relatives Came* (1985) by Cynthia Rylant is a personal narrative about visitors who came for the summer. With sparse, poetic language, Rylant establishes time of year and some of the setting in just three sentences on the first page: "It was in the summer of the year when the relatives came. They came up from Virginia. They left when their grapes were nearly purple enough to pick, but not quite." Students may notice that the first two sentences include information not only about the time of year, but also a bit of the geography of the two sets of relatives. The third sentence may inspire considerable conversation as students wonder why Rylant would choose to write about grapes on the first page. Rereading the book with an eye for Rylant's repeated use of grapes helps readers notice that the grapes appear to be a symbol for the familiar home they left as the relatives thought about the families they would visit and the "strange houses and different mountains" they traveled through on the way. You might also explore the illustrator's use of purple throughout the book and the final page, which features a single bunch of grapes on plain white paper without additional text.

Choosing Just the Right Word

Looking at books to find words that communicate particular moods or feelings can help young writers select just the right words to express their feelings as they write about visitors or the excitement of an upcoming birthday. *Max's Words* (2006) by Kate Banks is a picture book about three brothers with collections. Max's older brothers collected stamps and coins, respectively. Neither was willing to share their treasures with Max, but became quite interested when Max began collecting words and cutting them from magazines and newspapers. Max selected small words, bigger words, words that made him feel better, and words he liked to hear. But even more exciting were the discoveries Max made while arranging his words in different orders. Simple changes, such as switching words from "a blue crocodile ate the green iguana" to "the blue iguana ate a green crocodile" made a huge difference—especially to the iguana and crocodile! As Max began arranging and rearranging his collection of words into a story, he soon recognized the power of being an author. Max's efforts with and excitement in his word collection can help young writers think about the words they know and can draw on to tell their own stories.

As you read quality children's books, occasionally take the time to step back and admire some of the writer's word choices. Encourage students to do the same. You might create class charts of "Favorite Phrases" or "Exciting Words" or "Feeling Words" that help young writers appreciate the writer's craft and support their own writing. Looking at Barbara Cooney's words in *Miss Rumphius* (1982), students may notice descriptions such as "bristling masts of tall ships" Alice could see from her childhood home or how the "warm moist air wrapped itself around her" as she enjoyed the conservatory in the middle of the park.

Beyond noticing individual words and phases, young writers can use mentor texts to study the ways authors use techniques such a repetition, sequence, compare and contrast, or question and answer. Anthony Browne effectively captures Billy's character as a worrier through repetition in the first few pages of *Silly Billy* (2006): "Billy used to be a bit of a worrier. /He worried about many things. . . /Billy worried about hats, /and he worried about shoes. /Billy worried about clouds /and rain. /He even worried about giant birds." Repetition is one element in cumulative tales, such as *The Doorbell Rang* (Hutchins, 1986), with its repeated refrain, or in the predictable plot of Jan Brett's *The Mitten* (1989), as each two-page spread introduces yet another animal who enters the mitten to escape winter's cold. As Mole digs in Will Hillenbrand's *What a Treasure!* (2006), readers notice both repetition, as he gives away the treasures he finds underground, and a sequence leading to finding his most valuable treasure—a friend. The "steps" in learning to walk are the focus of *Walk On! A Guide for Babies of All Ages* (2006) by Marla Frazee. She offers helpful hints at the beginning of the book, such as staying away from "fragile stuff," then lists steps for how to move from crawling to walking. This book could serve as a model for other "how-to" books students may want to write about things they know how to do. Compare-and-contrast structures are a rich resource often found in nonfiction, such as Stephen Swinburne's *What's Opposite?* (2000). Other nonfiction books, such as Joy Cowley's *Red-Eyed Tree Frog* (1999), offer young writers a model for using question-and-answer techniques to write about their favorite animals, people, or places.

Studying Illustrations to Support Young Writers

Picture books are not only rich resources for studying the writer's craft, but also excellent models for thinking about the role of illustration during the writing process and in the final product. Capturing their stories first in drawing supports young writers as they make decisions about what to write. Students can draw on paper of various sizes without lines and also on sheets with one area for writing and another for drawing. Picture books such as *Rosie's Walk* (1969) by Pat Hutchins are wonderful examples of the ways that illustrations can support and enhance a story line. The drama of Hutchins' book, about a fox's efforts to capture Rosie the hen, rests on the combination of the minimal text and the illustrations. The danger in the plot is not found in the text, but is fully revealed only in the illustrations. In another book, *A Splendid Friend Indeed* (2005) by Suzanne Bloome, a pesky duck seems to be annoying his friend, the bear, with a barrage of questions: "What are you doing? Are you reading? I like to read. Do you want to hear me read?" Readers learn about the attitude and personality of the bear through his lack of responses to the duck and through his body language, which shows that he is clearly perturbed. Readers learn about the duck through the duck's actions, questions, and persistence.

As you talk about the contribution of the illustrations to books, young writers better understand the value of their own illustrations. For some, drawing a picture is a way of "holding on" to the story as they work through the writing process. For others, illustrations are opportunities to revisit the story to see whether additional text is needed to capture it. And for still others, illustrations complement the author's text in a way that leads to a fuller understanding of the story.

Immersion, Appreciation, and Instruction: Linking Quality Books to Children's Understandings As Writers

The ideas and examples in this chapter offer a range of instructional opportunities that can potentially build upon each other. First, immerse your class in wonderful words through daily read-alouds. Your role is to first to select just the right text for students to enjoy. Thinking carefully about just the right book to read aloud with your class requires both a deep understanding and appreciation of quality children's literature and the intent to be purposeful when selecting daily read-alouds. These interactive read-aloud times are not just to settle the students down after lunch or recess, but are powerful learning times when students are immersed in the words of exciting authors.

Invite children to appreciate the text by talking about favorite words, exciting sentences, or special words to think about. Your own excitement about words can help you develop a classroom culture where students are word detectives, learning to be authors by collecting words and phrases that they find interesting or exciting. These mentor texts contribute greatly to the quality of talk and writing in the classroom.

Finally, revisiting favorite books and stories as mentor texts for focused instruction based on the needs of students provides a high level of support for developing writers. These lessons may be large-group mini-lessons, small-group guided writing lessons, or individual conferences. These three—immersion, appreciation, and instruction—are centered on the conversations teachers and students have that become the link between writers' texts and students' writing. Thoughtfully selected books, read aloud repeatedly with new insights noted each time, become shared experiences that students can lean on as they write and develop as writers.

Suggestions for Professional Development

1. Invite your colleagues to join a book club that meets several times a month to talk about new books. Look carefully at the writers' and illustrators' craft to think about how the book's characteristics will influence your teaching. Think together about how to share each book. (The discussion questions for mentor texts in Appendix A may be helpful.) Later, share your students' responses to the book with the group to continue the discussion about the unique characteristics of the book and ways those characteristics can support students as readers and writers.

2. Schedule two meetings a year to read and discuss the award-winning books selected by the International Reading Association's Special Interest Group (SIG) and the National Council of Teachers of English, respectively. *Children's Literature and Reading* SIG (http://www. tcnj.edu/~childlit/proj/nbgs/intro-nbgs.html) lists Notable Books for a Global Society, announced each May, and the *Children's Literature Assembly's Notable Books for the English Language Arts* (http://www.childrensliterature assembly.org/index.htm) are announced each November. Both lists contain excellent books for elementary grades. ✦

CHAPTER 10

Story Structure as a Support to Meaning-Making

by Justina Henry

"Grandma, there's a monster in the bushes, and he's not saying anything." I looked down at Raegan, my three-year-old granddaughter. She stood very still, waiting for me to reply. "There is?" I asked. My eyebrows went up with my voice. "Yeah, and Uncle Tony put it in the trash."

Earlier that day, I had summoned my daughters, son-in-law, and Raegan to take a look at the empty hornets' nest nestled waist-high in a bush near the kitchen window. I had told them about calling the exterminator to get rid of the bald-faced hornets that had been living in the nest all summer. A round, little opening, the hornets' entry to their summer home, resembled a monster's mouth in a head about the size of a gray, cardboard-like bowling ball.

I thought about Raegan's "story"—really not much more than an explanation to herself—and how she was beginning to relate to others through personal narrative. Raegan's story, although very short, explained, in her mind, at least, the meaning of the "head" in the bush. To her, the "monster" was scary, and, she thought, "If I see a monster, then a grown-up will get rid of it." Like all of us, she was trying to make the world a predictable, reasonable place. She was trying to make sense of it all because it was too scary to think about events happening at random.

With the help of her family, Raegan, a meaning-maker from birth, is beginning to understand the rudiments of story. Through narrative, she constructs the meaning of her experiences. She learned to express herself by talking with family and friends throughout her preschool years. Eventually, she will enter into written language by writing about her personal experiences. Learning to write by putting a pencil to paper to capture her thoughts sets the stage for learning to write in other genres, for other purposes, for other audiences. She will learn to read by reading little books, simple stories about childhood experiences. To tell one's life stories and to see oneself in others' writing deepens our understanding of ourselves and the world.

Our stories attempt to explain our actions, and those of others, by linking cause and effect. We cope by looking for relationships—between people, events, and feelings. We make sense of the world, and ourselves, by telling each other our stories. But stories do more than that—they serve to satisfy a deep social need by connecting us with others while maintaining our personal identities.

Stories are by definition narratives. We all need narrative in our lives.

In this chapter, I describe aspects of narrative and implications for literacy learning and teaching. From kindergarten throughout the grades, children need daily, multiple opportunities to hear stories read aloud and discuss them with each other. Interactive read-aloud sessions form an important foundation for the development of writing. So, we use fictional narratives to help students learn to read, and we teach them to write through constructing personal narratives.

Leslie Evans reads to a group of students.

First, I visit Leslie Evans's classroom, where she reads *Old Henry* (Blos, 1987) to a group of students who have been involved in interactive read-aloud sessions for three years. Leslie uses "intentional conversation" (Fountas & Pinnell, 2006) to help her students understand the inner workings of a narrative text. Then, I briefly describe Leslie's use of *Old Henry* to help her students expand their own writing.

Understanding Story Structure

It supports our teaching to understand how narrative works, a phenomenon that varies by culture. (As our population becomes more diverse, we will need to learn several different kinds of narrative structures.) Stories in Western culture usually have a beginning, a rise in tension culminating in a crisis action, a turning point, and a resolution. Closure is achieved and the story ends. The ending may or may not be satisfying to the reader! Stories are more than events in chronological order; they are narratives about characters, their needs and desires, the obstacles they overcome to achieve what they yearn for, and the actions they take to remove the obstacles (see Figure 10-1).

Bill Roorbach, in *Writing Life Stories* (1998), writes that if you don't have a fic-

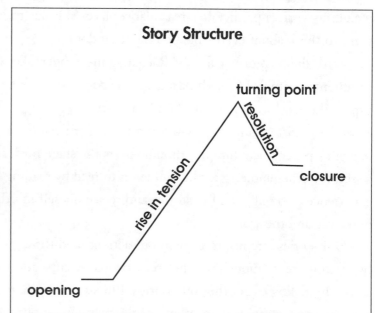

FIGURE 10-1. Story Structure

tion background (and most young writers don't), then you owe it to yourself to study the techniques of fiction, especially those related to creating characters. Understanding more about the craft of writing supports instructional decision making in reading and writing lessons.

We live in a literate society that reflects the need for meaning-making through narrative. Every day we are immersed in an ocean of stories, fiction and nonfiction, oral and written, transmitted by electronics, films, books, newspapers, and other media. Early in our lives we begin to develop a sense of story. As teachers of young children, we help them learn the reading and writing processes by tapping into their growing sense of how stories work. Perhaps deepening our understanding of story structure and writing techniques will make our reading and writing lessons a smoother bridge to literacy for our students.

When we read or listen to stories, we identify with characters through the emotions they evoke in us. Temporarily suspending our personal realities, we experience the characters' world through their actions and feelings. We have a chance to learn more about ourselves and life by witnessing how the characters change from the beginning of the story to the end. Janet Burroway, in *Writing Fiction* (2003), discusses James Joyce who wrote about how a character experiences an epiphany: the moment when he or she suddenly sees an event, person, or thing in a different light and is changed permanently. As readers, we, too, experience this epiphany. We become more aware of what it means to be human and to understand perspectives other than our own.

Interactive Read-Aloud: A Bridge to Thinking, Reading, and Writing

We will take a look at one teacher, Leslie, and how she thinks about fiction to teach her students about reading and writing. Knowing how most stories are organized helped Leslie in her teaching decisions. She knew that selecting, reading, and discussing interesting, high-quality stories helped her students learn the strategic "meaning-making" actions that are the foundation of comprehension. She also knew that these same texts were a rich resource for her students as they expanded their writing abilities. Readers and writers develop strategic actions for making meaning by attending to aspects of narrative, especially plot and character (See Figure 10-2).

The next selection, *Old Henry* (1987) by Joan Blos, helped Leslie meet her instructional goals over time. The main character of the story is Henry, a newcomer in town who has just moved into a house that is in need of repair. The story provides opportunities for discussing Henry and what he really wants. Interaction during the story-reading would give Leslie's students an opportunity to think about Henry's personality and how he makes decisions to achieve what he wants—to live in his new house in his own way rather than how his new neighbors want him to.

Leslie's goal was to read the story and support her students in making meaning through conversation. Discussing the story as it unfolded would enable them to think through the story events and understand the meaning at literal and inferential levels. The experience of thinking and talking together would help the students learn the strategic actions involved in meaning making. Readers take action to monitor

The Writer's Craft: Plot and Character

Aspects of Narrative	Reader	Writer
A story has tension or conflict that leads to the series of events and actions and is called the "plot."	Readers identify with characters' wants and the actions taken to remove obstacles to those wants.	Writers help readers connect with their stories by presenting conflict within and between characters.
"Plot thickens" before the turning point and is stretched out so the reader can fully experience the emotions of the characters.	Readers experience characters' feelings, and predict, based on what they know so far about characters and the story, what will happen next.	Writers strive to capture readers' interest by expanding the climax with more dialogue, actions, and/or feelings.
Characters are revealed by the writer's descriptions, what they do, think and say, and what others say about them.	Readers make connections to characters by attending to dialogue and actions of characters.	Writers help readers experience what characters are feeling and thinking by showing rather than telling.
Characters sometimes change from the beginning of the story to the end.	Readers can discover theme by using illustrations and/or the texts to analyze characters' feelings at the beginning and end of stories.	Writers often tell about personal experiences that changed their thinking by revealing characters' emotions throughout their narratives.
The ending of the story is satisfying to the reader.	Readers often make emotional connections to characters at the end of stories that often trigger understanding that goes beyond the text.	Writers often bring closure to narratives by describing characters' actions in a way that reveals significant ideas that readers can relate to.

FIGURE 10-2. The Writer's Craft: Plot and Character

understanding; connect to previous knowledge and infer new meanings; analyze plot, character, and theme; and then complete the circle to make deeper connections to their lives. Supported by the teacher, the students would draw on these interactive read-aloud conversations to form an understanding of what readers do, and to take a similar stance when they read and write independently.

Leslie's first teaching action was to read and analyze the story herself. She enjoyed it and responded to it deeply, relishing the insights into her own life. She read the story a second time and thought about her students and what the story could mean to them as readers and writers. She began to see possibilities for her students to learn how to discuss literature. Knowing her students and story structure helped her to select several "scenes" from the story where she could pause to encourage student response. A story, fiction, or personal narrative, is made up of scenes. In a well-written scene something happens and is vivid to readers. The root meaning of the word *vivid* is life. Leslie, as a teacher of reading, thinks through the stories she selects before presenting them to her students. She considers what the story is really about (theme), and which scenes might facilitate discussion and deep thinking. Her role is to guide thinking, not to get the students to "come up with the right answer."

Understanding Plot and Character

Leslie's goal was to stimulate high engagement in the story and facilitate discussion and thinking about the character and his wants and actions. She planned to help the students become more aware of the story's tension, created through the action and events, the conflict between characters, and the climax and ending. Let's see how Leslie addressed these goals.

Before Leslie began to read *Old Henry*, she and the students took a look at the illustration on the cover of the book. They talked about the house and its run-down condition. After reading a few pages, Leslie paused for the students to respond.

LESLIE: What do the neighbors want?

JAMES: They want Henry to fix things up a bit around his house, but Henry didn't think of it.

LESLIE: There seems to be a conflict in the story. How do you think Henry feels?

HANNAH: He thinks the house is interesting. He has a place for everything, like, one man's trash is another man's treasure.

PHILIP: He didn't think of it to clean up.

Leslie emphasized the relationship between the characters by pointing out significant details in the illustrations, like the messiness of the yard and house, and even Henry's clothing, and contrasting all that with the neatness of the neighbors' homes.

In this brief interaction, Leslie saw that students used both the text and the illustrations to understand the plot. Through conversation, they helped each other make meaning of the story as the character addressed his problem. At another point in the story, Leslie invited the students to think more about the characters' perspectives, their relationships with each other, and the conflict in the story. Leslie sharpened their awareness of the main character's dilemma by highlighting the conflict between him and the other characters. She prompted the students to think about what they already knew about Henry and to predict the actions Henry might take in response to the townspeople's requests to clean up his house. In a very brief, impromptu role play, two students took on the characters to dramatize the conversation between Henry and a townsperson.

LESLIE: The mayor suggests to a committee of neighbors that they talk to Henry and be nice instead. What would that look like? Who will come up here and do a little role play? [Maia and Hannah volunteer and come to the front of the group. Maia is the neighbor and Hannah is Henry.]
Hannah, use what you know about Henry to respond to Maia, who is a neighbor trying to be nice.

MAIA: [Role-playing] Hi, Henry. I was just wondering if you could fix up your house. Your house would match up the neighborhood. It would look nice. It would look like the rest of the neighborhood.

HANNAH: Sure, I'll fix up my house to make you guys happy. And thanks for saying it nicely.

LESLIE: Thank you. Hannah, why did you react like that to the neighbor?

HANNAH: Because Henry is easygoing. He doesn't really care about what the neighbor thinks, and would probably say yes to the neighbor because she was nice.

PHILIP: He has not cleaned it up yet. I don't think he will do it.

LESLIE: Well, let's read more of the story and find out what happens.

Leslie asked the students to use their ideas about the character to improvise a process drama through role play. To take on the characters, the students used the information they had gathered to predict how the characters would act and feel. Process drama provides opportunities for students to take on perspectives of others and come to new insights about the meaning of story (Fountas & Pinnell, 2006).

Notice that Leslie challenged the students' thinking. If conflict could disappear so easily, the plot might not be so interesting! Leslie read more of the story and the students began to realize that, at this point in the story, Henry does not agree to clean up his yard and house. This led to a discussion about compromise and how neighbors need to consider each other's wants if they are going to live in harmony. The students began to understand Henry better and to see both sides of the conflict. It is only when Henry leaves town that both he and the neighbors begin to miss each other. He returns to town, and, eventually, they all agree to compromise on the issue.

Through conversation, Leslie and her students negotiated meaning. They revised their thoughts as the story unfolded. The text and their interpretation created more information about the characters and events. Leslie sharpened their awareness of the main character's dilemma by highlighting the conflict between him and the other characters.

The opportunity to explain their reasons for what they made up in the role-play helped the students think and justify their beliefs and consider others' opinions. By attending to an important scene in the story, Leslie and her students thought and talked about theme and analyzed the characters. The discussion culminated with the students thinking about what the story was really about. The conversation throughout the reading supported the students thinking about and expressing possible universal truths.

Looking at Character and Dialogue

At another point in the story, Leslie drew students' attention to the dialogue between characters. Leslie understands that writers use dialogue to move plot along and that readers need to attend to characters' conversations to experience the full meaning of stories. Readers make connections to their own lives by inferring from the dialogue between characters. In the following example, Leslie and her students paused during the interactive read-aloud of *Old Henry*. They thought about the townspeople's conversations with each other after Henry realizes he would never please them and has left town for Dakota. In the scene, the townspeople come by Henry's abandoned house throughout the fall and winter.

LESLIE: [Reading] *They picked his apples and now and then someone would ask "Remember when…?*
Remember when…? Remember when…?"
What do you think they meant by that?

JAMES: Remember when he lived here, and look at it now.

LESLIE: What might they be feeling as they remember Henry?

HANNAH: Maybe they miss him.

JAMES: He might come back again.

LESLIE: How have the townspeople's feelings changed?

MAIA: They didn't like him at the beginning because he didn't clean his yard, but now they think they miss him. Maybe he could come back and clean up his yard and keep the inside of his house as messy as he wanted to.

LESLIE: Maybe that would be a compromise with the neighbors.

This brief interchange helped the students reflect on dialogue and the characters' feelings about Henry, and think about the theme of this story—that we are all different and we often need to compromise if we are going to get along with each other.

Leslie's intention was to draw her students' attention to aspects of narrative, especially dialogue. She wanted them to respond to the characters and to stimulate their thinking beyond the text. Attending to the dialogue between the characters helped the students make important inferences about plot, character, and theme. Figure 10-3 shows some uses of dialogue and actions readers and writers take.

The Writer's Craft: Dialogue

Aspects of Narrative	Reader	Writer
At the beginning of a story, dialogue can reveal both plot and character.	Readers connect to characters and their situations when dialogue is used to open a story.	Writers often use dialogue at the beginning to pull readers into a story. Conversation between characters reveals the direction of the plot and conflict between characters.
Dialogue moves the story forward.	Readers attend to dialogue to get a sense of the characters' traits and motivations. Readers look for revelations that indicate shifts in plot development.	Writers reveal characters through dialogue. Writers use dialogue to demonstrate relationships between characters, changes in tone, direction, and emotion.
Characters can remain silent rather than engage in dialogue.	Readers infer the meaning of a scene and relationships between characters when one character remains silent.	Writers reveal conflict or agreement between characters in scenes by keeping one character silent.

FIGURE 10-3. The Writer's Craft: Dialogue

At another point in the interactive read-aloud lesson, Leslie and the students paused to notice how the author used dialogue to show the personal differences and attitudes of the individual characters.

LESLIE: Listen as I reread this part. [Reading]

At last they decided to form a committee and went to him saying, "We are proud of our city. If you'd only help out, think how good it would look—"

"Excuse me." He bowed, and went back to his book.

Think about how the author uses dialogue to help us understand what the characters are like. The committee wants to persuade Henry to clean up his yard. Their language sounds nice but direct. The author wants us to think the committee is acting friendly and polite. Henry bows and responds, "Excuse me," and goes back to reading his book. What do his words say about his attitude? Think about the dialogue in this scene. What kind of a man is Henry? Why do you think that way?

Leslie wanted her students to notice how authors shape what characters say to convey meaning about who they are and what they need. There are subtle differences in word choice, syntax, and pace that provide information that readers use to comprehend meaning.

In this section, I have discussed only a few aspects of the writer's craft that children encounter as they hear and discuss stories. There are many more! But I will now illustrate how *Old Henry* became a resource for young writers in Leslie's classroom.

Using Fiction as a Resource for Writing Personal Narratives

Leslie, as a teacher of writing, supported her students in ways that helped them tap into their personal life experiences and view those experiences as scenes to learn the writing process. She helped her students look at their lives as drama and imagine themselves, and others, as characters in scenes. She encouraged them to think about their experiences, and to share their stories orally. Each student experienced how memories emerge in fragments: maybe images of wintertime and supper at the tiny kitchen table, mom at the stove serving up the meal, and the windows steamed up as a barrier between the family and the snowstorm. Sharing memories orally and then writing them as quick stories, or scenes, got her students started.

Young children take on oral storytelling and compose sentences, perhaps one at first, later a few that are connected, to communicate the images they hold of a life experience. We often prompt children to include a beginning, a middle, and an end to their personal narratives. Knowing how stories work may support students writing about a vivid memory to turn it into a narrative that is interesting to readers.

In writing workshop mini-lessons, as students shared scenes from their lives, Leslie encouraged them to "become storytellers"—that is, to connect with listeners by capitalizing on the character and the drama that unfolds when he tries to satisfy his desires, yearnings, or wants. Leslie used *Old Henry* as a mentor text, one that could help her students learn more about the craft techniques of the writer. In discussions during interactive read-aloud, Leslie and her students analyzed the story: How does the writer help us understand the character and what he wants? How is dialogue used to draw the reader into the story? How does the author show rather than tell? As they talked, Leslie helped her students become more aware of these writing techniques. In writing workshop mini-lessons, Leslie reread some of the story scenes and built on previous discussions to learn more about the craft of writing.

In one writing workshop mini-lesson, Leslie drew her students' attention to how writers maintain the interest of their readers by stretching out the tension of their stories. She had noticed that her students could talk about personal experiences, but wrote about them as lists of events, or statements, rather than as narratives that capture and hold readers' attention, like a storyteller might.

Leslie began the mini-lesson by rereading *Old Henry*. She pointed out that the author had used craft techniques to lengthen the readers' experience and enjoyment of the story. One technique is the use of dialogue to show what characters are like and to convey the emotions they feel throughout the story. Leslie's goal was to show her students examples of the use of dialogue in *Old Henry*, and to encourage them to try it in their own writing.

> LESLIE: In *Old Henry*, the author helped us understand the conflict between Henry and the towns-people. The author pulled us into the story—we wanted to know what would happen next. One way she did that was to include some conversation or dialogue between the characters. Listen to this part of the story again for the use of dialogue.

Leslie read several scenes that included dialogue and discussed with students how the author used dialogue to show that the conflict in the story was growing more emotional. They noted that as the tension increased between the characters, they, as readers, experienced similar emotions. As readers, they wanted to know if Henry and the townspeople would ever agree. Leslie pointed out that the tension in a well-written story is stretched out to help readers enter the experience of the characters. One way to increase reader involvement is through the use of dialogue. Then, Leslie used Hannah's unfinished piece to demonstrate how to make characters come to life through dialogue. She pointed out that one place to do this is at the emotional moments of their narratives.

> LESLIE: When you are writing about your life experiences, you will want to think of the people in your story as characters. You can help your characters speak for themselves if you think about the high points of your story. Hannah, will you tell us your story orally?

As Hannah told the class about her real-life experience, Leslie prompted her to share some of the remarks of the people in her story. The class discussed how adding these remarks to her written version would enrich her readers' understanding and enjoyment. Leslie concluded the lesson by encouraging the students to think about how they could effectively use dialogue in their narrative pieces.

Help Students Become Meaning-Makers

This chapter described aspects of narrative and implications for literacy learning and teaching. Gordon Wells, in *The Meaning Makers* (1986), reminds us that learning about the aspects of narrative will serve our students well as they strive to understand our world and their experiences in it. Understanding how narrative works will support students' constructing the meaning of the texts they read and write.

As teachers, we can use our understanding about the structure and demands of narrative to design lessons that will help our students learn to read and write. Our instructional decision making is guided by our intentions to support our students in becoming independent, meaning-makers. Teachers strive to do the following:

- Help students think about themselves as meaning-makers as they read and write
- Support their attempts to self-monitor for meaning in both reading and writing
- Explain and demonstrate strategic actions that will help students clarify and focus their writing and deepen their understanding of the texts they read
- Use mentor texts to help students notice how other writers make meaning

Conversations with students about narratives support their ability to understand and construct written text—and to make sense of their lives.

Suggestions for Professional Development

Working with other teachers in a group, explore some of these ideas to help all of you understand the significance of your life stories, both written and oral.

1. Have teachers work with a partner and ask each person to describe a memory of a personal experience to her or his partner. Then, have participants take a few minutes to write their personal narratives. Have teachers, still working as partners, read the written versions of their memories and then compare those versions to the oral storytelling. Discuss the role of oral storytelling as a support for writing personal narratives.

2. To understand story structure, ask participants to read a favorite picture book (fiction) to a partner. Analyze each book by determining its story structure, the main character's wants, the obstacles that emerge that challenge the main character, and the actions the character takes to overcome the obstacles. Discuss the craft techniques the author uses to build tension and resolve the character's dilemma.

3. To understand the role of conflict in fiction narratives, have teachers read aloud a picture book to a partner. Determine the conflict that emerges between characters and within characters as the story

unfolds. Discuss each character's emotions as a result of the conflict. What are the implications for planning interactive read-aloud lessons that support students in thinking within and beyond the text?

4. To understand how to use mentor texts in writing workshop mini-lessons, read aloud a picture book to a partner. Analyze the purpose of one or two examples of the dialogue, asking yourselves if the dialogue serves the following functions:

   • Introduces the characters and the plot?
   • Reveals characters' traits?
   • Shows the relationships between characters?
   • Demonstrates shifts in characters' attitudes?

   Discuss your examples and the implications for mini-lessons with students. ◂

CHAPTER 11

Creating School-to-Home Bridges Through Reading and Writing

by John McCarrier & Gay Su Pinnell

One of the most effective ways to motivate young children to read and write is for them to see adults reading and writing. Frequent models are a teacher or family member reading for themselves or reading aloud to a child. The latter activity is especially valuable because hearing texts read aloud expands children's knowledge of the structure of written language. They also learn how stories and other texts are organized; the texts *themselves* become models for the young writer. Children see adults writing less often, except for the routine lists and forms that accompany daily life. Adults seldom share the writing process with children at home, and even at school, teachers are more willing to share the writing of authors of children's literature than they are their own written products. Yet, a powerful way to help young children become writers is to share our own writing with them and invite them into the process.

We in the Literacy Collaborative (www.lcosu.org) kept this goal in mind as we developed KEEP BOOKS®, sets of small books designed to support beginning and more advanced readers. From children's first experiences at school, we wanted them to become engaged, *voluntary* readers, who gain information from reading, collect books, find themselves in the texts they read, and experience the real joy of reading. To be readers, children must do the following:

- Know the purpose of reading and writing
- Read with understanding and write to communicate
- Use reading and writing as tools for learning

The research is clear—the more children read, the better they get at reading (Anderson, Wilson, and Fielding, 1998). It is important for children to read successfully every day; it is just as important for them to read at home. All of this reading must be successful, interesting, enjoyable, and full of opportunities to learn more. Of course, most children cannot read when they enter kindergarten, and some are just beginning to read as they enter first grade; but with support and help, they quickly learn to read and enjoy very simple stories that usher them into the world of reading.

Since 1995, we have distributed more than 50 million KEEP BOOKS to schools, enabling an estimated 1 million children to build home collections of books that they can read and read again. (For more information about KEEP BOOKS, visit www.keepbooks.org.) In this chapter, we describe a new way of using KEEP BOOKS, one that reveals to young children the process of becoming an author of a *real book*. We have found that KEEP BOOKS raise children's interest and create greater confidence in reading (Gibson & Scharer, 2001). Through experiences with these books, children can develop knowledge of both the writing process and the structure of texts through talking with an author and writing their own books. We first explain the concept of KEEP BOOKS and then describe how one KEEP BOOK author invited children to become writers. Writing and sharing your own books is a process that you can use effectively in your own classroom; we guarantee that children will be delighted with it.

The Concept of KEEP BOOKS

We called our little books KEEP BOOKS because they are designed for children to read at school and then take home to keep. These 4¼-by-5½-inch books focus on everyday events that are familiar to children—such as eating pizza or catching a bug! Through experiences with KEEP BOOKS, children learn concepts such as these:

- You can get information from pictures, but you *read* the print. That's where the message is.
- Letters and sounds can help you figure out words.
- It helps to think about what would make sense.
- If you get stuck, it helps to start over and think what would sound right (and look right with the letters in the word).
- Punctuation helps you read better.

Seemingly simple ideas such as the ones above are only a part of the enormous amount of information that a young child has to acquire and coordinate in learning to read. During all of this learning, it's very important that the reading be fun and easy for the child. Without these qualities, learning will not be effective.

THE PURPOSES OF KEEP BOOKS

KEEP BOOKS serve a number of purposes, including the following:

- Providing a great deal of easy reading material, so children get lots of practice
- Including many high-frequency words that children read again and again, so they build up word knowledge
- Providing opportunities for children to notice how words "work" and learn phonics skills
- Making it possible for children to read on their own, rather than always depending on adults
- Motivating children to write

- Building a ready store of books at home that children can access any time
- Helping children learn to store, care for, and retrieve books
- Helping children build confidence in themselves as readers

KEEP BOOKS are not specifically designed for formal reading instruction. It is important to understand that a KEEP BOOK is a *different kind of book*. Children can write their names in these books, color the pictures, and keep them at home—this is all different from how they should treat other books. KEEP BOOKS do not take the place of children's literature, which should be included in every classroom library. They do not replace the books that teachers read aloud to children or the leveled book collection that teachers use for small-group reading instruction. Instead, KEEP BOOKS are "extra" reading that begins in the classroom and moves to the home and community.

THE DESIGN OF KEEP BOOKS

KEEP BOOKS are carefully designed to support readers as they progress in their ability to process texts. The very simplest KEEP BOOKS have characteristics such as these (see Figure 11-1):

- One or two lines of text
- Very easy high-frequency words
- Simple concepts
- Repeating patterns

Even the youngest readers, once they have heard the book or read it in a shared way, can process such simple texts independently. And, it is very good for them to read these texts over and over with family members. We would like for kindergarten and first-grade children to read a large number of these simple books, building knowledge of early understandings such as left-to-right directionality and word-by-word matching. As readers grow more sophisticated, they can progress to

FIGURE 11-1. *Trucks* (top) and *Look at Me!* (bottom)

KEEP BOOKS such as the following (see Figure 11-2).

As you can see, these texts are not so patterned; however, the language is natural and the topics are familiar. Also, there are easy high-frequency words, and readers are required to process simple dialogue. Even more challenging are KEEP BOOKS that present stories, such as the examples below (see Figures 11-3 and 11-4).

These texts have the following features:

- Variety of dialogue
- Many lines of text
- "Pre-paragraphing" through spaces between lines
- A full range of punctuation
- More complex stories

At the most sophisticated level of KEEP BOOKS, you will find simple chapter books and fiction and nonfiction pairs, for example. (See Figure 11-5.)

These fact and fiction chapter

I put my pencils and my notebook in my backpack.
2

I put my markers in my backpack.
3

"Please put your dirty tissue in the trash and wash your hands," said Mom. "Don't spread your germs."
6

"I will cover my mouth when I cough, too," said Cara.
7

FIGURE 11-2. *My Backpack* (top) and *Home Sick* (bottom)

books help children learn the characteristics of genre as well as conventions such as headings, graphics with additional information, and multiple paragraphs. They present the reader with extended dialogue, words in italics, complex sentences, and a variety of formats. If you examine the structure of KEEP BOOKS from the first very easy texts to the highest level (about second-grade level), you can observe a gradual increase in complexity. Each level demands more of young readers, and children can gain an implicit knowledge not only of words, but also of the ways texts are organized. And, this knowledge can support them as writers.

Of course, KEEP BOOKS are only a small part of a comprehensive literacy program that includes daily writing workshop, guided reading, and phonics and word study. In these classrooms, children are experiencing many texts each day, including those that the teacher reads to them as well as those they read for themselves. KEEP BOOKS provide clear examples, and if they are kept and valued at home, they add enormously to the school experience.

FIGURE 11-3. *Goldilocks and Baby Bear*

FIGURE 11-4. *Be Careful!*

The Literacy Collaborative has created several enlarged versions of KEEP BOOKS that correspond to many of the small versions. A BIG KEEP BOOK is 8½ by 11 inches and its print has been redesigned so it is easy for children to see. These enlarged books are helpful in introducing books through shared reading. Then, children read the little books for themselves. My Own KEEP BOOKS, 8½-by-5½-inch blank books, were designed to encourage young authors to write their own stories. These tempting blank books led to an idea for engaging children in an author-to-author dialogue in the process of becoming authors themselves.

Author-to-Author— The KEEP BOOK Way

Building on previous experiences with KEEP BOOKS, John, a KEEP BOOK author, designed a way to help beginning writers become authors. His goals were to help these young children understand the following:

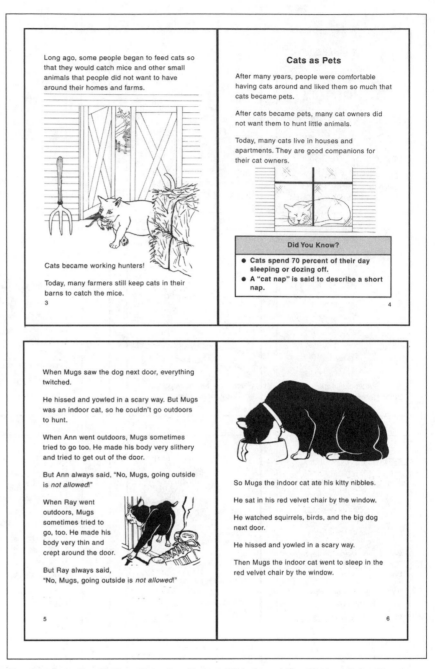

FIGURE 11-5. Nonfiction *Cats Are Hunters* (top) and Its Fiction Pair, *Mugs Indoors and Outdoors* (bottom)

- Adult writers follow the same process as beginners
- Writing from personal experience is powerful
- Perfection is not expected in writing, especially in a first draft
- Other texts can be a good source of ideas for writing
- The books they read in their classroom, as well as the books they take home, can be helpful as they do their own writing
- Everyone can write an eight-page book and illustrate it

Guiding K-3 Writers to Independence

In the next section, we describe the process John designed and has implemented in hundreds of classrooms he has visited as a guest author.

INTRODUCING THE MENTOR TEXTS

KEEP BOOKS were designed to be introduced at school (or in any other context that supports children's early literacy) and then to travel home with children. Teachers typically:

- Read the book to the child several times, inviting the child to "join in" as the story becomes familiar
- Read the book in a shared way (in unison, with the adult pointing to the words)
- Encourage the child to read the book independently

John uses a more personal approach. He begins by gathering the children on the carpet and showing them a mysterious box. He explains, "I am a writer visiting your school. I asked your teacher if she had any writers in her class that I could talk with. She said that you were all writers. Is that true? Oh, good—I love to talk with other writers about the stories that they are writing."

Then, he asks the children to talk about their own writing. He asks questions about some of the pieces of community writing (group writing) that are on the walls of the classroom and about individual pieces that are displayed. The children often talk about the writing that they keep in their writing folders and proudly show it to him. John then opens the box and shows the children a stack of KEEP BOOKS that he, his wife Andrea McCarrier, and their daughter have written—16 books altogether. When talking with older children, John points out that writers write different things for different audiences. He illustrates this point by showing them books and articles that he and his wife have written for older children and adults. Students immediately become interested in knowing more about John as a writer. You, as their teacher, can use the same strategy—you can write your own KEEP BOOKS and make the same claim. You can read the children a letter to the editor that you are drafting or an article you contributed to your church newsletter. Your students will be fascinated to hear about all of the writing that you do.

DESCRIPTION OF THE WRITING PROCESS

John tells the children that the steps he and other adult writers go through in writing books are the same steps that they are learning right now. Children will be using the writing skills they are learning in school for their entire lives, even when they are grandpas—like him! He asks, "What's the first thing that you do when you sit down to write?" Children always say, "think." John responds, "That's just what I do!" Then he tells them that he does the following:

- Writes about things he really knows about
- Thinks of the people who might read what he writes
- Asks other writers to talk with him about what he has written
- Rereads his writing and changes it

Next, it is time to get specific about texts. John introduces several books, or mentor texts, to the class. The first one shows children, in concrete and simple terms, how a writer proceeds to produce a book.

USING MENTOR TEXTS

Mentor texts can be a powerful influence on young writers, especially if teachers use them intentionally to foster writing abilities. John has selected four KEEP BOOKS as mentor texts that he uses with children in kindergarten and first grade. He has enlarged them to 8½ by 11 inches so the children can see the pictures and words as John and the children read them together. The typical process he follows is shown in Figure 11-6.

Sharing the Writing Process With Children

1. Introduces the book, showing the cover and indicating that he wrote it.
2. Reads the book to the children.
3. Gives each child a copy of the book and invites them to read it in a shared way.
4. Invites them to talk about the book by asking, for example, "What did this book make you think about?"
5. Tells why he wrote the book (personal experiences, something interesting).
6. Points out some of the decisions he made as a writer (as appropriate to the age group).
7. Asks children what they noticed about the writing.

FIGURE 11-6. Sharing the Writing Process With Children

Mentor Text—*My Brother's Motorcycle*

Of all the KEEP BOOKS John has written, *My Brother's Motorcycle* is his favorite because it

- Captures the children's interest with a topic they like: motorcycles
- Leads to a discussion of a more important topic, sharing by members of a family
- Is told from a child's point of view
- Shows that a complete story with a beginning, a middle, and an end can be told in eight pages (see Figure 11-7)

He introduces the book by saying, "This book is called *My Brother's Motorcycle*. I wrote this book because I wanted to write a book about members of a family doing things together. I was a big brother and I had a motorcycle, so I decided to write about something I knew, an older brother with a motorcycle who was nice to his younger brother."

He then gets children talking about their families by asking, "How many of you have big brothers or sisters? How many of you are big brothers or big sisters?" This always leads to the students talking about their families and also volunteering that various family members and their friends own motorcycles, snowmobiles, all-terrain vehicles, dirt bikes, and so on. After reading the book the class talks about their reactions to it: what they noticed about the writing, what they thought about the ending, how it made them feel. One child said the ending made him feel jealous because his older brother was not like the one in the book. A second-grade girl at a school in Minnesota declared, "I have an older sister. She has a snowmobile. I think I'll write a story titled 'My Sister's Snowmobile.'"

FIGURE 11-7. *My Brother's Motorcycle*

Then, John goes back into his box and takes out a stack of the blank My Own KEEP BOOKS described earlier. He tells the children, "I think that the people back at the book factory forgot to print the words and pictures in these books. Now I have all these blank books. What should I do with them?" Some children suggest that John use the blank books to write more stories, and when that suggestion arises, he says that he doesn't have time and points out that there are a lot of books. The children then decide that they can use the books to write KEEP BOOKS themselves. "You could give them to us! We can write our own KEEP BOOKS." John responds skeptically, "Are you sure?" "Yes!" the children reply. "We write all the time!" Finally, John gives everyone a blank book. But they do not begin to write just yet, because John says, "If you are going to write a book, you need to do a lot of thinking first. Let's look back at *My Brother's Motorcycle*."

John goes back through the mentor text, pointing out that it's really important to write about something you know. So, the children need to think hard about what they like, what's happening that they enjoy, and what they know about. He also points out that the pictures and words match and that he tried hard to make the ending interesting.

He finishes the mini-lesson by showing children a few examples of My Own KEEP BOOKS that other students have written, emphasizing that those children used their very best handwriting and

FIGURE 11-8. *Feeding the Birds*

spelling, but that these books do not have to be perfect. He also asks the children to whom they are going to read their books when they are finished writing them. If the children mention only their teacher, then John asks them if they will be reading to many people—family members and friends. In this way, he helps them think about an expanded audience for their written pieces.

Feeding the Birds

John wrote *Feeding the Birds* because he has several bird feeders on his back porch and enjoys watching the birds (see Figure 11-8).

Writing this book was a long process. He used the underlying structure of compare and contrast to tell about the birds. For example, two sets of pages use repeating patterns on facing pages for big and small birds and seeds and for square and round bird feeders. Often, when talking to a group of children, he particularly focuses on the ending of *Feeding the Birds*, saying, "When I first wrote the story, I ended it by saying that I always refill the bird feeder. But I read this ending to my friends, and they thought it was just a little boring. I wanted a more exciting ending, so they helped me think of all the times I chase raccoons away from the bird feeder. I put chasing raccoons at the end of my story, and that made it much better."

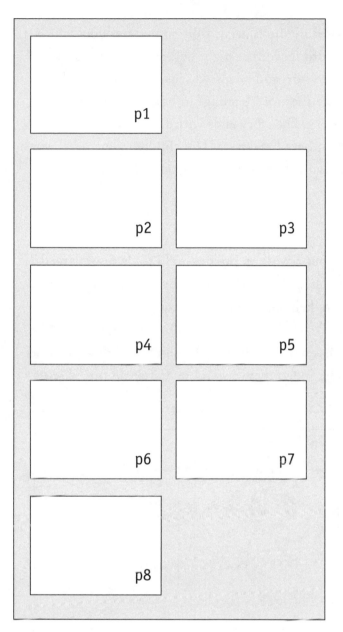

FIGURE 11-9. Layout Form for Advanced Writers to Plan My Own KEEP BOOK Story

With second and third graders, John uses a form that can help these more advanced writers plan a story (see Figure 11-9).

The form shows eight pages, with pairs of pages (in page layouts) facing each other. The writer can write a matching pattern on facing pages. John shows the children an example of the first draft of a story about the same bird feeders

FIGURE 11-10. *Clickety-Clack*

and the same raccoons but told from the perspective of Billy the Bluejay. Billy sometimes goes without breakfast because Ralph the Raccoon has emptied the bird feeder the night before. John shows the children how he drew illustrations and wrote text in each box, and he also discusses some edits that he made to improve the story. He emphasizes that he wrote the word "ending" in box eight to remind himself that he needed to have a good ending to the story. The story ends with Billy gently asking Ralph to leave some seeds in the feeder so that Billy can have breakfast. (The children generally favor a more confrontational ending.) John leaves these forms with the teacher for anyone who would like to use them.

A WORK IN PROGRESS

Another approach John uses is to talk with students about a work in progress. He reads his enlarged versions of *Clickety-Clack* and *Our Favorite Snowman*, KEEP BOOKS written by his wife and daughter, respectively, and talks about them as models that are helping him to write another book (see Figures 11-10 and 11-11).

John shows the children a draft of the new that he has written. He asks the children if they think he is finished with the story. They always say, "No!" Then he shows them two more drafts and they discuss

FIGURE 11-11. *Our Favorite Snowman*

Guiding K-3 Writers to Independence

the additions, changes, and improvements on each draft. He emphasizes that being a writer is about making decisions, and among the decisions he talks about are the following:

- Making the book eight pages long
- Having four lines on each page
- Having a kind of rhythm or "beat" to the book
- Using simple words such as "big" and "plain" with hard consonant sounds to maintain the "beat"
- Using a repeating phrase, such as "clickety-clack"
- Using natural language with unconventional spelling for the repeated phrase "whadda ya know"
- Having a beginning, a middle, and an end
- Having a transition into the end on the next-to-last page
- Tying the end of the story back to the beginning by repeating the phrase "pile of snow"

Then, he shows the children the final story and reads it to them. He discusses some of the decisions that he made while writing it and also talks about the title, "The Snowman Rap." Below are pages 1, 2, 7, and 8 from the story, which illustrate these decisions. Pages 2 through 6 repeat the pattern of page 2 with different locations in the house and articles of clothing for the snowman.

We built a big snowman but I don't know.
He looks too plain, just a pile of snow.
He needs decoration, some style and flair.
Let's look around the house and see what's there. (p. 1)

We looked on the coat rack and whadda ya know
We found a fur hat. Now where should it go?
On the top of his head. It sure looks fine.
Let's keep on looking to see what we find. (p. 2)

We looked in the hallway and whadda ya know
We found some old boots. Now where should they go?
He doesn't have feet. What should we do?
He looks pretty handsome. I guess that we're through. (p. 7)

Our snowman is finished and whadda ya know.
He looks really good, not a pile of snow.
He looks warm and cozy in his borrowed clothes.
He's all dressed up from his head to his toes. (p. 8)

Children's Writing

In this section we show some of the products that the author-to-author dialogue has inspired during many of John's writing workshop sessions with children. First, let's look at Aaron's book, *My Dad's Truck* (see Figure 11-12).

Notice that Aaron stays on the topic of his dad's truck, describing important characteristics of it.

Here is another good example from John's "author-to-author" talk with children—Haley's story called *The Fat Dog* (see Figure 11-13).

This text shows that Haley had internalized the idea of repeating patterns; yet, she includes a greater variety of sentences. Her informational book stays on the topic of the dog while providing a different piece of information on every page. She has numbered the pages, and several subtle characteristics indicate that she has learned a great deal from her experience with reading texts. For example, she begins page 1 calling her character "the fat dog," but she then uses a pronoun to refer to the dog on the rest of the pages. She begins

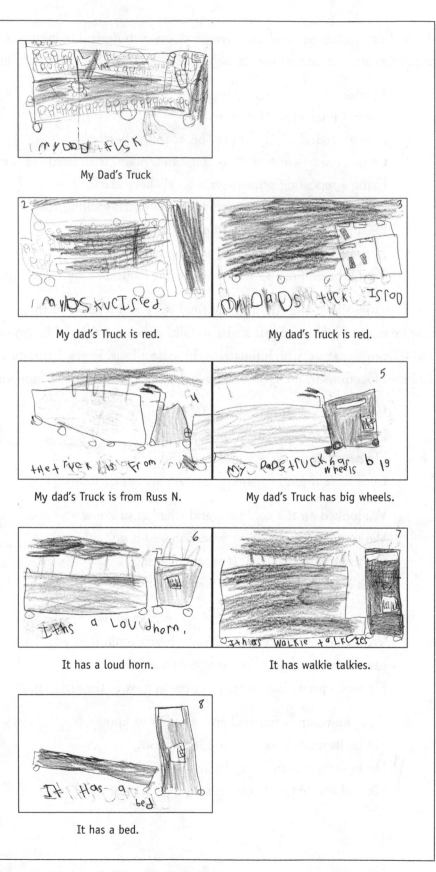

FIGURE 11-12. Aaron's Story, *My Dad's Truck*

Guiding K-3 Writers to Independence

her sentence on page 7 with the word *and*, creating a more literary feeling, and she has a conceptually satisfying ending.

We are not implying that this is the only kind of writing we want Haley to do, nor will her writing continue only in this vein. She will be exposed to a wide range of texts during her first-grade year and will use many of them as models, thus internalizing a variety of ways for organizing her writing. Right now, she is learning how to produce an extended piece of text on a single topic.

In the same class, Mackenzie produced the text below, which also shows awareness of pattern and variety in sentence structure. She also demonstrates memory of some high-frequency words, letter-sound knowledge, and ending punctuation.

[Page 1] I lik to swim.
[Page 2] I lik to go in the water at the lcc. (lake)
[Page 3] I lik to swim with the notls. (Nautilus)
[Page 4] The big bal is fun to pla with.
[Page 5] I lik to go don the slid.
[Page 6] I lik to go in the big pol.

The fat dog likes to lick you.

He likes to play.

He likes to bark.

He likes to jump and jump.

He likes to bite.

He likes to jump in the snow.

And he likes to be the king.

And he likes to be mine.

Figure 11-13. Haley's Story, *The Fat Dog*

[Page 7] It is fun to pla in the mishrom pol!

[Page 8] Swimin is fun!

In the example below, Emily shows that she can produce a highly organized informational text about her sister:

[Page 1] My sistr plas basktbl.

[Page 2] She plas fr the Sting.

[Page 3] Hr nam is Elizabeth.

[Page 4] She plays bast bl al the time.

[Page 5] She doesn't mak baskats.

[Page 6] She is on the tem.

[Page 7] She is a good drblr.

[Page 8] The end

Notice Emily's use of pronouns to refer to her sister as well as the capitalization of her sister's name. She uses ending punctuation except on the last page, when it is appropriate not to use a period. Across the text, you can see that Emily is working to get closer to conventional spelling.

Let's look at one more example from these beginning first graders: Figure 11-14 shows Jacob's exciting account of *The Race*, which is dedicated to "My Mom."

We love the way Jacob describes the action in an "it's happening now" kind of voice.
It is obvious that all of these young children are making progress in the conventions of written text, for example:

- Using letter-sound relationships to spell words
- Using high-frequency words that they know well
- Using punctuation, such as ending marks
- Using parts of words they know to spell other words
- Beginning to use capitalization
- Writing from left to right
- Differentiating between text and pictures
- Numbering pages

All of the above are important and represent essential steps in beginning writing; but even more important, they are learning some fundamental things that writers do, such as the following:

- Writing about things they know and/or are interested in
- Staying on a topic across a piece of writing
- Putting different and new information on each page (or in each section) of a text
- Creating a beginning, a series of events or categories of information, and an ending

- Making writing interesting by varying language

These young children are only beginning the long journey to becoming accomplished writers; but already they show some important understandings. For them, the process is whole; they compose and think while engaging everything they know about conventions. They are supported by access to texts that are highly supportive, by talk, and by dialogue with other writers. John's experience with hundreds of young writers reveals the power of sharing the writing process. Every teacher can write simple texts and use the computer and/or individual artistry to "publish" them for the children in the class, thus providing a powerful model that can give children access to the joy of being an author.

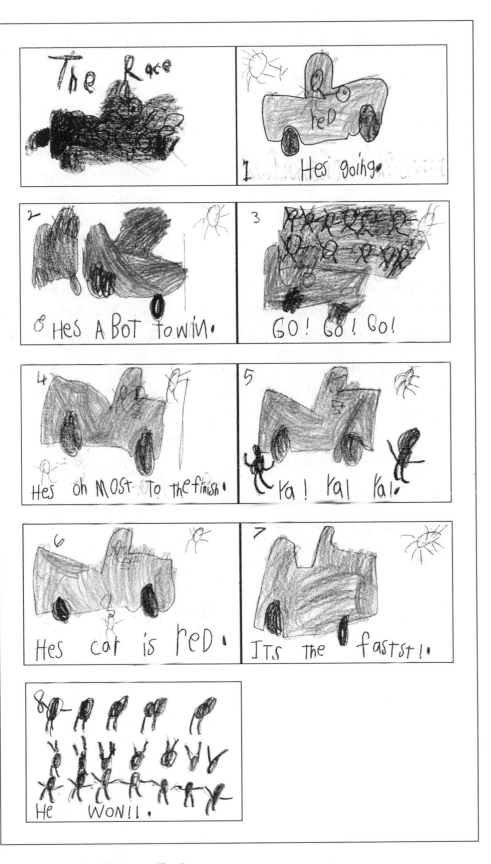

FIGURE 11-14. Jacob's Story, *The Race*

Suggestions for Professional Development

Work on these activities with a group of colleagues.

1. Have teachers pair up and then tell a story to each other that they want to write. Then, have time for them to draft their story, share it with a colleague, revise, and publish it using a My Own KEEP BOOK. Ask individuals to share their stories and also their thoughts about the writing process while working. Then, have each teacher share her story and the process she went through to write her story with her students as part of a mini-lesson on writing process. Share student responses to the lesson at a future meeting.

2. Help your colleagues find their voices as writers through a ten-minute write. First, read aloud one of the following books or start with one of the activities below. Then, model by telling and/or writing your own story. Finally, have teachers write their own personal narratives.

   - Introduce *Wilfrid Gordon McDonald Partridge* by Mem Fox with a memory basket and jot a list of ideas for additional items to include. Tell why.
   - Using *The Memory String* by Eve Bunting, create a list of big topics, such as vacations and families. Brainstorm many small topics that might trigger a memory. What buttons (memories) might you put on a string? Why?
   - Select an object from your purse/briefcase/wallet/pocket.
   - Write about a photo that is important to you. What story might come out of your relationship with the person in that photo?
   - Record the details of your life for the last 24 hours. Then, jot down some questions about yourself and your world. Think about which detail carries a story and write about it.

   Share your stories and then discuss these questions: What was involved in this process that led you to write? What are the implications for writing instruction?

Section IV

❧

Meeting the Needs of Individual Learners

"Meeting the Needs of Individual Learners" centers on how assessment and instruction merge to support the individual needs of young writers. Chapter 12, by Sherry Kinzel, provides an overview of writing assessment and draws particular attention to the importance of conversations between teachers and writers. The case study of Jesse by Rauline Morris in Chapter 13 is a fitting example of how teachers can move writers from reluctance to enthusiasm within a quality writing program that centers on students' individual needs. This section concludes with Emily Rodgers' chapter on the importance of providing writing instruction for students who struggle as a way to support their growth as both writers and readers.

CHAPTER 12

Assessment and Conversation: Powerful Tools for Teachers

by Sherry Kinzel

One of the most important things, if not the most important thing, that defines good writing teachers is that they are constantly learning about their students as writers. For good writing teachers, writing assessment is a habit of mind (Anderson, 2005, p. 2).

The Power of the Pen

Do you remember pouring your second-grade heart and soul into your two-page novel about your shiny red bicycle that you got for Christmas last year only to have the teacher return your work of art (your highest literary achievement to date) and find it covered with more red markings than your entire bike? You probably sat there staring at the paper with a steadily sinking feeling until you became aware that others might notice the red ink from across the room. Then you buried your paper, bloody from battle, under the stack of worksheets on your desk until you could give it a proper burial at home . . . in your trash can. You wouldn't dream of placing it on the refrigerator for all to see what a horrible writer you are.

The power of the marking pen is that it can inspire or demolish the human spirit. As teachers, we need to wield it with caution and care. Children of all ages consider their writing an extension of themselves, as do most published writers. As teachers of writing, we ask students to share their personal thoughts, feelings, memories, goals, desires, fantasies, fears, and accomplishments in their writing. We ask children to put themselves into their writing, so we must take care not to appear as though we are passing judgment on them or their lives when we assess their writing. There are many ways to

Assessing during a writing conference.

honor the writer's work while providing instruction and assessment that will ultimately benefit the writer.

In this chapter, I share the rationale for assessing writing—why do we do it? I also share practices and tools for effective assessment used by teachers in various grade levels.

Why Do We Assess Writing?

Every time you review, evaluate, and mark a student's writing, you are engaging in a form of assessment for one purpose—to give feedback to the student. In this chapter, I address several forms and purposes for the assessment of writing. In general, the purpose of assessing is three-fold: (1) to provide information about the writer's abilities; (2) to use as accountability; (3) to drive future instruction. Assessing written works is no different. You may notice that I have used the verb form—*assessing*—as much as I have used the noun form—*assessment*. We need to think of assessing as an active, ongoing process, not an end product.

Seeking Information

According to Richard Stiggins (1996), high-quality assessment starts with a vision of success. All writing teachers want their students to be successful writers. To ensure students' success, teachers need to have an understanding of where their writers are on the writing journey. When you use a map to find your way, the first information you need is to know exactly where you are. Only then do you have a good chance of finding the best path to your destination. Like using a road map, when you assess writing, you have to know exactly where you are in order to figure out the best path to take to arrive at your destination. Unfortunately, road maps are substantially easier to read at first than our students' writing abilities.

Think about the relationships in your life for a moment. Why are some deeper than others? Why does your best friend know more about you than your bank teller does? The teller may know your current checking balance, but your best friend has shared with you many more of the joys and pains of life than your cashier ever will. How does that happen? Two words form the answer—time and conversation. Just as we use these factors to build all relationships, time and conversation allow us to get to know our students as writers and to see students' strengths and challenges for ourselves. Time and conversation also help us develop mentoring relationships with our writers that, in turn, allow us to establish with them a collaborative vision that inspires progress.

Assessment must be an integral part of instruction. In fact, you can accomplish both assessment and teaching by observing and recording student behaviors during writing workshop. While the class is working independently on their writing pieces, teachers have one-on-one conversations with young writers. Individual conferring is a powerful component of writing workshop. In this one-to-one conversation, the teacher begins to develop the stance that "writing assessment is a habit of mind" (Anderson, 2005, p. 2). Before each conference prepare by asking yourself, "What do I know about this child as a writer?" During the conference and immediately following it, record the responses to these questions: What did I observe about this writer that confirms what I already knew? What did I learn? What is my learner's next goal? How can I support him in reaching his goal? The goals you and your student set will create a path of progress.

Collecting Information

You can collect assessment data in a variety of ways. Many teachers use individual conferences to record observations about a student's writing. While the student is sharing the writing, you have the opportunity not only to make quick notes about the written products, but also to record evidence of the student's self-awareness. These notes begin to build a picture of the developing writer.

We have found it helpful to use a master form in a way that makes it easy to monitor progress, plan future instruction, and share data with parents. You can house these materials in a binder with separate sections for each student or place them in hanging files. Tailor the master form to your own needs and purposes. The examples that follow are forms that classroom teachers have used successfully. You may want to use these examples as you develop your own form, realizing that sometimes it is very helpful for teachers across a grade level or several grades to use the same form. Above all, a recording form should be quick and easy to use. Also, you do not want the form to "take over" your conference time, during which the highest priority is your conversation with the student. The form should support the conferring process as well as allow quick notes that will help you use time effectively.

The recording form shown in Figure 12-1 provides space for brief comments about observations, as well as a section that allows you to keep track of which days and the number of days you have met with specific children. This information is helpful because it is easy to over-look an individual writer during a busy school week. The form also has space at the bottom in which to record the needs of writers in general terms; for example, notes on priorities for instruction based on patterns that are appearing in this writer's work that could be addressed with the whole class during mini-lessons. Using a form such as this one can help you notice when several students have the same needs. These observations

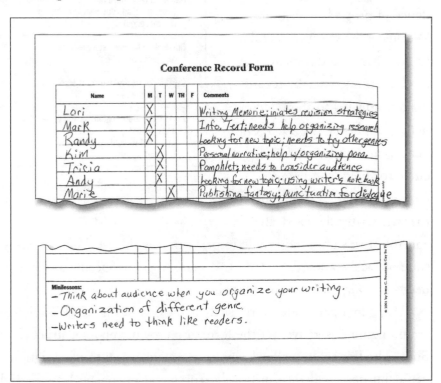

FIGURE 12-1. Conference Record Form

can be invaluable in informing your instructional decisions as you plan mini-lessons with the entire class, guiding writing with small groups, and conferences with individuals.

The recording form shown in Figure 12-2 was created by a group of primary teachers to collect specific information about their young writers. They began with their own understanding of the process of learning to write. To create the document, they made a list of recognizable early writing characteristics that, based on research, they believed would lead to successful writing. They used the form to help them find evidence of progress over time. While conferring with a child, the teacher would indicate the level of competence by recording a minus (−) to show "no evidence," a plus (+) to "some evidence," and a plus enclosed in a circle to show "competence." Competence in an area indicates that the writer demonstrates

NAME: Ben					2001-2002 YEAR/LEVEL: 1st		
WRITING PROCESS — Date:	9/3	11/10	1/21				
Knowledge of language organization (surface structure) Pictorial representation	+						
Scribble writing	−						
Random invented letters	+						
Linear invented writing	−	+					
Strings of repetitive alphabetic letters	−	+					
Strings of varied alphabetic letters	−	+					
Groups of letters with space between	−	+	⊕				
Copying sentences or words unrelated to stated topic	−						
Any recognizable word (own)	−	+					
Developing knowledge of sound/symbol correspondences	−	+	⊕				
Any simple sentence	−	+	⊕				
Message quality (deep structure) Identifies objects in picture	+						
One-sentence description of picture	−						
Tells a story about picture	+						
Has a concept that a message is conveyed (Tells message but what is written is not message)	+						
Correlation between story read back and piece of writing	−	+					
Correct (or nearly) words interspersed in right places	−	+	⊕				
Part of directional pattern is known — start top left move left to right return down left	−	+	⊕				

FIGURE 12-2. Recording Form Created by Teachers

control of this area and is able to perform it with ease. You can easily create a similar form using a list of state or local standards as a start. Be sure to get as specific as you need to be and tailor it to meet the needs of your students and school.

Using an open-ended form such as the one in Figure 12-3 allows you to make notes capturing evidence in an ongoing narrative, yet the form also provides enough structure to enable you to make later interpretations. The left column allows you to record what you think is significant about the piece (i.e., the title, genre, purpose, audience, areas of strength and/or concern). In the right column you can record the teaching point that is needed to support the writer with this piece or a future goal. Also, rubrics can be used as

Guiding K-3 Writers to Independence

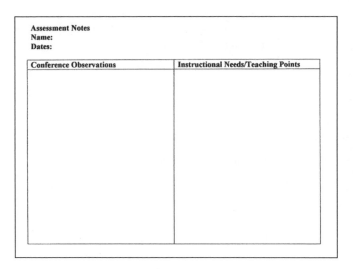

Assessment Notes
Name:
Dates:

Conference Observations	Instructional Needs/Teaching Points

FIGURE 12-3. Blank Recording Form

tools to support the assessment of specific qualities or traits of writing. Once you learn to use them, rubrics represent a quick way to collect information about your writers since the criteria for a rubric are set. More and more states are requiring the analysis of student achievement in writing using rubrics designed to measure competencies relative to various traits such as ideas and content, organization, voice, word choice, sentence structure, and conventions. The development of these traits supports your writers in many ways, as shown in Figure 12-4.

Such assessment may become the driving force behind the curriculum, so rubrics can be very influential. Teachers tend (or are required by administrators) to align writing instruction with these traits because many state assessments are analyzing students' progress in these same or similar traits and teachers want their students to be successful on state writing tests. In some school districts, committees are asked to survey the state standards in the areas of written communication and then create a standard-based tool for teachers to use during writing conferences. Evidence of progress toward meeting competency of a state standard can be noted with a point value, a date,

Rubric Traits

Ideas and Content	• Clear, well-focused message • Important details relevant to the topic • Interesting and easy to understand
Organization	• Beginning (lead) that hooks the reader and is easy to follow • Best way chosen to organize the message • Ideas link to main message • Strong conclusion
Voice	• Enthusiastic about topic • Sounds like writer talking • Holds the reader's attention
Sentence Fluency	• Easy to read • Sentences begin in different ways • Some long and some short sentences • Sounds smooth when read aloud (seems to flow)
Word Choice	• Some strong verbs or colorful phrases • Most precise words chosen • Any unique words • Avoids repeating common words too many times
Conventions	• Spaces between words and sentences • Title written correctly • Correct punctuation • Correct capitalization • Proper spelling • Proper grammar • Paragraph indented

FIGURE 12-4. Writing Traits Chart

Rubric for Academic Content Standard

Academic Content Standard
Language Arts—Fifth Grade
Writing Processes (Drafting, Revising, and Editing)

"Organize writing to create a coherent whole with an effective and engaging introduction, body and conclusion, and a closing sentence that summarizes, extends, or elaborates on points or ideas in the writing."

Introduction is . . .	effective and engaging 3	somewhat effective 2	not effective 1	missing 0
Ideas within the writing are . . .	well extended and elaborated 3	extended and/or elaborated some of the time 2	rarely extended or not clearly elaborated 1	not extended or elaborated 0

FIGURE 12-5. Rubric for Academic Content Standard

or a simple check mark. Figure 12-5 provides an example of using a state standard to create an assessment tool.

Ruth Culham encourages the use of rubrics with students and has developed several rubrics that are teacher-friendly and easily understood when used with students. You may find her book *6+1 Traits of Writing: The Complete Guide for the Primary Grades* (2005) to be a supportive resource. It

Advantages and Cautions About Rubrics

Ways Rubrics Are Helpful	Cautions About Using Rubrics
• Provide a way of collecting information or evidence of your students' learning • Quick and simple to use • Help build an ongoing picture of who your students are as writers • Cause you to continually reflect on your teaching	• Using them to grade (evaluate) but not using them to inform teaching • Using rubrics that do not have language that is accessible for students • Using rubrics that do not help students understand the expectations for performance

FIGURE 12-6. Advantages and Cautions About Rubrics

includes many examples of student writing to help you recognize the traits. Rubrics should not be used for grading or evaluating. As with all forms of assessment, their strength lies in their ability to inform your instruction. The advantages and cautions about using rubrics are listed in Figure 12-6.

The writing process is complex and multifaceted; so our assessments must reflect this understanding. You want to create a clear, well-supported view of their writing potential and progress, and using more than one form or tool to collect information on students as writers can help.

Getting Started

If you are new to systematic writing assessment and have not used tools such as those described above, you may be a bit uncertain about what you should record. Trust your instincts; they are usually right. When a child shares his work, the most pressing issues will pop right out at you. Make a note of them, but do not dwell on them. Assess the work to determine the learner's needs, but also look for evidence of what the writer can manage on her own and the degree to which she does it successfully. You will find that evidence of the learner's strengths is highly valuable and gives you a conservative view of what the beginning writer controls. Also, it is important to help writers use what they know to expand their learning.

Whichever tools you choose to use to collect information, make sure you remember that your goal is to "capture what students do well so they can do it again, and what they're not doing so well so you can help them do better next time" (Culham, p. 39). Communicating these ideas clearly to young writers has a much greater impact than any number or score. The ongoing process of conferring is a routine that develops a sense of accountability in young writers.

Building Accountability Through Conferring

All writers, even this one, live with deadlines. I am not referring to accountability as just the timely completion of a piece, however. A deadline is something much greater; it connotes expectations of progress for writing as writers. Confer regularly with your young writers to communicate and establish these expectations. For example, join me in a conference with Austin:

SHERRY: Hi, Austin. How's it going?

AUSTIN: Good.

SHERRY: What are you working on right now?

AUSTIN: I'm writing about a trip to the beach. I just started today, so this is my first draft.

SHERRY: Okay, so you're not worried about everything being perfect just yet.

AUSTIN: Nope. I'm just trying to get my ideas down.

From this brief exchange, I already know that Austin understands part of the writing process. He knows that the purpose of the first draft is to just get his ideas down on paper without worrying about grammar and the other conventions. He is focused on the story and the meaning that

Sherry and Austin confer about his writing.

he is trying to communicate to his reader. He realizes that he will have an opportunity to revise and edit as needed during another portion of the writing process.

SHERRY: Good thinking. Where did you get your original idea for the story?

AUSTIN: I found a page in my writer's notebook about stuff I did last summer. My family went to the beach with my grandparents, my aunt and uncle, and my cousins. They are younger than me.

SHERRY: So you're not writing about the whole summer, just the trip to the beach?

AUSTIN: Uh-huh!

Now I have further insight about Austin as a writer. He knows how to use resources such as a writer's notebook for ideas of things he can write about. He also can choose to narrow his topic or focus on a smaller topic, a common practice of published authors.

SHERRY: Austin, that's great! You know many writers choose to focus on a smaller piece of time when they write. It makes their writing more interesting and pulls their readers into the story. It's like the book we talked about, *Saturdays and Teacakes* by Lester Laminack. Mr. Laminack didn't tell us about the boy's whole life. He chose to tell us about one event in his life—going to his grandma's house on Saturday. Writers make a lot of choices. It sounds to me like this time you are making the same choice that Mr. Laminack made. You are planning to tell about a trip to the beach, not the whole summer vacation.

AUSTIN: Yep. I just want to tell that part.

SHERRY: Do you have any questions or concerns that you want to talk about as you start this piece?

AUSTIN: Well, I'm having trouble getting started.

SHERRY: A lot of writers struggle with that, including me. You said that you got your idea from your writer's notebook, right?

AUSTIN: Yes. I found it in a list of stuff I did last summer.

In this conference, Austin is able to recognize his need and communicate it well; he doesn't know how to generate or expand his idea. Even if students don't communicate as clearly as Austin, they will often give you an opening to support their learning if you listen carefully and notice their nonverbal cues. Based on Austin's comment about having trouble getting started, I chose to provide him with several options and let him decide which one he wanted to try out.

SHERRY: Okay. Well, let me give you some writer's advice. You could do several different things to help get your thoughts together. You could make another list, but this time your list would be just of things you did or saw at the beach. You could make a web with the beach vacation in its center, then connect your memories in other bubbles to the main idea in the center. [I modeled the web on paper.] You could make a sketch of how the beach or beach house looked to you. You could even talk to another writer about your trip to bring back important memories and get their reaction to what they think is interesting about your beach trip. Do you think one of these ideas might help you get started?

AUSTIN: Yes. I'd like to try talking to another writer and maybe sketching the place where we stayed.

SHERRY: Great! Why don't you get started on your sketch, and I'll see if Drew has some time today to listen to your thinking about your beach trip. You will want to keep your writing folder with you during your talk in case you get a great thought that you want to add to your piece or Drew gives you some feedback about what he thinks is really interesting as you tell him your story. I'll go ask him if he can spare a little time for you today. Maybe later you can do the same thing for him. How does that sound?

AUSTIN: Good!

After this conference with Austin, I recorded some observations on a form (see Figure 12-7). For example, Austin needed support with generating and expanding his thinking around a topic. I also noted that he uses his writer's notebook to generate ideas for writing. This type of conversation informs the teacher of what she can reasonably hold her students accountable for in their writing, and it allows the teacher to provide clear expectations for the students' writing in the future.

Assessment Notes for Conference With Austin

Writing Assessment Notes
Name: Austin
Dates: 9/21

Conference Observations (What do I notice about this writer?)	Teaching Points & Goals (How can I help this writer?)
• Working on first draft • Trip to beach • Personal narrative • Uses writer's notebook for topics • Values narrowing topic • Needs help getting started	• Offered suggestions for generating, expanding topic (list, web, confer w/partner, sketch); he chose to confer with Drew

FIGURE 12-7. Assessment Notes

Driving Instruction

We all have local and state requirements that motivate us on some level to evaluate our writers' finished pieces and compare them to writing examples of various degrees of quality, as established by local and state expectations. This process of comparison helps us establish a common vision for writing that exemplifies quality and measures progress toward it; it is the heart of accountability. Assessment is also an essential part of instruction, however. Only through close observation and analysis can you make good decisions about what to teach and when and how to teach it. As you look at an individual writer's work, look for quality. Identify what the writer is doing effectively and move from these strengths to what the individual needs to do more effectively. Next, look for patterns across students, and then decide whether the needed instruction can best be provided in individual, small-group, or whole-group settings—or should it be presented in different ways in all three? Let's look at a few examples across different grade levels.

Lila is a kindergartner who has written a story about going to her grandma's house (see Figure 12-8). I read the writing several times and viewed the supporting picture. Then I began to analyze by asking a question. What do I know about Lila as a writer?

FIGURE 12-8. Lila's Story

- She uses symbols to represent letters, words, and sounds.
- She understands the concept of directionality (shown by recording symbols in a left to right sequence).
- She attempts letter/sound correspondence (shown by writing "mi" for the word *my*).
- She knows that print should convey a message.
- She doesn't use spaces between words.
- She has some confusion about letter/sound correspondence. (She wrote "y" to represent /w/ as the beginning letter for *went*. Beginning writers commonly write the name of the letter that matches the sound they hear. She heard the name of the letter *y* as she began to say *went*.)

Based on this analysis I ask myself another question: What's next for this writer? The answer to my question will determine my future instruction. My analysis has revealed her greatest needs, and I reconsider these, looking for priorities. Then, I select two areas or concepts to focus on. One concept that I would choose to teach this writer is the importance of spaces between words. I know that this will make her writing easier to read and help her communicate her message more clearly. It also will support her understanding of directionality within words as she learns that most words have a beginning, a middle, and an end. Controlling this information will enable her to later take on more complex knowledge about how words work. I would also choose to help expand her knowledge of letter-sound correspondence. It is apparent that she has some ability to match letters and sounds; however, extending her understanding in this area will help her generate more writing in the future. The instruction provided to Lila could easily take place in various settings. In this case, I provide instruction in a whole-class setting during a mini-lesson at the beginning of writing workshop, because Lila was not the only student who needed to learn the importance of using spaces between words and letter-sound correspondence at this early point in the school year. These same concepts were repeated during interactive writing sessions. I knew that most of my students would benefit from instruction in these two areas; therefore, whole-class instruction was the best setting.

Let's take a look at a first-grade writing example from Michael (see Figure 12-9).

Again, I ask myself the same questions: What do I know about this student as a writer? (analysis) and What's next for this writer? (instructional decisions).

Analysis:

- He uses left-to-right directionality and a return sweep for text that continues beyond the edge of the paper.
- He uses spaces between words consistently.
- He uses known words correctly, such as *I*, *at*, and *my*.
- He hears beginning and ending sounds in words and can make appropriate letter-sound correspondence. For example, the /s/ and the /d/ in "stad" for the word *stayed*. He also recognized /t/ and /n/ in "tan" for the word *ten*.
- He hears and records blends, such as *stad* and *Granmo*.
- He uses vowels in words consistently.
- He uses punctuation properly.

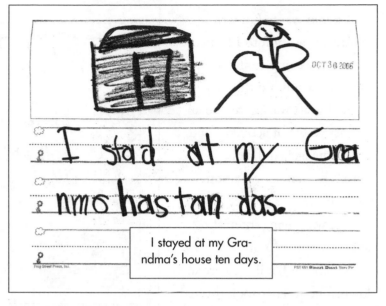

FIGURE 12-9. Michael's Story

Instructional decisions:

Based on my observations of the writing, I believe that Michael is ready to expand his thinking about onset and rime and learn about word families. Examining the writing, I notice that he can manage the beginning blend /gr/ (onset) in *Granmo*. I would ask Michael to think of other words he knows that begin like *grandma* and together we could list those words on chart paper. I could also draw his attention to the sounds at the middle and end of words (rime). After writing the word *ten* on a chart and showing him the part of the word that says –en, he and I could create a list of words that rhyme with *ten*. Being able to apply what he knows about a familiar word to another unknown word helps develop flexibility in the use of words and expands a writer's written vocabulary. This knowledge will support him in attempting to write words that may be a part of his spoken vocabulary but not his writing vocabulary.

This young writer had the same characteristics as two other advanced writers in our class. I believe that each writer makes progress when he is working at his own instructional level. Therefore, I chose to address Michael's instructional needs in a guided writing setting rather than a whole-class setting. So, I met with Michael and the other two advanced writers at my reading table. While the other students were working independently on their own pieces, I provided instruction similar to a whole-class mini-lesson to these three writers. The guiding writing setting is brief (five to fifteen minutes) and allows me to focus my instruction on a small group of children with similar needs. In guiding writing I am able to use my time more efficiently by meeting with three or four students instead of just one.

Lauren wanted to write about her vacation to Florida. During a writing conference, the teacher noticed that her original draft was more like an exhaustive list of activities and the events lacked details. Through their conversation Lauren's teacher noticed that Lauren was giving interesting details about the portion of the trip when the family car broke down. The teacher took this opportunity to share examples of ways to make a piece more interesting for the reader, such as descriptive words, voice, and dialogue. Together, they located parts of the writing where these strategies could be used. As a result of this conference, Lauren decided to narrow her focus for writing from a summer vacation to just the event of the car breaking down. The book that follows (see Figure 12-10) is a direct result of the conversation that Lauren and her teacher had about her writing.

As you continue conferring with students in your class, you may notice certain trends. Some areas may require additional instruction for the majority of students, some for

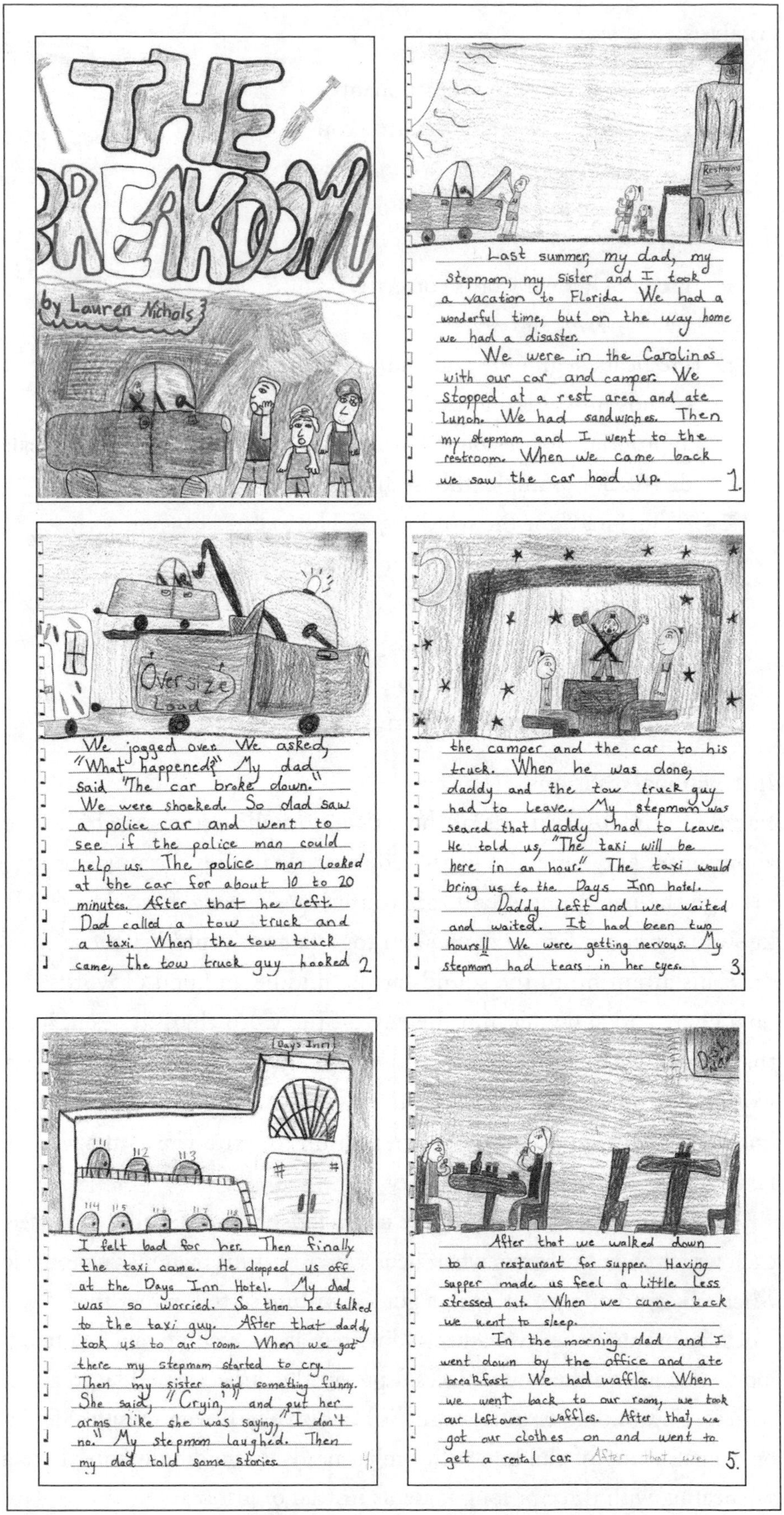

FIGURE 12-10. Lauren's Book

THE BREAKDOWN
by Lauren Nichols

Last summer, my dad, my stepmom, my sister and I took a vacation to Florida. We had a wonderful time, but on the way home we had a disaster.

We were in the Carolinas with our car and camper. We stopped at a rest area and ate lunch. We had sandwiches. Then my stepmom and I went to the restroom. When we came back we saw the car hood up. 1.

We jogged over. We asked, "What happened?" My dad said "The car broke down." We were shocked. So dad saw a police car and went to see if the police man could help us. The police man looked at the car for about 10 to 20 minutes. After that he left. Dad called a tow truck and a taxi. When the tow truck came, the tow truck guy hooked 2

the camper and the car to his truck. When he was done, daddy and the tow truck guy had to leave. My stepmom was scared that daddy had to leave. He told us, "The taxi will be here in an hour!" The taxi would bring us to the Days Inn hotel.
Daddy left and we waited and waited. It had been two hours!! We were getting nervous. My stepmom had tears in her eyes. 3.

I felt bad for her. Then finally the taxi came. He dropped us off at the Days Inn Hotel. My dad was so worried. So then he talked to the taxi guy. After that daddy took us to our room. When we got there my stepmom started to cry. Then my sister said something funny. She said, "Cryin'" and put her arms like she was saying, "I don't no." My stepmom laughed. Then my dad told some stories 4.

After that we walked down to a restaurant for supper. Having supper made us feel a little less stressed out. When we came back we went to sleep.
In the morning dad and I went down by the office and ate breakfast. We had waffles. When we went back to our room, we took our leftover waffles. After that, we got our clothes on and went to get a rental car. After that we 5.

only a small group. If many students are struggling in an area, instruction should take place in a whole class setting, such as mini-lessons, a great way to address similar needs in a time efficient manner. These brief lessons require about ten minutes and provide opportunities for immediate application. Figure 12-11 is a basic plan for mini-lessons.

You may discover that several students have similar instructional needs that are not shared by the majority of the class. In this

Basic Plan for Mini-lessons

1. Introduce the strategy or concept
2. Explain why it is important for readers
3. Demonstrate the strategy or share examples of concept
4. Explain the strategy of concept
5. Engage the students in guided practice or conversation about the idea
6. Summarize new learning
7. Provide independent practice

(Adapted from *Extending Our Reach: Teaching for Comprehension in Reading, Grades K–2*, Pinnell & Scharer, pp. 108–109)

FIGURE 12-11. Basic Plan for Mini-lessons

case, the efficient approach is to gather those students and provide explicit instruction. This small-group setting is often referred to as guided writing (Fountas & Pinnell, 2001). It is useful because it addresses the instructional needs of these few students while allowing the rest of the students, who do not need this information, to work independently. To provide a guided writing lesson, follow the basic plan described above for providing a mini-lesson to the class; however, in this setting, you will provide each student with more individualized attention. As often as possible, you can use examples of students' writing or published writing to support this learning. It is extremely important that writers have examples from actual texts that illustrate the strategy or concept that is being developed.

Assessment and Learning

It if often said that assessment and learning are two sides of the same coin—as we assess our writers we are building a body of knowledge that will enable us to become instructional decision-makers. The decisions we make and goals that we set with our learners will ultimately determine their level of success as writers. Effective teachers learn from their students daily. Teachers should view assessment as a way of learning more about their students, and students should view assessment as a way of learning what they are doing well and what they need to improve. It is important to communicate with our writers by providing them with feedback about their writing in a safe setting, which includes calling their attention to the progress they are making. Unfortunately, assessing is often confused with evaluating and is used only for determining a grade. We need to change our thinking about this. Most of us agree that a greater purpose is served when we follow the old adage of "teaching a boy to fish, rather than giving him one fish." The same principle can be applied to assessing. Simply assigning a grade for writing will not have the far-reaching effect that conferring and assessing a piece of writing with a child will have. With a new perspective, assessment can be thought of as a fact-finding process that leads us to greater discoveries about our students' writing and to critical opportunities for us as teachers to help all our students to step into the role of a true writer.

Suggestions for Professional Development

Work on these activities with a group of colleagues.

1. Ask each teacher to bring a copy of one current writing sample each from a high-, a middle-, and a low-progress writer in his or her class. Have the teachers form grade-level groups, and then place some of the samples on roll paper to form a continuum from early to more sophisticated writing. (You may not need to use all the samples, but include those that represent a distinctive characteristic.) Write a specific description for each sample on 4-by-6-inch cards and tape each of these below the sample it describes. Think about the patterns of writing progress you notice from low- to high-progress writers. What patterns seem to emerge across grade levels over time? Share your findings with the whole group. (Later, the charts can be combined to form a schoolwide continuum that can be used for reference and revised to reflect new learning.)

2. Using your state standards and school district writing assessments, rubrics, or guidelines, ask each grade-level group to generate a short list of benchmark writing behaviors/characteristics they would like to see in writers by the end of the year. Compare this list with the descriptors and samples analyzed in the last session. Have each grade discuss and chart the following:

    *   Where are our students in their development as writers?
    *   Where are the gaps?
    *   What focus areas do we need to address in our teaching this year? (Keep your list short and prioritize the goals.)

    Share your end-of-year benchmarks and instructional focus goals with the whole group.

3. Again, have teachers work together by grade levels to develop an assessment tool that would support their collection of information about their writers. You could create an easy-to-use tool, such as a rubric or checklist, by reviewing state or local standards to clarify grade-level expectations and to use as guidelines. This tool could be used to note progress over time, as well as assist in decision making about future instruction.

CHAPTER 13

From Reluctance to Enthusiasm

by Rauline Morris

Jesse is a first-grade boy with lots of energy and interests in outdoor activities. He enjoys playing soccer and basketball, and he wants to sandwich all the physical exercise he can into a regular school day. Academically, Jesse struggles in the areas of reading and writing. His journey, the focus of this chapter, carries him through the school year and demonstrates a teacher's professional decision making that empowers Jesse to transition from a beginning writer to a more systematic, confident, developed writer. Here is Jesse's story.

Jesse as a Writer in September

Jesse began grade 1 in the fall with limited writing behaviors and abilities. A quiet child who rarely let you know what he was thinking, Jesse easily blended in with the other 22 students. He did what was asked of him and often survived by emulating what other students were doing. He managed to stay unnoticed by his teacher, Judy, until the day she and Jesse sat down together. At that time, Judy administered some one-on-one assessments. Her sensitive observation of what Jesse did, her careful attention to his responsiveness, and the data she obtained from the formal assessments informed the instructional program that was needed to move Jesse ahead both as a reader and a writer.

Figure 13-1 shows Jesse's performance on the Writing Vocabulary subtest from Marie Clay's Observation Survey (2002). To administer this test, Judy gave Jesse a pencil and a piece of paper and said to him, "I want to see how many words you can write." He

Jesse
SUN
MI
cat
Dog
Ran

FIGURE 13-1. Jesse (Sept. 11, 1997)

was given ten minutes to write as many words as he could. She asked him, "Can you write your name?" and Jesse wrote his name. Jesse also needed the teacher's prompts to write the remaining words, *sun*, *my*, *cat*, *dog*, and *ran* (see Figure 13-1).

Jesse's strengths, as shown by this test, were his left-to-right directionality, making and recognizing some of the visual symbols (letters), some letter-sound connections, and five words spelled correctly. Jesse's scores were the lowest in the class on all of the subtests of the Observation Survey. Because Jesse was one of the older students in the class, Judy was concerned about his small repertoire of words and his difficulties in the other areas shown by the data. Jesse scored in the second stanine in Letter Identification (the highest stanine is nine) and the first stanine in each of the other subtests areas: Concepts About Print, the Ohio Word Test, and Hearing and Recording Sounds in Words.

In the Letter Identification test, Jesse had to identify all of the capital and lowercase letters of the alphabet, plus the letters *g* and *a* printed as we often see them in books. The Concepts About Print test gave Judy a window into what Jesse recalled about the written language in his environment. For this test, Jesse was given a designated book and asked to identify specific concepts on each page. These print concepts included left to right, return sweep, one-to-one matching, concepts of first and last, and many other indicators of a student's progress in becoming a successful reader. The Ohio Word Test is a list of designated words indicating which words Jesse had accumulated as he began his reading vocabulary. During the Hearing and Recording Sounds in Words test, a sentence was dictated to Jesse and he wrote the sounds that he heard. This test showed Jesse's ability to hear sounds and write what he heard. Jesse's scores in the lowest stanines for all of these tests was an indicator of a potentially struggling reader and writer.

Jesse avoided writing. During the daily writing time his reluctance was evident by his hesitation. In fact, he would "do anything" to not write. He spent extra time trying to find his writing supplies, even though they were in conspicuous places. While other students had their pencils and writing folders on their desks, Jesse searched his desk and book bag trying to locate the things he needed. When other students began working on a current piece, Jesse said he didn't feel good or needed to go to the restroom, to sharpen his pencil, to use different paper, or to leave the room for any reason. Writing was "work" and seemingly an unattainable task to Jesse.

Meeting the Challenge

Judy was frustrated at the beginning, because she wasn't sure how to help Jesse or how to get him started as a writer. But, as she analyzed the information from the Observation Survey and continued to observe Jesse, she learned both what he knew and what confused him about putting print on paper. As she looked at her assessment data and compared Jesse to the rest of her class, she determined that immediate intervention was needed. Jesse knew very little about print and had difficulty putting any type of information on paper. He did not want to draw pictures to communicate his thinking, nor was he interested in looking at any books.

Judy discussed Jesse's difficulties with colleagues and with the school's literacy specialist, and she continued reading the professional books and articles she found about early writers. As a result of the conversations with colleagues and of her research and reading, she thought deeply about instructional decision making that would support Jesse's learning. Informed instructional decisions surfaced as she learned more about writing and read about how to help reluctant writers. Judy felt she needed a "hook" that would actively involve Jesse in the enjoyment of writing and that involved the enjoyment of reading. She looked at her daily schedule to see when she could "cast hooks and bait" to "catch" Jesse. She decided to interest him in the world of print both through reading to him and through deliberate teaching of what authors do when they write.

INTERACTIVE READ-ALOUD

One of the first hooks that Judy cast for Jesse was getting him interested in books. She decided to expose Jesse to as many books as possible. She chose her daily read-alouds from a variety of genres—fantasy, realistic fiction, informational books, fairy tales, tall tales, biographies, and/or humor. These books could have included *The Pig in the Pond* by Martin Waddell, *Stellaluna* by Jannell Cannon, *From Seed to Plant* by Gail Gibbons, and many others. Judy also chose from a variety of topics—animals, people, magical characters, places, and/or things that interested her first graders—and read books such as *Do Animals Dream?* by Joyce Pope, *Jack's Garden* by Henry Cole, and *George Washington: A Picture Book Biography* by James Cross Giblin. As she read daily to her students, she observed Jesse's interest in her reading and watched for his response.

Many times, the hook was ignored and new bait (a genre or topic) had to be cast. With each new read-aloud, Jesse sat closer to the book; his eyes seemed more focused on the pictures, and he participated in conversations about the book. Judy felt that he never really "took the hook," however, until she read nonfiction, informational books such as *Under the Sea From A to Z* by Anne Doubilet, *Look Out for Turtles* by Melvin Berger, and *A Tree Is Growing* by Arthur Dorros. Jesse started to request informational books, and his choices at the book center were the collections about animals, hobbies, and sports. Judy's large collection, containing a wide variety of books, finally hooked Jesse. Each day, he looked at the books for 20 to 30 minutes. Over time, his attentiveness to books improved and his hesitation to look at books disappeared. Jesse was still reluctant, however, to put print on paper.

Engaging students during interactive read-aloud.

GUIDED READING

As Jesse worked daily in his guided reading group, Judy decided to use as many nonfiction books as were available in the book room, such as *Animals at the Zoo*; *Animal Babies*; *Seeds, Seeds, Seeds*; and *Rocks*. Jesse continued to express interest in this genre and began to contribute to the conversation about the book after the reading. His conversation deepened over time as he described connections between animals and his own experiences or between rocks and his adventures outside in the backyard or walks in the woods close to his house.

Working with a small group of students during a guided reading lesson.

He was fascinated with the pictures of real plants and of animals and their habitats, and asked if they were going to read more books about "real things." With daily practice, he became more successful at reading unfamiliar words and understanding the author's purpose in the book. His attitude about reading was now one of anticipation and he was disappointed if something happened and he did not have his guided reading group.

SHARED READING

The science units (from the adopted science curriculum that the school purchased for the teachers) provided many big books on animals, weather, the human body, and other science concepts. Utilized in a shared reading setting, these texts provided meaningful reading interactions for the teachers and the students. The information was presented in a logical, well-organized format that enabled teachers to model the work of reading informational texts while the students listened to and discussed the information. The format of these books gave Jesse the opportunity to recognize print in varying formats, from captions to a few

Experiencing shared reading.

lines to more and more lines of print on each page. While reading, Judy emphasized the pictures and how they related to each type of text on the page. As science ideas and concepts were explained, Jesse shared his thoughts and questions—which, to this point, Judy had not observed him doing during other shared readings.

INDEPENDENT READING

After the science trade books were read several times, they were placed in the science center, where students reviewed the books individually or in small groups. Classmates reread these books as readers, as writers, and/or as scientists. Using the big books as the "hook and bait" was successful for many of the first graders, including Jesse. He

Enjoying a book during independent reading.

demonstrated interest in reading the words of the books, spent time looking at the pictures, and asked questions about what was happening in the photographs. His conversations evidenced that he was connecting what he saw with his own experiences. Judy found Jesse engaged as he reflected on the texts and connected the big book concepts with those of other books he had heard or read. Judy realized that the "hook and bait" of the science big books was a turning point for Jesse. Further, his need to focus his new enthusiasm for nonfiction on how authors communicate their message arose clearly in the context of shared reading.

SHARED WRITING

Shared writing is the instructional tool used for intentional and explicit teaching of types of sentences, organization of the piece, word choice, and formatting of the informational genre. Using the informational books as a whole and then examining them in parts made it much easier for Jesse to understand the purpose and format of this kind of writing. Each day, Jesse analyzed books through the lens of a writer both independently and with the support of the whole class. Judy led class conversations about what

Shared writing as an instructional tool.

the class had read and recorded the new learning using shared writing as the instructional tool. She modeled her thinking for Jesse and his classmates while she was writing. For example, they read a big book on the human body and then composed a summary of it. Judy discussed and scribed the information the students gave her as she explicitly taught students about the types of sentences, word choice, and organization appropriate for the piece. The science content area and the materials she used meshed expertly with her literacy teaching. These were not isolated pieces of literacy instruction, but, rather, intricately crisscrossed writing behaviors that all students could thread together during their learning experiences. Judy masterfully wove reading and writing into her instruction throughout the entire day.

INTERACTIVE WRITING

Interactive writing is the activity of collaboratively composing a text on chart paper and then sharing the pen with individual students to scribe that text on paper. Judy used interactive writing as an instructional tool on a daily basis. This decision was a crucial part of writing instruction and an extremely effective tool to use with her first graders. Through interactive writing, Judy directly and deliberately taught the features of print as well as the writing process.

Students are actively involved as scribes during interactive writing.

When Jesse came to the chart, he either began a new sentence or ended the sentence that they were writing, sometimes adding a beginning or ending sound to a word. Judy decided which aspect of the composition or individual word would benefit Jesse the most in his learning. Then, she invited him to add that specific part to the writing, providing an opportunity for herself to observe and evaluate his understanding of putting print on paper. Because the children were at different levels in their understanding of writing, continuous and specific teaching was needed throughout each interactive writing experience.

WRITING WORKSHOP

Daily writing workshop, which usually lasted about 45 minutes, provided time for Jesse to examine the science books as a writer. Judy frequently taught mini-lessons on what types of information to include in nonfiction writing. An integral part of Judy's instruction was how an author chose a topic and then how the author began his or her work. Judy showed the class specific places in books where the authors moved from one idea to the next. An example of this was the book *The Pumpkin Patch* by Elizabeth King. King begins the book by describing the season of autumn and writes about how the days are cool and crisp. She details the setting of the pumpkin patch and presents the farm and the farmer. Then, she writes about how the pumpkins grow. Judy taught sequential order using this text, which helped Jesse and his classmates to construct their thinking as writers. Judy also planned individual conferences with students during writing workshop to converse with them about their writing. Discussions during writing time and in individual conferences emphasized writing for a purpose in a sequential, organized way.

One-on-one conversations are a necessary part of writing workshop.

After several weeks of purposeful teaching and continual reading of informational books, Jesse acquired a purpose for his writing. He drew pictures of the animals presented in the science books and watched as the teacher modeled writing sentences for informational work. His purpose was telling others what he knew and what he thought was interesting about his favorite animals. Constructing texts with his pictures became more attainable and much more desirable. Jesse had learned much about animals and wanted to tell others about his learning. He talked to his friends about the things that fascinated him about different animals, and his enthusiasm for animals, especially ones that could run fast, became evident in his conversations with classmates. Judy then provided instruction about how authors used the skill of organization within their work, using several of the nonfiction read-alouds as mentor texts. Once again, Jesse looked at the science big books through the lens of an author. Jesse continued to work throughout the year in writing workshop and produced steady growth as he moved toward creating a nonfiction piece.

Jesse as a Writer in May

Reflect again on Jesse's abilities in September and compare them with what he was able to do in May:

MAY

Jesse's writing in Figure 13-2 is evidence of the considerable growth that he made throughout the year. He constructed this piece of writing during independent writing time in writing workshop. As Judy analyzed this writing, she concluded that many of the writing difficulties that Jesse displayed in September had been mastered: He created a text that was readable by others; used mostly phonetic spellings and appropriate spacing between words; wrote in multiple sentences; shared details and complexity of thought; spelled many of the high-frequency words correctly; used new words; and demonstrated an understanding of punctuation. Jesse exhibited logical, sequential thinking and an understanding of informational writing. Clearly, Judy's instructional decisions and the "hook" of nonfiction had made a big difference for this child. "WOW, look what he did!" was her expression of enthusiasm and reward for the accomplishments that she and Jesse had achieved over the course of the year.

Tracing the Decision-Making Progress

Let's take a look at instructional decisions Judy made to transition Jesse from September to May.

EVALUATING THE CLASSROOM LIBRARY

One of Judy's first instructional decisions was to evaluate her classroom library as she thought about her students, especially Jesse. Obtaining new books was often a challenge due to limited school budgets. To meet the needs of her students, Judy began by completing an inventory that identified topics, genre types, and the various levels of difficulty of texts already in the library. Judy used the inventory of the existing classroom library to request new books and kept in mind topics of interest for her students. With the inventory completed, it was easier to identify which books she needed. As money became available through various sources, such as book clubs, parent/teacher organizations, and the school budget, she began to efficiently order books to augment the classroom library.

One of my favorite animals is the jegwyr the jegwyr can run fast. It is fowd in tree. And his uieyes glowe in the drach. And he jups fre. And he can klim. he has sum htrep klous. He is shtou. and he can Swim. and he has a bigr tuning thin me. And he sleps on a tree drah. It has goblin fr. And he has htik fr His teht aru big. He is dist lik a regir cat. Jist bigr. He es met.

One of my favorite animals is the jaguar. The jaguar can run fast. It is found in tree. And his eyes glow in the dark. And he jumps far. And he can climb. He has some sharp claws. He is short and he can swim. And he has a bigger tongue than me. And he sleeps on a tree branch. It has golden fur. And he has thick fur. His teeth are big. He is just like a regular cat. Just bigger. He eats meat.

FIGURE 13-2. Jesse (May 1998)

USING THE POWER OF DISCOVERY

Guided by conversations about books and daily observations, Judy learned about Jesse's abilities as a reader and writer. She recorded these observations and conversations in her anecdotal notes. Based on this information, Judy designed purposeful, deliberate teaching and learning opportunities to support Jesse's next step as a writer. She frequently and intentionally used big nonfiction books after Jesse took the "hook" of animal stories. Discussions with him about what interested him about the topic and the organization or formatting of the book followed the read-alouds. Jesse began to notice the pictures of real animals, nature, and other details. He made comments about the things he had seen outside and how they compared to what he saw in the book. He showed interest in how the author had shared his information and how words and sentences were placed on a page. Judy's instructional decisions created rich contexts that provided opportunities for Jesse to discover his love for nonfiction and his abilities as a reader and writer.

ENGAGING IN CLOSE EXAMINATION OF TEXT

Judy's decision to get the whole class closely examining books set the stage for the discovery of specific characteristics of print and genre. She began by having the class study big books, read-aloud books, and books from the book center. One day, for example, Judy gave the class a picture book and asked them to look at it closely. Students worked in heterogeneous ability groups to describe what they noticed. Here are some of the questions Judy asked the students:

- What did you notice about the books?
- What did you like about it?
- Who would want to read this book?
- How did one book compare to another?

Judy closely observed the students' discoveries as they identified features of the texts and led the conversation during sharing time around concepts such as:

- What information did the author choose to tell us in this book?
- What kinds of sentences did the author use?
- How are they placed on the page?
- What details did the readers take with them after they read the book?

As her first graders spent more time with books, Judy observed closely for evidence that the conversation made sense them. The confused look in Jesse's eyes meant he was having trouble understanding what he was expected to do. To clear up his confusion, Judy considered the terminology she used. For example, did Jesse understand what a sentence was? Did he understand the word *details*? As Jesse continued to look at books, he learned to identify the beginning and ending of sentences, recognize punctuation showing what type of sentence the author used, and describe details of the pictures in the book. These experiences deepened his learning of the technical words that were used when talking about writing. As students looked at the features of print, Jesse and his classmates learned about the following:

- Titles
- Where the pictures are on the page
- Where the words are on the page
- What kinds of sentences the author used
- How long the sentences the author wrote were
- What types of pictures (photographs or drawings) were used
- What sort of information was included in nonfiction writing

Intentional teaching about each of these characteristics improved students' writing, including Jesse's. Judy's instructional decisions using power of discovery and examining features of the text were effective because they helped students begin to pay attention to what authors really did. Her first graders grew as writers, and Jesse specifically developed confidence in himself as a writer. He saw that there were different ways to communicate and present information and he was eager to try his hand at writing about a jaguar.

TAKING TIME TO SHARE

Judy was sometimes tempted to skip time at the end of writing workshop for students to share their work, but then she remembered the value of students' talking about their writing. Sharing was the time when Judy and the classmates listened to each other's observations and when there was no pressure to find a "right" answer. Instead, the focus of the conversation was discussion about the learning from that day's writing workshop. Jesse looked forward to this time each day as he frequently had something to share, either about his writing or about what he had found in a book that related to his writing. Jesse's participation in sharing moved him forward as a writer. It gave him the chance to talk about his thinking and new learning. He began to show interest in books and to show signs of wanting to write more and more. He became a communicator of his new learning through pictures and conversation about those pictures. As Jesse and other students shared things they noticed in the books, Judy recorded their comments on her clipboard. This information became the basis for her instructional decisions about mini-lessons, guided her shared writing experiences, and informed Jesse's participation during interactive writing.

A Year's Worth of Instructional Decisions

In May, Judy saw the results of her effective and thoughtful instructional decision making. Jesse showed interest in animals and frequently read about them. His trips to the school library included checking out a nonfiction book about wildlife. Students were encouraged to find an animal that interested them and to begin gathering information. They wrote about their new learning and placed their writing in a display in the hall for the spring science fair.

Jesse wrote about the jaguar because it could run fast. He beamed from ear to ear when his completed piece was put out for all to read. His use of invented spellings in the final copy revealed that he had made significant progress in both communicating his ideas and representing them in ways that showed his new understandings about how words work. Jesse used descriptive words and exhibited writing behaviors and conventional writing techniques more than he had done before. He wanted his readers to know as much about the jaguar as he had learned. Since September, his reading had improved; his writing had improved; his science knowledge had improved; and most importantly, his enthusiasm for reading and writing had become the foundation for additional learning. The instructional decisions Judy made through the year enabled Jesse's transition from a reluctant writer to an enthusiastic writer.

Suggestion for Professional Development

Do a yearlong case study of writing progression for three students from your class (it is recommended that you choose one low, one average, and one high student). Acquire baseline scores for these writers by using a scoring guide, and then record the scores. You could use a guide such as *Seeing with New Eyes* (Northwest Regional Educational Laboratory, 1999), which uses the Six-Trait Writing Model at the primary level, or your school's standardized guide or model, if it has one. Also, observe the students within a scheduled writing time during your day and note the writing behaviors of both the struggling writers and the more proficient writers.

After you have made several observations of students, discuss your notes with your colleagues. Discuss questions such as:

- What can this particular student do independently as a writer?
- What can these students write for themselves?
- Who will need more support and less support?
- Where did the students get their ideas for the writing?
- What can they verbalize about what they want to write about?
- What kind of small-group and large-group instruction will support these writers?

CHAPTER 14

Write Now! Don't Wait to Teach Struggling Readers About Writing

by Emily Rodgers

We have learned so much during the last 40 years about young children and their writing. Following the publication of Marie Clay's book *What Did I Write?* in 1975 (and reprinted nearly every year since), we could no longer think of children's early writing as mere scribbles. Clay's description of children's writing development, and the memorable examples of their writing that she included in *What Did I Write?* clearly demonstrated the emerging nature and growing complexity of children's early attempts to use print to record their ideas, thoughts, and messages.

In the same volume, Clay theorized about the link between children's writing and reading development. Writing, she thought, contributed to children's developing phonological awareness and helped them understand that letters represent sounds in spoken language. Clay concluded that writing helps children learn to read because of the reciprocal nature of the reading and writing processes.

In this chapter, I briefly describe the relationship between reading and writing and then discuss how writing helps young children learn to read, particularly those children having great difficulty learning to read. I also discuss how teachers can scaffold children's learning about print during writing instruction, including the kinds and amounts of help teachers can provide and when they can provide it.

The Relationship Between Reading and Writing as Different Processes

Children sometimes puzzle us when they have difficulty writing a word that they have read many times before in books or on word cards. We think, "I thought he could write the word *said*; he just finished a book and read *said* accurately on every page." While children should, indeed, be developing a visual memory for words that they encounter during reading, particularly high-frequency words that they see repeatedly, it is not surprising that early on, there are words that children can read but not write and words that they can write but not read.

In fact, this difference between reading and writing vocabularies continues, though to a lesser degree, into adulthood. Think of words that most of us can read but would have difficulty writing, such as *jewelry, commitment, accommodate, knowledgeable, reminisce, license,* and *remembrance,* to name just a few. Those are common words. There are plenty of examples of less common words that you could probably read fairly successfully but would struggle to write; such as *serrefine,* this year's winning word at the Scripp's National Spelling Bee.

Children also provide us with examples of words that they can write but not read. Philip, a Reading Recovery student of mine, demonstrated this to me clearly and memorably. This occurred during our second session working together, and I knew from my Observation Survey (Clay, 2002a) assessment that Philip could write one word—his name. Here is our exchange from that lesson.

ME: Philip, you can write your name. Write it here. (pointing to the chalkboard)

PHILIP: (writes his name slowly and carefully on the chalkboard)

ME: Great! (erasing his name) Now, write it over here.

PHILIP: (writes his name again, this time a little faster)

ME: Great job, Philip. Now, what did you write?

PHILIP: (looks at his name, then slides his finger under the word) Me!

I had asked Philip to read his name without for a moment thinking he would say anything but Philip. It was only when he read the word *Philip* as *me* that I realized he had learned to write his name but he could not read it.

These two examples, words that are easy to read but hard to write, and Philip not being able to read his name even though he could write it, demonstrate that reading and writing are different processes. If they were the same, then we would be able to write everything we could read and read everything we could write. In fact, in Clay's update of Reading Recovery instructional procedures (Clay, 2005), she included two record-keeping forms—one to keep track of a child's reading vocabulary, and the other to keep track of writing vocabulary. These separate records for teachers underscore Clay's point that reading and writing start out fairly separately and that we should expect a child's reading vocabulary and writing vocabulary to initially contain different words.

Even though reading and writing are different, they are also related; they share many common features about print such that learning about one can help with progress in learning about the other. In the remainder of this chapter, I describe the reciprocal nature of reading and writing, and make the case that writing instruction should not be postponed when children are having difficulty learning to read.

Writing Helps Young Children Learn to Read: Reading and Writing Are Reciprocal Processes

Writing plays a critical role early on in a child's reading development. The implication for children having great difficulty learning to read is that writing cannot be ignored or minimized or treated as an expendable instructional activity if time runs short. Instead, time must be allotted for daily writing instruction so that the child has an opportunity to write with the teacher's support.

This implication is clearly supported by DeFord's (1994) research in which she found that students with higher literacy outcomes at the end of their series of lessons in Reading Recovery had spent nearly twice as much time on writing early in their lessons than the lower-outcome students in the same period. Time spent on writing, it seems, matters to reading progress when children are learning to read and write. What is it about learning to write that helps children learn to read?

Reading and writing share a reciprocal relationship, meaning that what one learns while writing can help with reading and vice versa. Clay described the reciprocal relationship between reading and writing in this way:

> Before school, reading and writing have rather independent lives but they are most interactive at the point where instruction begins in school. *For about two years they appear to share a great deal of common ground.* (Clay, 2002b, p. 17, italics in original)

Reading and writing do appear to lead independent lives when children are very young and, developmentally speaking, for a very good reason. Young children read their favorite stories with beautiful phrasing and fluency, but pay little attention to the print on the page. Their reading is carried by their memory of the story and their knowledge about the structure of their language, an important milestone as they continue to emerge on their individual developmental paths to more conventional reading. Perhaps they know a word here or there and recognize some familiar letters, but they almost certainly do not use letter-sound relationships to read at this early stage.

In contrast, however, young children operate on a finer level of print analysis when they write than when they read. Early on, their attention goes to sound-and-letter relationships in order to record their messages for others to read. Just like the young children in Clay's *What Did I Write?*, they learn to say words slowly and to code the sounds they are saying into letters and words. They do not always choose the right letters to spell the words correctly or even form the letters correctly, but, even so, their writing attempts bring them to a finer-grained analysis of print than the one that they use to read their favorite memorized stories.

Research supports the view that young children work with letter-sound relationships in writing before they do in reading. DeFord (1994) noted in her review, for example, that there is little evidence that children use grapheme-phoneme information when they begin to learn to read; instead, it seems likely that children's first encounters with the phonemic code comes through their early writing experiences when they are introduced to the idea that sounds can be represented as letters.

Even though reading and writing start out leading separate lives, children very soon begin applying what they are learning about print in writing to reading. For example, they learn in writing that sounds can be represented by letters, and this understanding is soon applied to reading so that children come to understand that letters represent sounds. They also begin to apply to reading their growing awareness about the arbitrary demands of print, including the directional rules that must be followed (Clay, 2002b). DeFord described the reciprocal relationship between reading and writing as follows:

- Initially, reading and writing develop as separate systems of knowledge.
- Soon, the systems of knowledge that develop across encounters with reading and writing merge so

that children simultaneously learn about both processes.

- Eventually, children learn more about complex orthography through reading. (DeFord, 1994, p. 53)

In the section that follows, I describe specifically what young children are learning about reading through writing. I divide this learning into two categories that fit theoretically with Clay's theory of literacy development: items of knowledge and problem-solving activities.

READING AND WRITING SHARE SIMILAR ITEMS OF KNOWLEDGE

In order for a child to successfully write a word that someone else can read, Clay noted that the child has had to learn "how to visually analyze words, and what to study in a word so as to be able to reproduce it, and how to organize his own actions to achieve this writing goal" (Clay, 2000, p. 71). All of these understandings help with the visual scanning needed for reading. Readers and writers must learn about print and how it operates in order to read and write. The following items of knowledge about print are common to both reading and writing:

- Letter recognition
- Letter-sound relationships
- Reading and writing vocabularies
- Rules about directionality

Letter Recognition

Reading and writing both require children to be fluent with letter knowledge. They need to be able to recognize letters quickly and be able to discriminate one from another in the strings of letters that make up words. Children also need to be able to form letters quickly and easily in order to write them and construct messages.

It is easy to forget just how complex these visual and motor tasks are because as proficient readers we learned a long time ago how to perceive, discriminate, and form letters quickly and easily. The Chinese characters in Figure 14-1 help remind us about the complexity of learning to look at print. Pay attention to your brain's scanning work as you find these features:

- Two that are exactly alike
- The three characters that have one side that is the same
- Two other characters that have one side that is the same
- One character that is different from the others

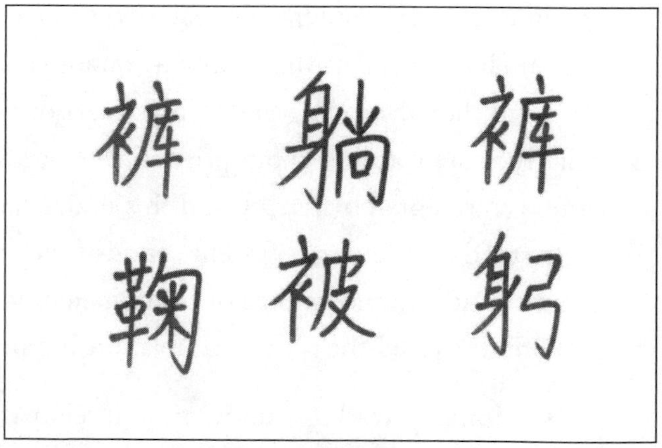

裤 躺 裤
鞠 被 躬

Figure 14-1. Chinese Characters

Did you find that you began to look at the characters in a more systematic way the more you searched? At first, you may not have known what to attend to or how to look, but gradually, your brain began to find order among the symbols and your scanning became more efficient.

Now, imagine how much easier your discrimination of the print would be if you practiced writing one or more of the characters. Writing a character requires you to pay attention to all of its details. In this case you would soon discover that each character has a left side and a right side; a fact that no doubt would support your visual analysis of the characters as you compared one to another and looked for differences. Writing the characters would also lead you to quickly notice that some of the characters have the same left side and this would speed up your discrimination and production of those characters.

Children who learn to read in English have learned to scan characters that are just as complex. Think about the letters *n*, *h*, and *r*, for example. The difference between each of them is just one short stroke, yet children learn how to discriminate each from the others in words. Learning to form the letters in writing brings a child's attention to these tiny differences that might otherwise be hard for the brain to notice as it scans an array of visually similar characters.

Letters and Sounds

Reading and writing both involve visual and auditory sources of information; the difference is the direction you work in—going from letters to sounds in reading and from sounds to letters in writing. The next sentence is written in Italian; try reading it aloud.

Questa frase è dura affinchè me legga.

In order to read that sentence, any sentence in fact, you pick up visual information first (the print) and then attach auditory information to it. The amount of visual information you picked up would vary from reader to reader (letter by letter, clusters of letters) but the processing involved is still the same: picking up the letters and then attaching sounds to them.

Imagine how the task would be different if I dictated the sentence instead. As you heard the words being dictated one at a time you would need to use your very good phonemic awareness to analyze the individual sounds, make the connection between the sound and the letter that would represent it, and then record the letter.

In writing, your brain starts with auditory information, and then you need to go in search of visual information. In reading, you begin with the visual pickup of information, and then your brain needs to go in search of the sounds. Even though the direction of the processing is different, from sounds to letters or letters to sounds, reading and writing inform each other in that children learn that sounds can be represented by letters and that letters represent sounds.

Of course, we cannot reduce the complex activities of reading and writing to processing individual letters and sounds. The perceptual work is vital (just try reading in the dark!), but reading and writing involve much more than auditory and visual processing, as I discuss in the sections that follow.

Reading and Writing Vocabularies Need to Be Developed

The writing sample in Figure 14-2 is a page from a story written independently by Connor, a first-grade student whom I taught in Reading Recovery. The story is about two aliens, the main character in a series of little books that Connor enjoyed reading. Think about what Connor is learning about print and about the reading process.

Even from Connor's small writing sample about the aliens putting on their helmets, we can hypothesize several things. Connor knows that print carries a message and that pictures have a special function in a story to help convey the message. He also is developing a

Figure 14-2. "He Took off His Helmet."

core vocabulary of words that he can write independently; he knew the words *off*, *his*, and *he*, fairly well, but the word *took* was less well known to him.

Writing provided Connor with a slowed-down exposure to print in which he had to pay attention to every detail of each word in order to write a message. When he meets the word *off* in a story, for example, he can draw on his encounter with it in writing to help himself. If he does not make the connection, then the teacher can do it for him. "You wrote that word in your story. Have a good look at it."

DeFord (1994) calls this work "digging ditches" in reference to the fact that the child needs to learn that he can go to his writing vocabulary as a resource to help with reading and vice versa. If he doesn't, the teacher can "dig the ditch" between the two vocabularies and remind the child about what he knows that can help.

Rules About Directionality

Based on Connor's placement of the word *helmet*, we can also hypothesize that he may not yet have internalized the rules about directionality that govern how the English language is written and read. Connor seems to be still developing his understanding of at least one aspect of directionality—return sweep. Return sweep means that at the end of a line the reader or writer automatically moves left and down to continue. This rule does not apply to every written language, but it does apply to English, and children need to learn the rule such that their visual scanning of print becomes automatic.

Children who have internalized return sweep would never break the rule and move up a line to write a word. They either would have anticipated the upcoming space problem because they know the constraints of writing down the English language and they know where they are headed, or they would have written the word in tiny letters below and squeezed in the word *helmet* where it belonged. It just would not occur to children who have directionality under control to move up a line as a solution to the issue of space.

Connor's willingness to solve the problem by breaking the return sweep rule suggests that he may not yet have internalized rules of directionality in reading either. It is as though what Connor is producing in writing suggests how he might be attending to print in reading as well. Indeed, it was around this time that Connor encountered a double-page spread with text on two sides and instead of starting on the left-hand side, he began reading on the right page.

Each time he wrote a little story in our daily Reading Recovery lessons, Connor practiced the movements needed for reading: going to the top left of the first line on a page to begin, moving left to right across words and lines, and moving down and to the left at the end of each line. I did not talk about return sweep with him; talk would have likely been confusing. Instead, I was ready to prevent him from abandoning the rules of directionality as he wrote and to intervene when it appeared he was uncertain about which way to go next.

It seems likely that the practice in writing helped Connor bring directionality in reading under control as well. Without the writing experiences, directionality would have remained an abstract concept, confined to very tiny eye-muscle movements during reading. Instead, writing made the directional movement bigger and more concrete and it slowed down the movements needed for reading. These writing sessions provided opportunities for Connor to rehearse the directional movement needed for reading and opportunities for me to teach him.

READING AND WRITING INVOLVE SIMILAR PROBLEM-SOLVING ACTIVITIES

Reading and writing also share common problem-solving activities. Both the reader and the writer need to learn how to do the following:

- Monitor
- Search
- Problem solve

In the sections that follow, I describe how these problem-solving activities occur in writing as well as in reading.

Monitoring the Output and Searching for More Information

Both readers and writers monitor the output to ensure that the message makes sense, looks right, and sounds right. If they detect an error they go in search of more information in order to fix the problem. Clay called this error-detecting behavior (Clay, 2002b). The paragraph below provides a good example of error-detecting behavior in reading that Clay described. Pay attention to your own problem-solving activities as you read.

> My nephew Travis began to read at a very young age. From the time he was a toddler he
> seemed to enjoy handling books. He would turn the pages and look at the pictures while

listening to his grandfather read the story to him. Soon he started reading the stories himself. On his first day at nursery school his preschool carers expressed doubt that he could read. Perhaps he had just learned to memorize some favorite books. To test whether Travis could read or not, a teacher picked up a book and handed it to him and invited him to read it.

Did you have to do some problem solving around the word *carers*? If you deduced that the word is *care-ers* and that it means caregivers, then you would be right. In some English-speaking countries the word *carers* is used instead of *caregivers*. The problem-solving activities that you engaged in before settling on that decision probably went something like this:

- Reading accurately and well
- Noticing the unfamiliar word
- Hypothesizing that the word might be a misspelling of *careers*
- Going back several words to reread and test the *careers* hypothesis
- Eliminating *careers* as a possibility because it did not make sense nor did it fit the sentence structure
- Taking a closer look at the word *carers* to do a slower visual analysis
- Hypothesizing that the root of the word could be *care* and that the word could be *care-ers*
- Rereading to see whether *care-ers* would fit
- Deciding that everything now looks right, makes sense, and sounds right and continuing to read

And all of this processing of print happened in a matter of moments.

Writers work in a similar way to construct messages, because the same kinds of problem-solving activities take place in writing. As I write these words, I am monitoring the message. If I think I have lost the idea of my message, I take action to correct—I reread to see where the meaning might have broken down.

At the same time, I am monitoring the production of the words themselves. I notice when a word does not look right or when I have too many spaces between words or not enough. Sometimes I postpone the action to go back and fix a mistake, but in any case I eventually do fix the errors. These actions of noticing and finding errors in order to fix them are common to reading and writing. The writer who has composed a story has practiced the same activities that a reader needs to engage in. The added value comes in the fact that writing a story also provides an opportunity for reading because writers reread their message to monitor the output.

Problem Solving in Reading and Writing

Proficient readers and writers also problem solve once an error is detected, just like you did when you detected the problem with the word *carers* in the previous example. Problem-solving activities are at the heart of Clay's theory about the reading process and they apply equally well to the writing process. Noticing and taking problem-solving actions, such as searching and rereading until there is a satisfaction that all sources of information now fit together, are the kinds of activities that proficient readers engage in; writers do it too.

One specific kind of problem-solving activity that proficient readers and writers undertake is using analogies to known words to read or write unfamiliar words. Using an analogy refers to the idea that you can think of a word that sounds or looks like the one you are trying to read or write. A student who can write the word *can*, for example, can use this knowledge to write an unfamiliar word such as *cat* or *candy*. My student Connor, for example, was writing a story when we had this exchange:

CONNOR: I don't know how to write *play*.

ME: You can write a word that sounds like *play* and that will help you. Can you think of it?

CONNOR: No.

ME: You know *day*

[writing *day* on the paper].

And because you know how to write *day* you can write *play*

[writing *play* underneath *day*].

In my example, Connor is just learning how to use analogies to problem solve new words and he needed a lot of help from me. Gradually, he was able to work with more independence and think of words that he knew to help write new ones.

Larry Sipe (1998) provides a delightful case study filled with examples of a first-grade student, Mikey, learning how to use analogies to write new words. In some cases, his teacher helps him, as when she told him that the word *like* was written like his name—*Mike*—or that the word *paper* ended like the word *better*, which he already knew how to write. In other cases, he can be heard making connections to known words himself, as when he thought of the word *please*, a word he knew how to write, to help him write a new word, *piece*. Such problem-solving experiences in writing prepare a child for problem solving by analogy in reading. DeFord writes:

> As [the child] encounters the same information in new texts, the knowledge about print is expanded and the child works to fill out and extend the categories being built, hypothesizing new relationships about print, language, and meaning. As the child continues to read and write, what he or she knows as a reader and writer begins to expand and become integrated. (DeFord, 1994, p. 52)

One can imagine that in this writing context of slowed-down attention to print, the child has an opportunity to really explore how what is known can be used to write a new word. Such experiences in writing will prepare a child for problem solving by analogy in reading.

In the final section, I discuss how teachers can scaffold students' writing attempts by adjusting the kind and amount of support they offer in order to help students learn more about item knowledge and more about problem solving during writing.

Scaffolding Item Knowledge and Word Solving During Writing

Scaffolding simply means teaching, providing just enough help so that a student can complete a task that would otherwise be too hard to do independently (Wood, Bruner, & Ross, 1976). Teaching like this on a student's cutting edge is not as easy as it sounds, as anyone who has been helped or tried to give help knows. If you think back to any learning experience in your life, you probably can recall some frustration about the help you received at the time; perhaps you did not get enough help or you did not get the help when you needed it.

Wood, Bruner, and Ross (1976) coined the term *scaffolding* in their early research as a way to describe how mothers varied the amount of help that they provided in their interactions with their children to carry out a toy-building task. The researchers found that the parents who were more successful at teaching their children to put together the toy on their own seemed to follow what Wood, Bruner, and Ross came to refer to as a tutoring rule—give more help when the child runs into difficulty, give less help when the child is successful. This tutoring rule is the essence of scaffolding learning; it sounds simple, but it is actually very challenging to make teaching decisions in the moment about the amount of help needed for a child to complete a task successfully and as independently as possible.

Hobsbaum, Peters, and Sylva (1996) described the interactions between child and teacher during writing in Reading Recovery lessons as being in keeping with the features of scaffolding, which meant that the teachers responded to what children were attempting to do in writing, rather than imposing upon the child a preconceived plan for teaching. Wong, Groth, and O'Flahavan (1994) also found that Reading Recovery teachers used teaching prompts flexibly, in response to the child's reading. When reading was more difficult for the child, teachers increased their modeling, prompting, and discussion comments.

These studies suggest that it is the nature of the talk during writing or reading instruction that may account for the intensity and effectiveness of instruction. Teachers are scaffolding children's reading behaviors by using language effectively; by this I mean that they are responding to the child's reading behaviors with talk that is designed to bring the child a little further along.

I have studied teacher-student interactions during reading in my own scaffolding research and categorized the amount of help provided by the teacher when the student reached difficulty (Rodgers, 2004). I based my analysis on Wood, Bruner, and Ross's research and their categorizations of help as provided by the mothers in their study.

In the section that follows, I describe the four kinds of help that the teachers in my study seemed to offer when the student encountered difficulty while reading: telling, demonstrating, directing, and questioning. Then, I provide examples of how teachers can vary the kind of help they provide when students encounter difficulty while writing. Keep in mind that in order to scaffold learning, the teacher needs to assist performance at difficulty but give just enough help as is necessary for the child to complete the task. Too little help will leave the child floundering and frustrated; too much help can be just as frustrating.

KINDS AND AMOUNTS OF HELP, AND WHEN TO OFFER IT

I categorize teacher help in four ways arranged here from most amount of help to least.

- **Telling.** When the student encounters difficulty while reading or writing, the teacher can tell the student what to do next. Telling is the most amount of help that the teacher can offer, and it is sometimes the fastest and most efficient way to move forward.

- **Demonstrating.** At other times, the teacher can help the student by demonstrating what the student needs to do. In these instances, the teacher takes the student's role and does what the student needs to do at difficulty. A common example of a demonstrating move by the teacher is to reread at difficulty or slowly articulate the first letter or letters of a difficult word that the student is trying to write. The teacher is showing the student what the student needs to do. This is less support than telling because when the teacher tells the child a difficult word or writes a word for the child, there is no expectation for the child to be able to do it.

- **Directing.** When the teacher provides this kind of help, the child is directed to some piece of information that would help solve the problem, such as saying, "You know a word like that." Or "Go back and reread and see what would make sense and look right." Directing provides less help than telling or questioning. A directing move provides a hint to the child. Drawing boxes to represent each sound in a word or using spelling boxes to represent each letter (Clay, 2005) is a good example of a directing move. The teacher provides some hint to the student about what is needed to write a word, and the student has more involvement in the problem solving.

- **Questioning.** A questioning move provides the least amount of help of all. An example of this kind of help might be, "What do you know that can help you?" or simply "Were you right?" after the child has made an attempt.

The teachers in my study of teacher-student interactions while reading (Rodgers, 2004) varied the amount of help that they provided when their students encountered difficulty. Depending on the student's response to the amount of help offered, the teachers provided more or less help within the interaction. The following examples occurred during reading of the same book, but on different pages. In the first interaction, the teacher provides some help, but not much, by questioning the student who is reading the sentence *James said, "Wake up, Dad."*

STUDENT: James said, (pause)
TEACHER: What do you suppose he said to Dad? (questioning)
STUDENT: "Wake up, Dad"

In the next interaction, the teacher starts out by questioning, but then immediately offers more help by demonstrating for the student how he could say a word slowly in order to check it. The same student is reading the text *Kate said, "Wake up, Dad."*

STUDENT: Kate is, Kate said (pauses)

TEACHER: Are you right? Could it say *said*? (questioning)

    Sssaid. (demonstrating)

STUDENT: said, "Wake up, Dad."

The teacher calibrated her help in the moment by shifting from questioning the student to demonstrating. No doubt the teacher analyzed that the student would need more help than what she provided with her questions ("Are you right? Could it say *said*?"), so she added a demonstration of how to say the word slowly ("Sssaid"), thereby providing more help.

The examples discussed in this chapter are presented in the following two tables in terms of the level or amount of help contained in each example of support. The goal is to offer the least amount of support that a child needs to accomplish a task successfully. Figure 14-3 has ideas for scaffolding item knowledge in writing.

Placing your hand on top of the child's or having the child "take a piggyback ride" atop your hand, is an extreme form of help that should be used rarely and only in special circumstances when a child needs that much help. Clay noted as long ago as 1975:

> There are several research reports which suggest that children of five years learn faster if they are able to organize for themselves a sequence of movements than they do if their hands are passively moved through that sequence (p. 14).

Ideas for Scaffolding Item Knowledge in Writing

Level of Help	Kinds of Help	Examples of Scaffolding Item Knowledge (letter recognition, letter-sound relationships, vocabulary, directionality)
Most Amount of Help	Telling	• Writing the letter for the child • Telling the letter needed to record a sound • Writing the unfamiliar word for the child
	Demonstrating	• Showing how to form a letter • Using sound boxes, the teacher slowly articulates whole word for the child and writes in a letter or letters to record a sound
	Directing	• Giving a hint, saying, "You can write that letter." • Drawing Elkonin boxes for the child to use to write a word
Least Amount of Help	Questioning	• Asking, "What letter is making that sound?" • Asking, "How is that letter made?" • Asking, "Where do you go next?" or "Where should you start to read/write?"

FIGURE 14-3. Scaffolding Item Knowledge in Writing

Ideas for Scaffolding Problem-Solving Activity

Level of Help	Kinds of Help	Examples of Scaffolding Problem-Solving Activity (monitoring, searching, problem solving)
Most Amount of Help	Telling or Showing	• Showing the child where an error occurred • Writing the unfamiliar word while the child watches
	Demonstrating	• Rereading a sentence for the child and failing to move on at point of error • Writing the whole analogy (both the known words and the new word) while the student watches
	Directing	• Directing the child to reread and find something that does not look right • Giving a hint: "You know *let*; that will help you write *yet*."
Least Amount of Help	Questioning	• "Do you know a word that sounds [or looks] like that?"

FIGURE 14-4. Ideas for Scaffolding Problem-Solving Activity

In addition to scaffolding items of knowledge, the teacher also scaffolds problem-solving activities while the student writes. Figure 14-4 presents ideas for scaffolding monitoring, searching, and problem solving.

Scaffolding a student's performance in reading or writing requires the teacher to vary the amount of help offered when the student is at difficulty, with the goal of providing just the right amount of help needed in order for the student to be successful. This does not mean, however, that the teacher will always be able to respond with exactly the right amount of help every time with each interaction. Sometimes, you will unintentionally give more help than what the student actually needs; at other times, not enough help. The important point is that you continually work at calibrating your teaching; if you thought you gave enough help but the student was not successful, then come in with a little more help.

Conclusion

Reading and writing share a reciprocal relationship such that engaging in writing can help students with reading, particularly those having great difficulty learning to read. Features of print that are abstract for the young reader, such as directionality, letter-sound relationships, analogy-making, letter recognition, and discrimination, become tangible and concrete during writing. Problem-solving activities, such as monitoring meaning, searching for more information at difficulty, and problem solving by analogy, are easily practiced in writing and transferred to reading.

Teachers can scaffold students' item knowledge and problem solving in writing by calibrating the kinds of help they offer students at difficulty. Scaffolding is not a straightforward, easy task. It requires contingent teaching characterized by providing more or less help in the moment in response to what the student is trying to do at difficulty.

In her 2002 volume, *Change Over Time in Children's Literacy Development*, Clay repeated her view first expressed in 1975 that educators need to incorporate writing instruction with reading instruction. Just as she did in 1975, Clay based her recommendation in theory, but this time, there was a sense of urgency in her message. Perhaps she expected more progress in 30 years. Perhaps she was impatient that, after all this time, our tendency is still to postpone writing instruction until children have learned to read, particularly children having great difficulty learning to read.

The theories that Clay reviewed in 1975 and her updated research in 2002 underscore the reciprocal nature of reading and writing. Learning to read can be supported and accelerated through writing experiences because they share common items of knowledge and involve similar problem-solving activities. Reflective teachers who examine how they are scaffolding students in writing will be well prepared to help students who are having difficulty learning to read.

Suggestions for Professional Development

Try some of these ideas with your colleagues.

1. Organize a Read and Talk group with teachers at your grade level. Read and share Mary Lose's 2007 article about contingent teaching.

2. Audiotape yourself during writing instruction when you are working with a student one-to-one. Listen to the tape afterward and analyze the kind of help you are providing to the student at difficulty. Categorize the help you provide as questioning, directing, demonstrating, or telling.
   - Are you providing more help when the student encounters difficulty and less help when the student is successful?
   - Do you favor a certain kind of help, such as questioning? If you do, think about varying the kind of help you are providing. What could you have said instead?

3. Identify one or more students in your class who are receiving assistance through an intervention such as Reading Recovery or Special Education. Arrange to observe the student during the intervention teaching, and invite the intervention specialist to observe your teaching of the child. If schedules do not permit, then exchange videotapes of your teaching. Collect and compare the students' writing samples from each setting. Are there any surprises? Debrief with each other about what the student can do in each setting. ❧

Section V

Taking Action

"Taking Action" offers a set of resources to help teachers plan their writing program. Reading Lynda Hamilton Mudre's "Fifteen Ways to Help Young Writers" is a succinct way to think through important aspects of writing instruction in the primary grades. The final chapter, by Lynda Hamilton Mudre and Gay Su Pinnell, focuses on handwriting, a skill some might argue is often neglected. Their approach to handwriting ensures appropriate attention to this skill as a way to foster fluency as a writer and clarity for the reader without compromising attention to the writing process. Six appendices round out this book. Bibliographies, frequently asked questions, and teaching ideas can be found in the first five appendices. The sixth appendix contains information about KEEP BOOKS available through the Ohio State University, with an order form for interested readers.

CHAPTER 15

Fifteen Ways to Help Young Writers

by Lynda Hamilton Mudre

Let's approach the teaching of young writers by first thinking of ourselves as writers. The reasons we write and the benefits writing offers us are similar to those of our students. So—why do we write? Writing shows who we are. Most of us have experienced the satisfaction of completing a piece of writing, for any purpose, perhaps after returning to it to make it just right. Even for the most functional and everyday ways of writing, when we pick up a pen or sit at a computer, we intuitively want what comes from the ink or keyboard to represent our own way of thinking. We want the words we compose to say what we want to say in the ways only we can say it. Often, without realizing it, we want the message we write to express who we are.

Writing helps us conduct our lives and search for what is meaningful to us. Of course, writing is useful in helping us get along in the world. In addition:

> Writing is one of the ways we explore our understanding of the world and discover the meaning of our experiences. Writing contributes in its own special way to the growth and realization of self, and enables us to discover, make clear, and share personal interpretations of events and ideas. (New Zealand Ministry of Education, 1992, p. 21)

Writing helps us think. "Unlike the spoken word, writing allows you to literally look at your thoughts. When we speak, our thoughts exist for the moment we say them. When we write, our thoughts are recorded and can be revisited and reflected upon" (Bodrova & Leong, 1995, p. 108). Vygotsky (1978) believed that writing is a cognitive tool. Like all forms of language, it guides our mental processing to construct new paths. Through representing our thoughts symbolically with letters and words, we discover new thoughts and ways of connecting one idea with another. The very act of putting thoughts on paper expands our capacity to create new avenues for what is possible.

Finally, writing is art. What makes the cadence, the imagery, the structures—the music of the composition—pleasing can grow and be nourished by artists and teachers of art, by those who know something about what makes art beautiful, clever, fun, balanced, or purposeful. As teachers of writing, we can learn all we can about good writing. We can ride on the coattails of writers who inspire us, show us endless possibilities, and teach us by the work they have crafted.

And this is what we want for our children. To help them discover who they are through the very act of writing. To help them pursue and preserve the carefree dreams of childhood. To help them feel the power of writing in the creation and reconceptualization of ideas. To help them experience the joy of something clever or lovely or meaningful coming from their own minds and hands.

During one of my visits to a first-grade class, I discovered Zack. His teacher was nourishing his authorship with rich writing models and productive conversation. She was encouraging him to write with his own voice and soon would show Zack how writers can create memorable closings. Zack was already well on his way to discovering the power of writing. (See Figure 15-1.)

My purpose in this chapter is to capture some of the energy and substance from the body of work on the teaching of writing, along with my own 30-plus years of experience working in classrooms as teacher and with teachers and children. What is exciting is that all of us who write with children are contributing to this endeavor—by writing alongside our students and allowing them to teach us, by reflecting together on our practice, and by searching for productive ways to make becoming a writer as memorable and meaningful as it can possibly be from the very beginning.

FIGURE 15-1. Zack's Writing

Guiding K-3 Writers to Independence

1. Be a Writer Yourself

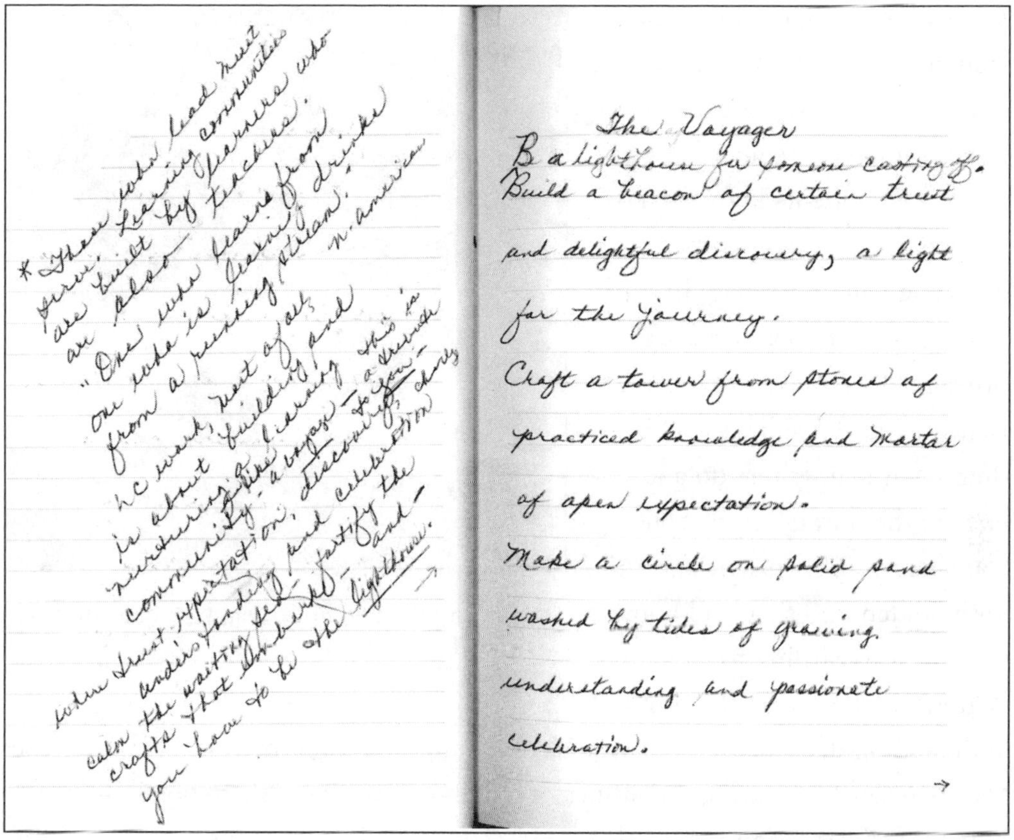

To teach writing well you need to write often for many purposes, not necessarily with the goal of formal publishing, but to reflect, present, and clarify ideas, or to capture special moments and memories. Because you have lived the process, you can offer your assistance to children as they encounter some of the same decisions during their own process. Beyond the mechanics of writing, children must learn what it is to be a writer. If we already appreciate what writing has done to make our own lives richer, we can convey this appreciation with sincerity. If we are writers ourselves, we can make the writing experience richer and clearer for our students.

In the midst of my hectic schedule of teaching and working with teachers, staff developers, and administrators, pausing to invest in my own writing leads me in positive directions. Collecting ideas and trying them out in a writer's notebook clarifies my thinking, captures what is really important in my life, and helps me discover more about who I am. In this entry, I am wrestling with metaphors that relate to supporting teachers through building a trusting community of learners. (See Figure 15-2.)

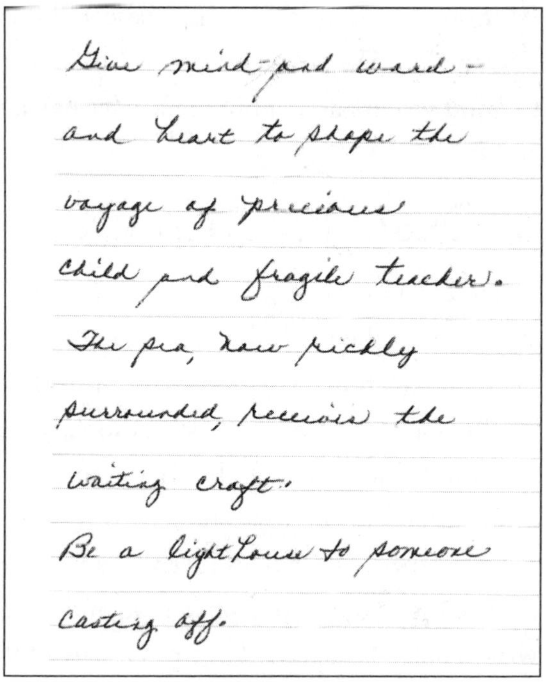

FIGURE 15-2. Writer's Notebook

2. Build a Community of Writers

Issue a joyful invitation to your students to join the classroom circle of writers you are assembling. Preserve a regular time to write. Let students know that every day, at the same time, everyone will be writing. In writing workshop and through other reading and writing experiences, you can show the children what real writers do and engage them in doing it. You can share your own writing with students so they will know you are still learning to be a writer, too. Involving them in

Teacher and children in writing workshop circle.

your writing decisions can provide clear examples of high interest. While we encourage young writers to "be themselves" within the confines of childhood, we show them possibilities that will make their writing better. We introduce them to the world of authors through our writing.

Sometimes we mistakenly expect children to talk and act like writers before they know how writers talk and act. When we invite our students to join a community of writers, we take time to introduce them to good writers and show them what it's like to be a writer.

3. Design Multiple Literacy Contexts to Support Writers

There are a number of opportunities across the day for exploring the writing process. A good place to start is with the read-aloud experience. Help your students appreciate what writers do by modeling your own appreciation. As students are introduced to the best books you can find, they also get to know about the lives and craft of the best authors. In the beginning, you might look for authors whose work parallels the simple narratives of childhood and is clear and memorable enough to become templates for the children's attempts at authorship.

Students will read and write across several genres during the year. For example, if you begin poetry read-aloud the first day of school, and continue it for a few minutes every day, the children will begin to write poetry because it becomes a part of them. The same principle applies to any genre. Through artful interaction with the children during the read-aloud time, help your students deepen their thinking and appreciate the craft of the writer.

By echoing your instructional focus across several contexts, you can achieve greater shifts in learning. For example, in community writing (shared and interactive writing) with the whole group, or in small groups, you can model for, scaffold for, and engage your students in much of the writing work you want them to take on independently. As you teach through shared and guided reading, study the literary characteristics of the texts you have chosen. If you help children understand what the author is doing—how the author reaches the reader—you will not only strengthen their awareness of craft as writers, but you will be building a firm foundation for comprehension. Of course, a powerful context for teaching writers is writing workshop, where you engage the children in a life of authorship. If you create a variety of literacy experiences to teach for writing work that students need, you increase your chances of seeing forward progress in learning.

One teacher's experience is an example of how a teacher might use a literacy framework to strengthen an instructional focus. He has observed that many of his second graders need to learn how to compose more interesting closings for their personal narrative pieces. Through interactive read-aloud, he helps the children notice how authors create memorable endings for their stories. Through shared writing, he involves the children in planning and writing an appealing closing for a class story relating a common experience. In guided reading with small groups of children, he again draws attention to the closings of the stories they are reading. This focus echoes in multiple contexts across the week, and by the time he is ready to begin a series of mini-lessons on closings in writing workshop, the children have a rich background of experience that he can build upon.

Meeting favorite authors in read-aloud.

Teaching a writer during conferring.

Learning about a new genre in guided reading.

Composing as a community of writers.

Reading class stories independently.

Learning about print through interactive writing.

4. Help Students Find Their Voices Through Oral Storytelling

Help children value the stories of their lives as the best raw material for writing. Invite storytelling about things that matter most in their world, so that their spoken voices can propel their voices on paper. Tell the stories of your life well and model writing them down, and the writers listening and watching will be able to use a powerful mediator to begin the writing process—their own oral language. Build bridges from oral to written language by writing with the whole class or a small group to show how a shared experience can first be told, then written down in an interesting way.

If we aim to teach writing well, our classrooms must be filled with the voices of children and teachers telling their life stories and finding ways to preserve their oral quality. When you confer with writers, you can help them capture their voices on paper by tuning in to the unique way they are verbalizing thoughts and delights. Say something like, "Wow, that's great storytelling. You need to write that down, just the way you are saying it."

Encourage young students to capture their own voices by showing them how to use something concrete to hold the words in their heads. They might tell their stories across several fingers, touching a finger for each part, sketch the parts, or touch one page at a time for each section of the story being told. From the beginning, you can show students how they can stretch one small happening that is very meaningful across several pages (Calkins, 2003).

In Figure 15-3, Rob, in the fall of second grade, is writing about a walk in the woods, where he discovers a deer skull. This event is important to him because his father is a hunter, and he wants to be one too. The moment when he finds the skull is rich with description of how it looked and a high point for the writer. However, he has placed it at the end of the piece, almost as an afterthought.

The teacher shows him how he could make these few minutes come alive for readers by capturing them as the centerpiece for his story. He could place his description of the old dirty skull, with its gold teeth, near the beginning of his piece. During the next few writing workshops, he could do what writers often do—cross out the writing that is repetitive or doesn't seem to align with his focus, then add more detail to the centerpiece to bring readers into the experience.

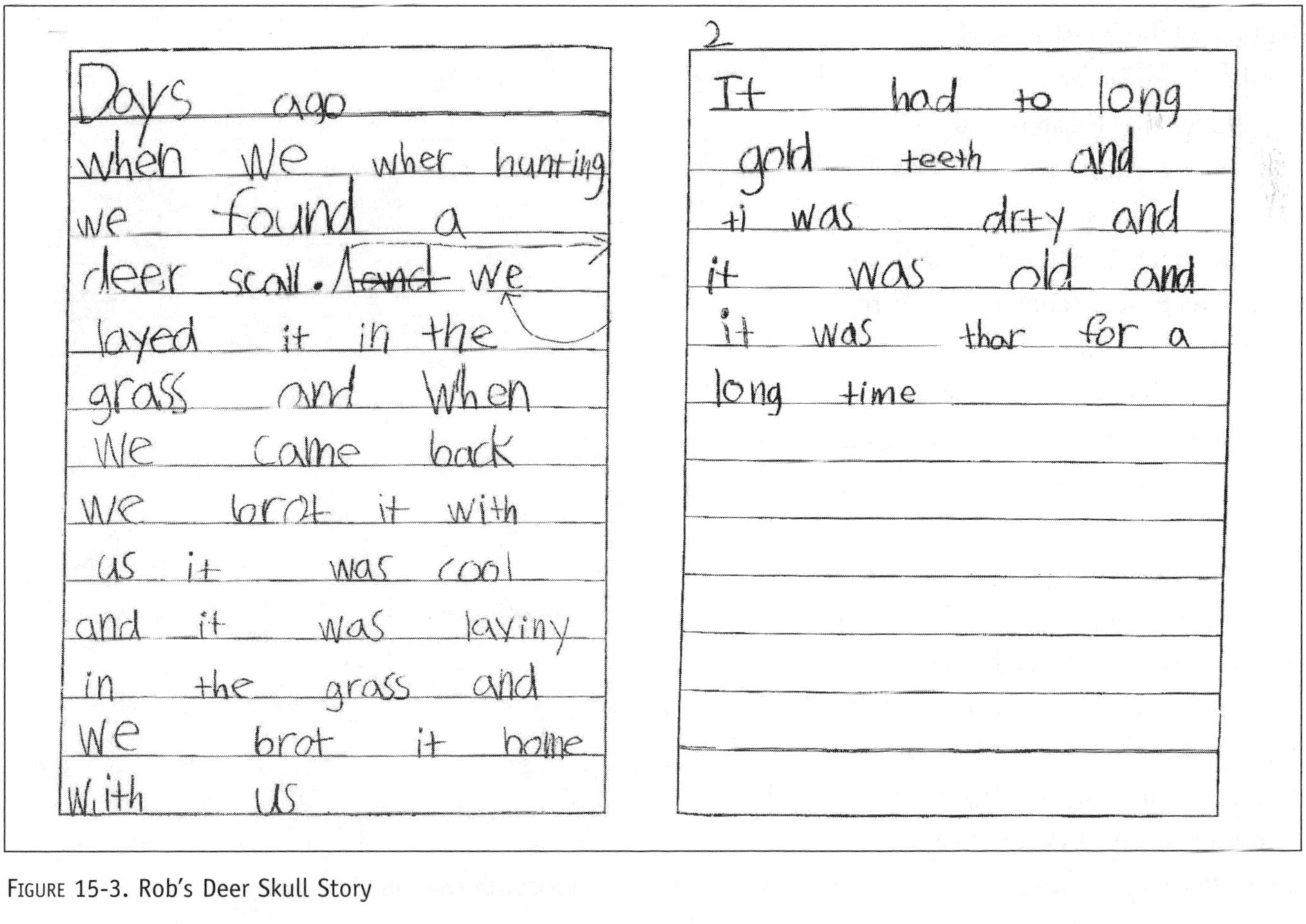
~~Days ago~~
when we wher hunting
we found a
deer scall. ~~And~~ we
layed it in the
grass and When
We came back
we brot it with
us it was cool
and it was layiny
in the grass and
we brot it home
With us

2
It had to long
gold teeth and
ti was drty and
it was old and
it was thar for a
long time

FIGURE 15-3. Rob's Deer Skull Story

5. Develop Voice Through Choice and Personal Investment

Show the children how authors choose to write about things that really matter to them and encourage your students to do the same. Find out the things they love most, and encourage the children to pursue them in writing. Excellent teachers of writing know their students well. They are constantly listening for what is important in children's lives and encouraging students to write their peak experiences in ways that readers can experience them too. Consider Dejah's piece in Figure 15-4, written after she was given a typical writing assessment prompt to determine if she had reached the district's fall "benchmark" for second grade.

Notice that Dejah is well on her way in the use of conventional spelling, capital letters, and punctuation. In addition to helping her learn the print conventions writers necessarily need to learn, her teacher can provide opportunities for her to share herself with readers by choosing a meaningful focus and using her voice and personality to develop it.

Listen now to the voice of Abby in Figure 15-5, also a second grader, when she was encouraged to make free choices about things close to her heart.

Unlike pieces motivated by story starters and assigned topics, voices of writers echo in topics children have chosen because they are meaningful to them.

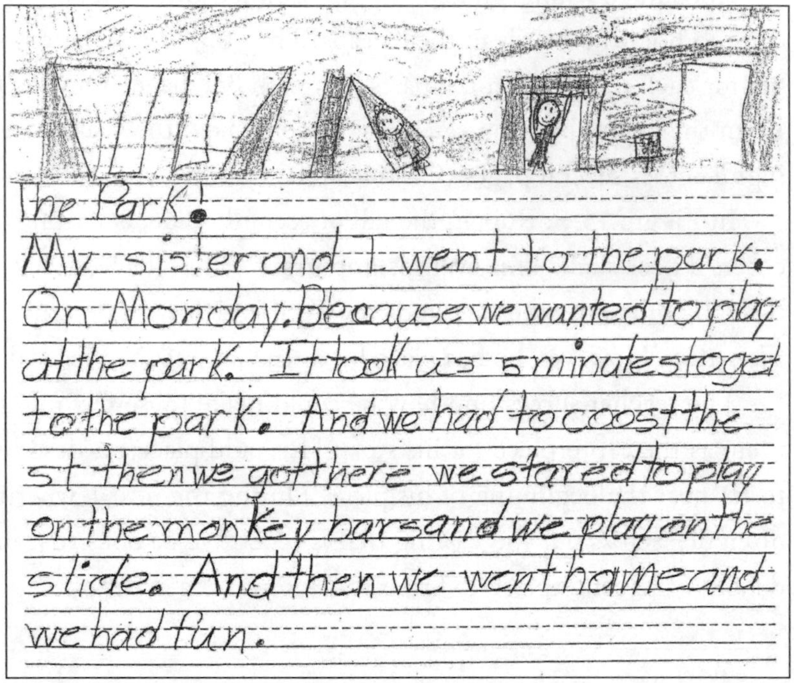
The Park!
My sister and I went to the park.
On Monday. Because we wanted to play
at the park. It took us 5 minutes to get
to the park. And we had to coost the
st then we got there we stared to play
on the monkey bars and we play on the
slide. And then we went home and
we had fun.

FIGURE 15-4. "The Park" by Dejah

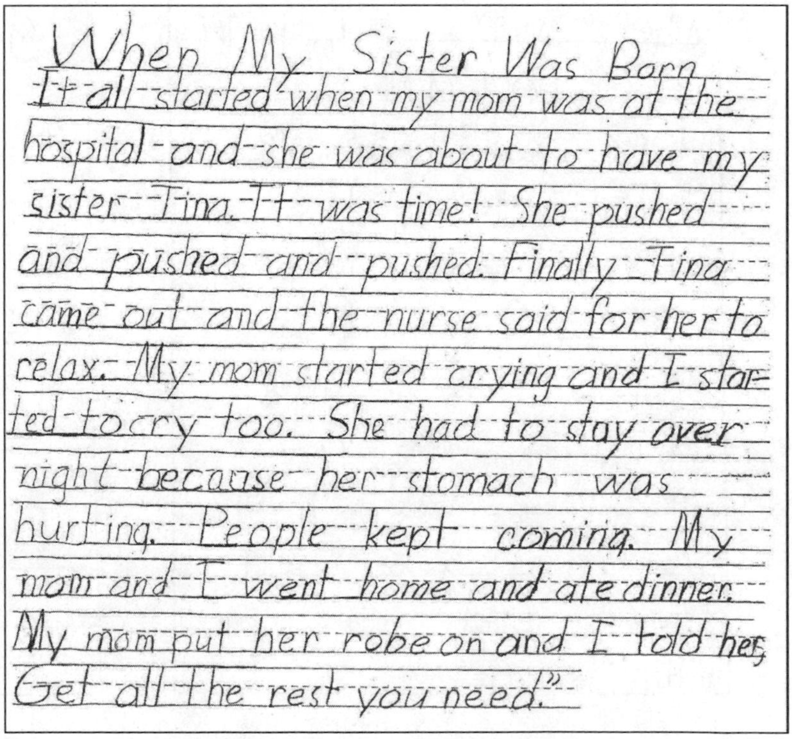
When My Sister Was Born
It all started when my mom was at the
hospital and she was about to have my
sister Tina. It was time! She pushed
and pushed and pushed. Finally Tina
came out and the nurse said for her to
relax. My mom started crying and I started to cry too. She had to stay over
night because her stomach was
hurting. People kept coming. My
mom and I went home and ate dinner.
My mom put her robe on and I told her,
"Get all the rest you need."

FIGURE 15-5. "When My Sister Was Born" by Abby

6. Help Children Learn to Read Like Writers

We often first read an article, a poem, or a story to get information, seek meaning, or enjoy it. If we are writers and teachers of writers, however, we go further. We begin to notice the ways the author uses craft to awaken our interest, help us get to know a character, or make it possible for us to experience feelings or events as though they were real. Noticing in this way is called "reading like a writer" (Ray, 1999). Early in a young writer's life we can begin to plan "reading like a writer" experiences that guide the noticing. Students who are tuned in to an author's technique find it easier to apply that technique in their own writing.

French artist Edgar Degas has said that he developed his craft through the study of the great masters. Like Degas, we do not need to develop our art in isolation—we needn't teach writing alone. We can have many teachers of writing in our classrooms. All we need to do is to make their work visible, familiar, and accessible to our students. If we guide the ways that students experience the work of fine writers across the day, children will begin to think of familiar authors as partners whose writing can guide them.

7. Use Mentor Texts to Teach About Craft

A mentor text for our youngest writers is a fine piece of literature that is close to the children's lives and simple in writing style. Read the story several times and students will have an opportunity to experience it on different levels. Depending on the genre, at first they might be attending to the story line, information, or meaning of the text. As time goes on they may become interested in word meanings or more detail in the illustrations. As these books become more familiar, you can use them to help students become better writers.

The text you choose on a particular day will address a need you have noticed in your students' writing—the use of dialogue; an inviting lead; an unforgettable closing; how writers can reveal feelings, thoughts, and characters; or how writers create tension, get ideas, and use a variety of language structures. You can highlight a part of the book to illustrate how the author reaches readers or some writing the author has tried to make remarkable. Choose two or three clear examples, keeping in mind that you can also showcase an instance where a child has tried the same technique. Figure 15-6 describes Cathy Speeg using an exceptional mentor text alongside the children's work in her mini-lesson on leads with first graders.

Bev Roberts uses a familiar text to support a young writer.

It is helpful to keep a basket of mentor texts at hand in the classroom to use for different purposes—in mini-lessons, conferring, and as examples when you are writing with groups. It is better to keep the collection small and know the books well than to use materials not familiar to you and your students.

Cathy's Mini-lesson Using Mentor Texts: Learning More About Leads

Cathy begins by telling her first graders that today they will learn more about leads. She reads enlarged copies of lead sentences from two students. Juan has written, "This weekend something good happened." Mark began his story with, "Valentine's Day is a day that makes kids happy."

TEACHER: Now, if you read these lead sentences, what would it make you do?

CHILD: Read on!

TEACHER: Yes, you would want to read on and find out what was good, or what makes kids happy. Now, we've also read some very good books that have lead sentences, and one is *The Relatives Came* (1985).

Cathy holds up an enlarged print version of Rylant's lead and invites the children to read with her, "It was the summer of the year when the relatives came...."
So that makes us want to read on. Why did they come? What did they do?

CHILD: Yeah, you'd want to know what happened.

Cathy quickly shares leads from two other familiar stories, holding the books up, along with enlarged print versions for students to read. Her language is clear and simple, as in the explanation of the other examples.

TEACHER: So, okay, today when you get your writing workshop stories, I want you to go back to an old story, where maybe you need to write a better lead sentence. Think about your audience. Your lead sentence is what they are going to read first, and if it's good, they are going to want to read your story. So I want everyone to go back to an old story, and I'm giving you a sticky note to write a good lead sentence. If you need more, I'll put them right over here, at the writing center.

Cathy has used a tangible reminder to scaffold the transfer of the behavior she has demonstrated and requested. She will be looking for opportunities to guide writers in composing leads during conferring, and she will use the work of students beginning to take on this craft to teach during the share session. Note that in this mini-lesson, all the children could try the technique demonstrated. In other mini-lessons this direct approach might not be possible, but dependent on where the children are in their own writing process. Cathy's mini-lesson does not stand by itself, but is one of many focused on leads.

FIGURE 15-6. Cathy's Mini-lesson

8. Teach the Writer

We often hear the statement, "Teach the writer," attributed by Donald Graves to Mary Ellen Giacobbe (2004) and endorsed by many scholars and teachers of writing. And, it may be overused without careful consideration. What does it mean? How hard is it to do? Perhaps an example will make the concept clearer. A teacher has just completed a mini-lesson in writing workshop with her first graders about the ways writers can use the language of the senses (how things feel, look, smell, sound, or taste) in their pieces, and she has given two clear examples, one from a child's writing, and one from a familiar piece of literature. She later pulls in beside Tyrone to confer and finds that he has not tried any "sense" words in his writing. In fact, he is having difficulty holding his story together. He can't seem to retain his thoughts enough to write them down. It would be tempting for her to engineer the placement of some sense words in Tyrone's writing, but what would Tyrone learn about what he really needs? She would be fixing the piece rather than teaching the writer. At this point Tyrone needs her to show him how a writer can plan a message and hold on to it, so he can write it down (perhaps by repeating it to himself several times, retelling to a friend, sketching, using fingers, or touching pages to "hold" his words.) If she teaches Tyrone an action to follow and helps him get started, she will be "teaching the writer" something he can use each time he writes.

When we confer with children, we want to follow their lead and intentions as much as possible. If children live in the world of Disney or Power Rangers, it is natural for them to write about what they know. We will continue to show them the work of real writers and to talk about the reasons they write and the ways they choose topics from what is important to them. Eventually, our students will realize that rehashing a cartoon, choosing characters unlike those they know in their lives, or fantasizing events not true to life is not interesting to readers and not the work of a writer. This guidance is not an edict, but a gentle lead.

We nudge our students to explore the path a writer takes by reaching into their own thinking and experience to help readers think and experience in richer ways. Helping writers to become invested in their topics involves encouraging our students to pursue their passions and interests. These passions and interests evolve naturally into different forms of writing as children gradually learn about writing their messages in different genres. It often begins through read-aloud and community writing in different genres.

We can encourage writing about real experiences, often by listening for them. "We need to help writers find those big important things to say in their lives.... Their writing should say, 'This is who I am, this is what I wish for, and this is what I care about'" (Ray, 1999, p. 7). We must not be afraid to teach, yet we would not ask children to try a new technique or alter their writing unless the trial or alteration yields generative learning. It is far better that a student learn a useful action writers can take to make their writing better than it is to produce a polished piece.

9. Teach Young Writers Productive Ways to Get Messages on Paper

When you write as an adult, a large portion of the writing process can center on what you want to say because you have internalized, for the most part, the conventions of written language. However, emerging writers must learn about the complexities of their language in its written form. Children bring their amazing capacity for oral language to this new learning about how print works, but they must master the alphabetic system, concepts of word and letter, directionality, voice-print match, and many actions that will help them in the construction and solving of words. They must learn to generate a meaningful mes-

---

Ida's Mini-lesson Modeling Getting Messages Down on Paper

The kindergartners in Ida's fall class have been using a name chart to link some of the sounds in their names and in classmates' names to letters they represent. They have had daily practice composing pieces as a group on the easel through interactive writing, and have a few known words on a chart. On this day, Ida is showing her students how to get messages down on paper more independently.

TEACHER: I'm going to write first, then ask you to write. First I have to be sure I have my pencils and crayons and a nice clean page. Then I have to think of an idea. Hmm...

I'm thinking of an idea of what I want to write. (Long pause; finger to head.) I know what I'm going to write. I'm going to write about the weather on Saturday. I can remember what the weather was like because it rained so much! It was so rainy!

I'm going to write: *It was raining on Saturday*.

CHILD: *r*, rain

TEACHER: Yes, you hear an *r*. I'll say the story out loud so you can hear what my brain is thinking. *It was raining on Saturday*. I'll start here. *I-t* (says slowly)

CHILD: Spells *it*. I-t

TEACHER: I'll start here. (Writes *It*, and mentions the capital *I*.) I'll go back and read. *It*— (pause)

CHILD: *was*

TEACHER: *w-a-s* (says slowly). I can hear this *w*. (Repeats *was* slowly.)

CHILD: *s*

TEACHER: (Using pointer under each word) I'll read again. *It was*—

CHILD: *r*

TEACHER: Let's say *raining* slowly. (Children and teacher say the word very slowly.) Are you right?

Ida continues to demonstrate actions she knows children do not yet control and allows students to offer what they know. She reminds them that in their own writing today, they can say what they want to write to themselves, then say each word slowly and write the letters they hear.

FIGURE 15-7. Ida's Mini-lesson

sage, hold it in memory, and find ways to characterize it graphically.

Emerging writers must learn to combine letter-sound actions with the visual memory of a core of high-frequency words, and later, to use a word, or word part they know to form a new word. So, in the beginning, you will be spending a good deal of time teaching writers how to build and draw upon these resources to compose what they want to say. In a mini-lesson, Ida Potacca, a master teacher, is thinking aloud and demonstrating an early writing process for her kindergartners. Here is a snippet of her language. (See Figure 15-7.)

We teach powerfully to help our students develop and internalize efficient ways to represent their language in writing. Fluent responding is more likely to occur in children who understand and practice how words work. Brief word study mini-lessons, followed by guided and independent practice, helps word-solving responses to become more automatic. Lessons are guided by what you see in the children's reading and writing. You can also free your students to attend to the meaning of what they want to write by teaching them efficient, fluid ways to form letters. Take five minutes with young students for whole-group instruction in handwriting, again followed by guided and independent practice (see Chapter 16). Because you know your students and study their writing, you can strike an instructional balance, in addition to procedural lessons, between craft lessons and lessons that support strategic actions young writers need.

10. Do More Showing Than Telling

Children need clear examples coupled with active engagement. They need to be shown how to do something new and guided through trying it out, rather than being prompted to do something they have never done. Think about the following levels of teacher support (see Figure 15-8).

How might these levels of teacher support guide you in teaching young writers? Here is an example: A teacher has observed that her first graders need to understand the concept of focus in their writing. Their pieces have a beginning, middle, and end. They are gaining control over a number of words they can write fluently, and the length of compositions is growing, but, unfor-

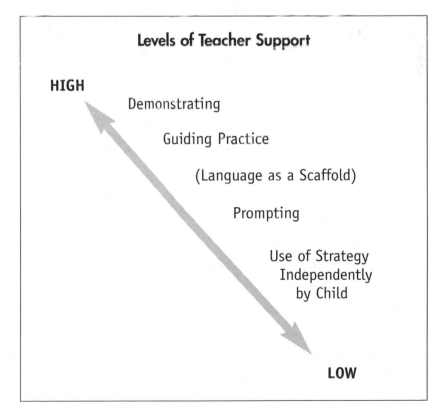

FIGURE 15-8. Levels of Teacher Support

tunately, growing into list stories that chronicle events rather than capture an experience. She wants her students to understand that they can write about one small piece of the topic in order to help the reader experience it more fully. Ralph Fletcher (1993) suggests that specificity is one of the most essential qualities of good writing. He calls this technique "writing small."

Because this concept is new, the teacher decides to start with a demonstration. She begins with her own writing. She thinks aloud a walk in the park, from beginning to end, then shows the children how she decides to focus only on one special part of her experience: the Mallard duck family that she saw in the pond area. She is careful to make the task of describing the ducks short, simple, and clear, well within the reach of her students as writers.

She closes her eyes and remembers how the four ducklings follow the mother duck in a straight line, joining in a chorus of quacking with mom. "Quack, quack!" She begins to make four quick sketches on four pages of chart paper, then writes in large print under the sketches. She remembers how the father mallard brought up the rear, showing off his bright green neck and guarding his children, and how they all glide into the water, one at a time, with the ducklings swimming as though they had been practicing for weeks, paddle, paddle, paddle. She ends her story by revealing her thinking—by posing a question. Were the ducklings just born knowing how to swim, or did the parents teach them?

On successive days, in workshop mini-lessons, the teacher uses several examples of how familiar authors develop an experience for readers around one focus and arranges for students to discover examples at read-aloud and guided reading times. When the children begin to apply the technique in their own writing, she seizes the opportunity to use their stories as examples for teaching during sharing. She helps the children practice the concept she has demonstrated by engaging them in group writing with a narrow focus, and during conferring helps children choose one small "pearl" to expand. Over time, she will be able to guide the children's actions more with words, and one day, the idea of focus will be internalized. It will become part of the decision making the students do as writers.

Determining an Appropriate Level of Teacher Support

Observation	Level of Teacher Support (HIGH → LOW)	Teaching
Child is: • uncertain • passive • confused		Demonstration
Child has made an approximation		Share the task
Child has partial control		Guided practice High support prompts Clear, specific language
Child is becoming more consistent with desired response		Gradually withdraw scaffold Low support prompts
Child initiates strategy independently		Specific praise Withdraw support

FIGURE 15-9. Determining Appropriate Level of Teacher Support

222

When do you know how much support to give a child when conferring, or the whole class when planning literacy lessons? The following guide should be helpful (see Figure 15-9).

Keep in mind that we use demonstration frequently when working with young writers because the concepts we are presenting are new. For many children the action we are suggesting for making their writing better continues to be "new" until it is guided, approximated, tried with greater success, then internalized.

11. Help Students Use Writing to Preserve the Memories of Childhood

Shelley Harwayne (2001) writes that if we are to nurture writers, we must enter the world of children and see it through their eyes. We must honor the unique ways they choose to use language to reveal their thoughts, feelings, and cultures. We must preserve the worlds that emerge on paper from a child's lens. Bailey, a beginning second grader, is starting a story about "bangs." Someday she and her family will cherish this memory. Relish the freshness of Bailey's words (see Figure 15-10).

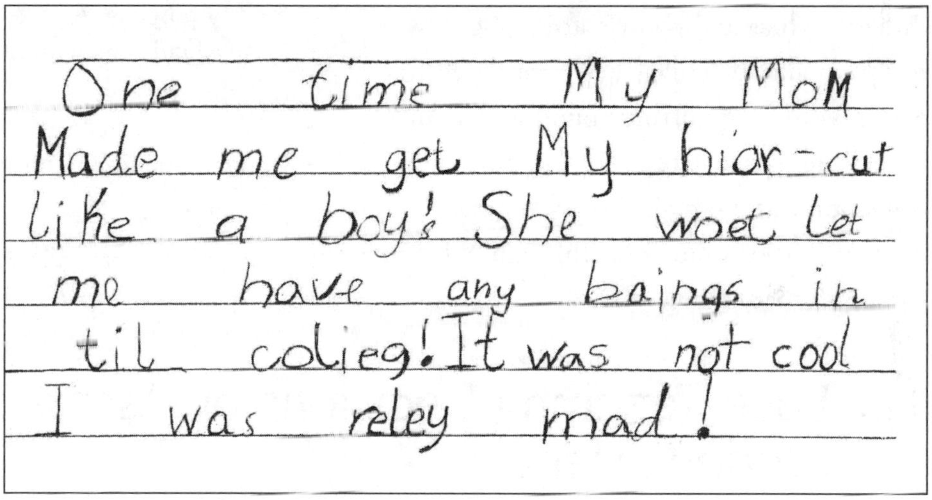

We avoid the temptation to elicit adult writing from the pens of young writers—whether it is word choice, language structures, or perspective. In addition to work across content areas, we will gradually introduce students to the registers of fine written language and the world of experience beyond their experience through literature and conversation.

> One time My MoM Made me get My hiar-cut like a boy's She woet Let me have any bajngs in til colieg! It was not cool I was reley mad!

FIGURE 15-10. Bailey's Writing

You will, at times, encourage a child to try a technique an author has used well, or an action that will expand his repertoire of choices for writing work. You are using the expertise of good writers as a scaffold so that writers can try on a particular craft. Your job is to help children find their own voices within the craft they want to try, to express themselves by finding just the right way to show how they feel or think, and to choose an approach that will help them be themselves. Often it is the child's own oral language that helps capture the world of that child.

Harwayne (2001) suggests that a piece of chosen writing is "published" when the writer has found an authentic purpose for it and has completed it for that purpose. Figure 15-11 suggests some ways to help children preserve childhood memories and publish their writing. These suggestions are not whole-class assignments, or an inclusive list, but examples of ways to help students discover an audience and purpose for a particular piece as you confer with them.

These types of pieces are considered published when they meet the child's purpose and provide a useful service for someone, even for peers in the classroom library. Ray (2004) and Calkins (2003) also suggest that children feel a sense of celebration and accomplishment as authors if they engage in "fancy publishing" of a few chosen pieces. The revision process is kept simple in the primary years and provides an opportunity for learning and orchestrating a few new things, such as adding or rearranging text, to make the child's best writing even better. When supporting young writers in the editing process, teach one or two new conventions, then make it easy for students to "make a memory" through publishing in some form.

> **Guiding Writers in Preserving the Memories of Childhood: Forms Children Might Choose**
>
> - Annotated mini-scrapbook of special event
> - Framed poem of peak experience, secret place, favorite pet
> - Word and picture portrait of influential person or beloved pet
> - Birthday memory book with descriptions and photos or drawings
> - Illustrated storybook of life-changing experience
> - How-to manual by class expert about hobby or interest
> - Historical log, or biographical journal of family member's life or journey
> - Letter to a very good friend or close family member for any purpose, e.g., to recommend a good book
> - Persuasive letter presenting arguments for a needed change
> - Story written from an interview with family or friend
> - Informational book presenting a chosen content area inquiry

FIGURE 15-11. Guiding Writers in Preserving Memories

12. Base Teaching Decisions on Assessments of Student Need

By studying your writers and their writing, you will know what they need to learn next. First, you need a good idea of where you want to take your students as writers. Calkins (2003), Ray (2004), and others have in recent years worked in classrooms with our youngest writers. They have conceived the notion of units of study throughout the year. A "unit" is a series of lessons through which children can learn what they need to know in order to grow as writers. Looking at these units, your school district's curriculum or required benchmark writing behaviors, and books on the teaching of writing will be helpful as you set goals for what you want your students to learn about writing. List the goals and keep them in front of you as you plan your teaching.

Second, carefully observe your students in the process of writing. As you collect and analyze samples of their writing, jot down what you might need to teach them next. Sometimes simple descriptive phrases with tally marks are better than elaborate assessment systems and checklists that require a large amount of time. Looking at what the children need and planning from your assessment is far better than following a sequenced program or series of mini-lessons. If you use units of study or suggested lessons, see them not as recipes, but as resources for gathering approaches and ideas. Work with your colleagues to look at children's writing to clarify what you might teach. The ultimate guide for instruction is whether or not what you are teaching is appearing in the children's independent writing. But then we must ask, "Is what is appearing what is needed?"

13. Teach "Test-Writing" as a Separate Genre

Yes, children need to learn how to write to a prompt, because this kind of writing is required in many districts and states as part of proficiency or achievement testing. The concern is that children begin to think that this kind of writing is authorship. Therefore, be very clear that writing in response to a prompt or assigned topic is something students need to learn to do for tests, and that you will help them learn to do this kind of writing well, but not in writing workshop. Even if you have to omit workshop occasionally, teach test-taking strategies that do not relate to real composing during a separate time, with a separate label. Writing workshop is about choice.

Most states now offer online practice tests in each curriculum area being tested during a particular year. You can analyze the tests for specific requirements they ask of writers and teach students how to address and check on themselves for each requirement. Some states require students to write a summary statement in addition to marking a correct main idea statement for passages on reading tests. Involving students in analyzing the test and making a checklist raises their awareness of key features to remember when taking reading and writing tests.

Demonstration, followed by guided practice on items similar to those on the test, is an effective means of helping children learn these skills. This process can begin as a shared writing lesson. If students have had rich and varied literacy experiences, they tend to do well on tests. However, it helps to show them what is in store for them during testing situations and involve them in practicing for the kind of work they will be expected to do on the test.

14. Engage Children in Writing From the Beginning of Their School Experience

Children's early approximations in writing are a window through which teachers can look to assess the child's present understandings about how print works and to plan what they will teach the child next. In addition to the benefits mentioned at the beginning of this chapter, writing helps young children learn to read. All writers practice reading as they construct messages. A child's early contact with writing presents many opportunities for exploring the features of print. Active composing and self-directed motor movement as children construct letters and words provide a plan or scheme for other vital responses and assist the integration of the message, language, and graphic systems so necessary for reading. Thus, the role writing plays as an organizer for reading behavior is an important contributor to early reading success in programs where reading and writing are taught side by side from the beginning (Clay, 1975; 1991).

15. Set Expectations High

The longer I teach, the more I marvel at the amazing things young children can learn. I no longer speak to children as though some of the goals I have for their learning are to be accomplished in the distant future. I expect them to learn important and complex things, and I challenge myself to teach so clearly, choosing just the right language and examples, that they will learn. It is so exciting, and humbling, to see our youngest children becoming authors whose work is so fresh and alive. What a contribution they are making to the field of literature! Our efforts in teaching them yield fruit that is delicious!

My gratitude to Bev Roberts and the teaching
staff at Kae Elementary, Whitehall, Ohio,
as well as Ida Patacca and Cathy Steeg for
exceptional teaching examples.

Suggestions for Professional Development

1. With a group of colleagues, review the 15 ways to help young writers, mentioned in this chapter. Then, discuss which ones an observer would find implemented in your school and which could be strengthened. Identify several ways that you can better support young writers, and then determine which of those interest you most. As a group, design a plan for achieving these goals. Plans might include reading and discussing professional articles, chapters, or books; viewing videotapes of classroom practice; or trying new ideas in classrooms and sharing the results with the group.

2. Lean on the format used in this chapter to design a session and/or handout for parents that describes the work teachers are doing to support young writers. Include ideas about ways parents can support their writers by encouraging their children to write and illustrate their own books at home. Share your work with parents during conferences, at a parent meeting, via the school Web site, or through notes sent home.

CHAPTER 16

Learning About, From, and Through Handwriting

by Lynda Hamilton Mudre & Gay Su Pinnell

At one time in our educational history, the curriculum area labeled "writing" was nearly synonymous with the term *handwriting*. Writing with elegant penmanship was the mark of an educated person—and this was at a time when alternative spellings of words were considered "creative" and "individualistic." Students practiced long hours with copybooks. Even within the last 30 to 40 years, copying in order to practice penmanship was a daily activity. Children in kindergarten seldom wrote at all, and first graders copied, sometimes laboriously, from the chalkboard as part of their independent work. Only after handwriting was mastered did children begin to write their own stories. Teachers devoted a portion of each day to handwriting lessons—first in manuscript and then in cursive.

As a result of research on emergent literacy and the writing process, the tedious drill of handwriting instruction waned, and rightly so. Children began composing and producing their own pieces of writing, resulting in an amazing change in perception—even young children could do far more in writing than previously thought. An unfortunate side effect of this productive new direction was a dramatic decrease in handwriting instruction. As teachers, we all know that there is just not enough time in a school day. When new requirements arise, old ones get shoved aside.

Nonetheless, while we advocate an emphasis on purpose-driven writing, we need to save some time for handwriting. We do not advocate a return to daily handwriting drill or to extensive copying, of course, but we believe that young children have much to learn from and through handwriting.

You might be thinking that your students are learning to form letters because they are writing more. You might be thinking that if you are dealing with letter formation as the need arises, it will be enough to teach children how to write legibly. We agree that teaching letter formation in these ways supports children in learning how to write letters and words, yet we should also consider this question: *Is there more we should do?* In this chapter, our answer is Yes, and we present the what, how, and why of providing brief yet consistent lessons in handwriting.

The Place of Handwriting Instruction

As curriculum content has increased and demands on the curriculum have grown, educators have found it increasingly difficult to find time for handwriting instruction. It may seem that with the expansion of technologies (for example, all kinds of computers, pen-based interfaces, and the prospect of voice recognition), handwriting will continue to decrease in importance. Researchers have noticed an increased emphasis on cognitive and self-regulatory aspects of composing, as well as a general de-emphasis on transcription skills (handwriting and spelling) during the 1980s and 1990s (Graham & Weintraub, 1996). The degree to which transcription skills are developed is a good predictor of quality and quantity of written composition in the elementary grades (Graham, Berninger, Abbott, Abbott, & Whitaker, 1970).

The de-emphasis on handwriting is reflected in the fact that in the last decades of the twentieth century few researchers were interested in examining handwriting speed, legibility, or the relationship between the two (Peck, Askov, & Fairchild, 1980). These researchers ended a review of the decade of the 1980s with this statement:

> Although seemingly almost an archaic tool, handwriting remains one means of individualized expression. Its relationship to the development of the other language arts has been demonstrated to some extent by research, so we encourage the perpetuation of handwriting instruction supported by scholarly research (Peck, Askov, & Fairchild, 1980, p. 297).

Research has not indicated a superior style in beginning writing, although in 1974, Barbe and Lucas suggested that manuscript writing should be maintained throughout life even after cursive writing has been learned. This suggestion is interesting, because manuscript writing was a new and controversial technique at the time of its introduction to the U.S. educational system in the 1920s (Hildreth, 1963). Prior to that time, children, even beginners, were taught cursive writing exclusively, and as late as the 1970s, George Early (1973) again urged the exclusive use of cursive writing in the elementary grades, with manuscript writing being taught only to college freshman involved in fields such as engineering.

Fisher and Terry (1990) weighed in on the manuscript print side of the argument with the following claims:

1. Manuscript and cursive forms of writing can be produced at the same rate if practice time is equal.
2. Manuscript is the most legible form and the goal of instruction is legibility.
3. Developmentally delayed children could benefit from continued practice with manuscript as a reinforcement for beginning reading success.
4. The time spent in transition from manuscript to cursive could be better spent creating, composing, and expressing content. At the end of elementary school, students will have transitioned to technology and/or may take on cursive writing.

Whatever the style of writing, there seems to be a strand of research about it indicating that effortless legible handwriting is related to the ability to engage in the writing process. Laborious handwriting, on the other hand, may be so demanding that it constrains children's ability to compose, elaborate, plan, and revise. Berninger, Mizokawa, and Bragg (1991) suggest that difficulty in handwriting may lead children to avoid the act altogether or engage in it only when required.

Graham, Berninger, Weintraub, and Schafer (2006) reviewed research on speed of handwriting, although the studies were scarce (only four since 1980), and they also examined research on legibility. Based on this research, they expected that the speed and legibility of handwriting would increase across the grades but progress would be uneven. Their study of 900 children in grades 1–9 indicated that speed typically increased from one grade to the next, but that the pace of change was more rapid from grades 1–4, slowed in subsequent grades, and leveled off in grade 9 as students achieved the speeds typical of adults. They also found that girls were faster writers than boys (this superiority is limited, however, to grades 1, 6, and 7) and that right-handers wrote faster than left-handers, possibly due to the placement of paper students were being taught. Legibility also increased across the grades, but there were long periods with little or no change, and girls generally wrote more legibly than boys. For primary-grade children, handwriting was more legible when children copied than when they composed an original text, indicating that dividing attention between writing neatly and engaging in the writing process leads to deterioration of legibility. Finally, the researchers discovered little relationship between speed and legibility; in fact, there may be a "trade-off" between the two.

It makes sense that improvement in speed and legibility would contribute to a student's ability to compose texts. This claim is supported by researchers who studied first graders who had handwriting problems (Berninger et al., 1998). Graham et al. (1998) suggest that difficulty in getting language onto paper may cause a writer to switch attention in a way that will limit the capability of memory and interfere with the generation of content and recall of ideas.

For the last four decades, Marie Clay's (2001) research and theoretical works have directed educators to attend to the reciprocal relationship between early writing and reading—and this relationship includes the mechanics of producing letters and words. According to Clay (2001), when young children write, they search for "visual forms to represent the sounds in the messages they have composed. When they check visually by reading what they wrote, they find out whether it says what they intended to write" (p. 20).

Writing helps young children do the following:

- Attend closely to the features of letters (the tall and short sticks, the tunnels and circles, the dots and tails)
- Become aware of the sounds within the words they are trying to write
- Begin to represent sounds with letters
- Build up a repertoire of known words that can be written with increasing speed and ease
- Develop a system for "learning how to learn" words

Clay rests her theory on a broad base of research, including her own. She refers to the seminal research by Charles Read (1971) that documented the ways children began to record sounds even before they had learned traditional spelling. Read made no claim that children would learn English spelling by themselves, but did document the power of writing in beginning literacy. Clay's recent work (2005) places a greater emphasis on helping children, especially those who have reading difficulties, develop the ability to scan print left to right—not only lines of print but words and letters. This linear directional movement is very different from the kind of visual scanning most children have been required to do prior to school, and it is a huge advantage to young children to learn directional rules early.

Teaching Handwriting in the Early Years

As we observe young writers at work, we notice that much of their time is spent in the process of forming letters. After all, getting letters down on the page is an important task if you are going to relay a message to a reader. Some children seem to cope fairly well in figuring out how to transfer the form they are visualizing (or sometimes copying) to paper. Others are practicing—and habituating—inefficient and time-consuming actions. Some forget what they want to say because their attention is focused on letter formation. Some are even "drawing" letters.

Letter formation can be frustrating and time consuming for many students because they have not internalized where to start, which way to go, and how to make letters fluently in the easiest way. This confusion robs them of time they could be spending in thinking about what they want to say and how to say it. What if our students could write letters more easily and fluidly? More automatic control would free them up to attend to one of the primary goals we have for them as writers—thinking about the meaning of what they are trying to write and writing it in a way that an audience can read and enjoy. It seems logical to provide the kind of handwriting instruction that will not only result in fluent transcribing, but also facilitate the craft of writing.

WHEN CHILDREN ARE LEARNING HANDWRITING, WHAT ARE THEY REALLY LEARNING?

When children copy letters and words, they coordinate eye-scanning movements with hand movements. If they are recalling the letters without using a model, they mentally scan their memory of the word or shape of the letter and translate this visualization into a sequential pattern of movement. The visual analysis and motor response is a brain activity that must be developed through involving students actively in the process. The goal is that the child will be able to initiate and control smooth, consistent, and sequential movements automatically and independently (Clay, 1975).

Clay writes that "writing can contribute to the building of almost every kind of inner control of literacy learning that is needed by the successful reader" (1998, p. 130). If the act of writing is self-directed, the resulting "visual exploration behaviors" (Clay, 1975, p. 73) become a support system for learning to read. Writing slows the visual analysis process and encourages children to notice particular features of print—how certain forms are alike and different.

As children bring a vast knowledge of their own oral language and of the world around them to the reading process, they must learn to perceive and manage print in efficient ways. Fostering this visual control is one of the major challenges of reading instruction in the primary years. Writing, if it is concurrent with reading from the beginning, enhances children's ability to work on print resources in the books they are reading (Clay, 1998). Of course, *writing* is much more than handwriting. The formation of letters is only a part of the whole process of authorship. A writer uses multiple resources in flexible ways to produce a message.

The reciprocal benefits of teaching writing alongside reading are logical. All writers must undertake the activities that a reader does. They must use the words they have produced to guide the writing of the next word just as readers use the context of the sentence or story to decipher the words an author has written. Writers must often reread; check on their use of visual, semantic, or syntactic information; and sometimes correct it to fit the message being composed. Like readers, writers must keep meaning in their heads as the ultimate check on the composition. Teaching children how to form letters is part of becoming a writer because writers need efficient ways to encode their thoughts. And automatic eye-hand response frees them to compose.

HOW CAN WE HELP CHILDREN DEVELOP EFFICIENT AND FLUENT HANDWRITING?

Our instructional goal is to help our students internalize the visual forms and directional movements necessary to produce letters. Using language to direct this movement helps. When the eyes, ears, mouth, and hand are involved together in performing a task, they can support and check one another. Seeing, hearing, saying, and moving concurrently is an especially effective way for our youngest writers to learn. For many children, this learning needs to occur before we expect them to use their eyes alone to act on print (Clay, 1975; 1998).

Often, learning something new begins with someone physically showing us exactly how to do it. For example, swimming lessons often begin with a demonstration from the instructor. Then the instructor invites you to move your arms and legs in the same way she does, using verbal descriptions of the movement. She might physically guide your limbs for a while, and usually directs the correct motion with the same words each time. As you try to swim, you begin to internalize the instructor's words in your mind and guide your own moves. Finally swimming becomes a routine that you don't need to think about a great deal.

Think about what learning to swim required you to do. You first had to attend closely to what the instructor was doing and saying. You then had to be actively involved in moving your arms and legs in appropriate ways. It was important to make her language your own because it finally directed your moves from within. Internalizing the language was the key to the self-direction of your movement—to your independence as a swimmer.

This swimming lesson example can help you design handwriting instruction for your students. Your language can act as a scaffold for children until it becomes internalized by them, enabling them to self-direct their moves. How does this process work as we teach handwriting? Here is an example from a kindergarten lesson (see Figure 16-1).

Formation of the Letter *h*

Procedures	Your Language
• Be sure you have your students' full attention. Slowly demonstrate writing the letter in large, bold print.	• Let me see your eyes right up here. Watch very closely. I'm going to show you exactly how to make the letter *h*. Start at the top. Pull down, back up, over, and down: *h*.
• Use the same brief and specific language each time to guide your movement while you are producing a clear visual model. Name the letter.	• Down, up, over, and down: *h*.
• Ask students to watch your writing, use your language, and move in exactly the same ways you do. The children's writing of a letter is done in the air, then later, on paper.	• Try it with me now in the air with your writing finger. Pull down, up, over, and down: *h*. (Repeat several times, until the children are verbalizing the movements without your voice.)
• Ask the children to try the writing on their own and guide their attempts verbally and physically as necessary.	• Now, you try it. Say and make the moves. Show me how you can do it by yourselves. Good. Let me hear and see you again. Again, etc. Now trace it in the box with your finger and whisper. Again. Now use your pencil, and I'll come and watch—and I'll listen to your words.
• When you are satisfied that the movements are firmly established in a sequential, fluent pattern, create opportunities for the children to practice independently. Demonstrate each independent activity and involve students in guided practice before they do it on their own. Verbalizing is gradually discontinued.	• At the ABC center make the letter very slowly in each square and whisper the words that tell which way to go. Then, check on yourself by finding a magnetic letter just like the one you made. Tell a friend the name of the letter you made.

FIGURE 16-1. Formation of the Letter *h*

Notice the gradual release of the teacher's control as the children take on the new behavior (see Figure 16-2).

This lesson could be taught across a week, or a bit longer, in the beginning. As children gain control, you might demonstrate and practice several letters that are similar in shape and movement, such as *h*, *m*, and *n*. Be sure to name the letters after forming them. Independent work could be part of the ABC/word study center, or each child could practice for a few minutes before moving on to other independent activities. After the forma-

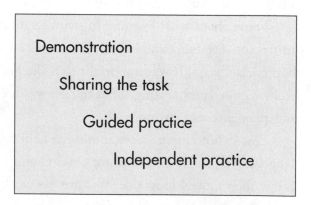

Demonstration

Sharing the task

Guided practice

Independent practice

FIGURE 16-2. Teacher's Release of Control Based on New Behavior

tion for a group of letters has been learned, fluent writing of two- and three-letter high-frequency words containing those letters can be practiced, along with manipulation of magnetic letters to form the words.

INSTRUCTION CHANGES OVER TIME AND ACROSS GRADE LEVELS

How does this instruction change over time and across grade levels? The answer to this question is dependent on the teacher's knowledge of what students need. If children in a given class have had little formal instruction in letter formation, we suggest following a routine similar to the one above, and as students gain more experience, instruction can be less frequent and more self-directed. Of course, you will use language appropriate for the level of your students, and older students will need less time because they have had more experience with print. Some may need a little more practice to "relearn" efficient movements and overcome habits. Whatever you decide, you will want to keep lessons very short, about five minutes, because you are planning many other important learning opportunities throughout the literacy block.

Observation is key. How are the children forming letters? Is the movement fluent, choppy, confused, or too slow? Is getting letters down on paper interfering with meaning-making?

Lessons for More Experienced Learners

GRADE	PROCEDURES
1	• Assess the class by observing students in the process of writing. • Decide the type of instruction that is needed. • Whole-group instruction might follow procedures similar to those suggested for kindergarten. The children might progress more quickly, because print features are more familiar. • When students are reaching fluency in formation of a particular group of single letters, teaching for fluency in writing high-frequency words containing those letters can be undertaken and practiced. • Attention to individual needs might mean adjusting both expectations and the type and amount of support you provide.
2	• Assess the class by observing students in the process of writing. • Decide the type of instruction that is needed. • Whole-group instruction might be a more rapid presentation of the language and movement for letter formation. Several letters formed in the same way might be presented at a time (for example, *a, g, d*). • At first, you might provide practice pages with the written language for directional movement for each letter in the set. You will want to discontinue this support as students become independent. • Whole-group lessons probably will become less necessary and practice more occasional until cursive writing is introduced. • To introduce cursive writing, we suggest you adapt the process presented above as an example for kindergarten because the learning is new. • In teaching cursive writing, it is important to demonstrate and practice how to connect one letter to another when writing words. • Teach letters in groups that are formed in similar ways and provide practice exercises for connections (for example, *h* and *n*).

FIGURE 16-3. Lessons for More Experienced Learners

How much support do they need? If many of your students are not forming letters in a smooth efficient way, or if letter learning is new to students, whole-class lessons, beginning with demonstration, make good sense. Small-group and individual teaching will provide additional support for the children who need it. (See Figure 16-3 for sample lessons for grades one and two and suggestions for children having difficulty.) If students have had a consistent program for handwriting instruction, and you are satisfied with the result, handwriting might receive occasional practice. Be cautious about assuming that all students have internalized directional movement patterns. Identify those children who need more help as you observe writers and review the language and movement for letters.

WHAT GUIDELINES SHOULD I KEEP IN MIND AS I TEACH FOR FLUENT HANDWRITING?

A few guidelines can help to make handwriting instruction effective.

Begin With Children's Names

Writing their own names is a highly motivating activity for children, and it is a good place to start when teaching them about the features of letters. Make a name card for each student. For the mini-lesson, select one child's name card. Show one side of the card with the child's name written clearly. Emphasize the tall letters and how the letters are placed right next to each other in an exact order. Show the other side of the card. First with your finger and then with a dry-erase marker, trace each letter using efficient movements. Show the other side of the card with the name in dotted print. Trace each letter and use words to describe the action. You may want to say something like, "Your name is always written the same way and you can write the letters in your name." Children can then use magnetic letters to make their names, using the fully written name on the card as a model. They can then trace the dotted outlines of the letters on the other side of the card, first with a finger and then with a marker or crayon.

Use Specific and Consistent Language

Earlier we described the use of a verbal path for the formation of letters (see Fountas & Pinnell, 2003). This very specific use of language helps children form letters, especially if they learn to "talk their way through" a letter by saying the directions themselves. To teach this skill, you might say something like "I'm going to make an *h*. To make a lowercase *h*, you pull down, up, over, and down." Have children make the letter slowly as you demonstrate on the board, a chart, or a MagnaDoodle®, and have them say the name of the letter with you. Teach children to use the verbal path every time they are practicing handwriting the letter. After efficient movements are learned, it will not be necessary to say the words. You can create your own verbal path directions or find examples in Fountas and Pinnell's (2003) *Phonics Lessons, K & 1*.

Provide Opportunities for Guided and Independent Practice

Children can practice on one letter at a time. They may trace sandpaper letters, trace letters on laminated letter cards, write the letter in salt or sand in a flat tray or box, or write the letter on paper with a crayon or marker. They may also want to make "rainbow letters." Write a letter in pencil on a large piece of chart paper and place dots and arrows on it with black marker. Then each child, in turn, while saying the verbal path, traces the letter on the newsprint using a different-colored crayon. At the end of the day, you will have a large letter written in about 20 different colors. One child can take it home—perhaps someone whose name contains the letter.

FIGURE 16-4. Independent Writing Activity

In Figure 16-4, you see an independent writing activity. In the first column, the child makes a word using magnetic letters. This is easy to do once the model has been placed in the middle column by the teacher. Then, the child traces the letters in the word several times with different colored crayons. Finally, in the third column, the child writes the word, using a verbal path to make each letter. The directions at the bottom are for the purpose of helping the parents understand the directions. Teach this task through a mini-lesson and children can practice letters during independent work time.

ASK CHILDREN TO NOTICE THE SPECIFIC FEATURES OF LETTERS

Use magnetic letters to help children notice specific features of letters, including:

- Letters with tall sticks (*h, d, l, k, b*)
- Letters with short sticks (*r, n, m, a, u, r, i*)
- Letters with tunnels (*m, n, u*)
- Letters with dots (*j, i*)
- Letters with tails (*p, q, g, j*)
- Letters with a slant (*k, x, w*)

Children need some time finding and sorting letters by feature to notice these distinctions, but when they do, it will help them immensely. They can then write letters in different categories.

USE UNLINED AND LINED PAPER

Often, teachers face a dilemma as to whether to use lined or unlined paper. When young children are have difficulty perceiving the distinctive features of letters (what makes a letter different from every other letter), then the lines on a page may be a source of difficulty. Some children may find it difficult to separate the lines on the page from the lines that make up the letter. Also, the task of making the letter with its distinctive features is a difficult enough motor task for some young children. Requiring them, at the same time, to make the letter a certain size and "sit" on a line actually makes the task even more difficult.

FIGURE 16-5. Writing on Lines

When children are just beginning to make letters, you may want to use plain, white paper and dark markers or pencils. Erasing is unproductive because some children will simply dig holes in their paper. Teach them to cross out, rather than erase, when they want to do something over. If you want to provide some guidance for children's use of the space on the page, consider folding the paper into three to six long boxes. The children can use the folds as a general guide, and the folds help them to organize print on the page. As they gain control, you can demonstrate and teach how to make letters and at the same time touch lines (see Figure 16-5).

It will not take a long time to teach children to write on lined paper, but most will need explicit teaching and some concentrated practice.

USE A HANDWRITING BOOK

Create a large version of a handwriting book (see Figure 16-6) to show your students what you want them to do. Select an easy letter that most children know and can make. Use the verbal path as you write the letter on a whiteboard, chart paper, or a MagnaDoodle. Then, show children how to write the letter in the handwriting book. Demonstrate it several times and then say, "Now I'm going to choose the best *c* that I have made. I'm going to circle it with a colored marker." Then, close the book.

Give the children a letter to practice in their own handwriting books—perhaps one row of letters. Guide them to use the verbal path and say the name of the letter. Then, have them choose their best letter. Help them understand why this letter is "best." This self-evaluation will gradually become routine as children learn to evaluate their own handwriting. These handwriting books can be used several times a week, because it takes only a few minutes for children to write a row of letters and pick their best.

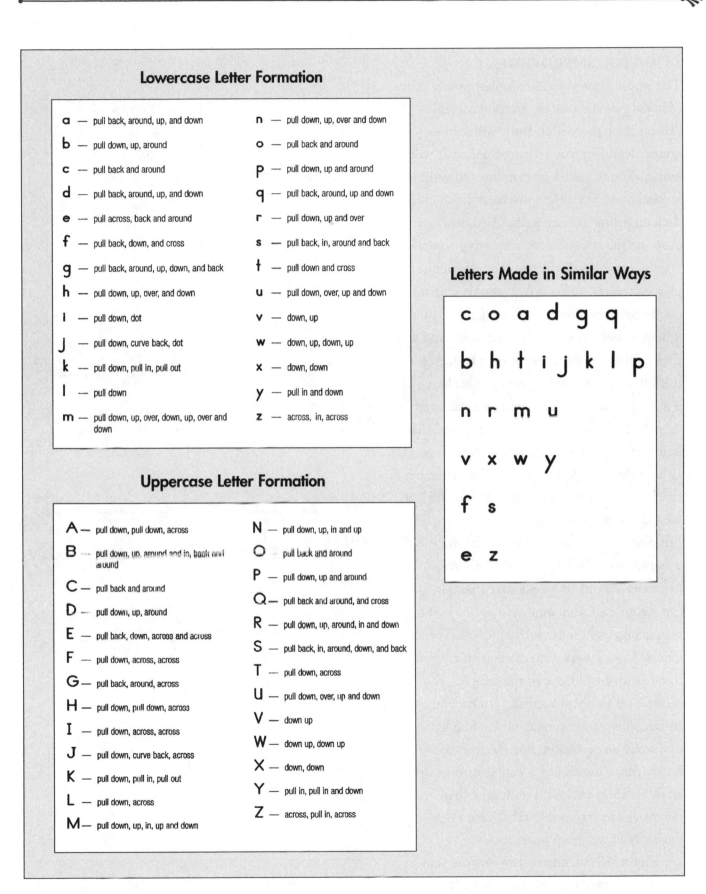

Lowercase Letter Formation

a — pull back, around, up, and down

b — pull down, up, around

c — pull back and around

d — pull back, around, up, and down

e — pull across, back and around

f — pull back, down, and cross

g — pull back, around, up, down, and back

h — pull down, up, over, and down

i — pull down, dot

j — pull down, curve back, dot

k — pull down, pull in, pull out

l — pull down

m — pull down, up, over, down, up, over and down

n — pull down, up, over and down

o — pull back and around

p — pull down, up and around

q — pull back, around, up and down

r — pull down, up and over

s — pull back, in, around and back

t — pull down and cross

u — pull down, over, up and down

v — down, up

w — down, up, down, up

x — down, down

y — pull in and down

z — across, in, across

Letters Made in Similar Ways

c o a d g q

b h t i j k l p

n r m u

v x w y

f s

e z

Uppercase Letter Formation

A — pull down, pull down, across

B — pull down, up, around and in, back and around

C — pull back and around

D — pull down, up, around

E — pull back, down, across and across

F — pull down, across, across

G — pull back, around, across

H — pull down, pull down, across

I — pull down, across, across

J — pull down, curve back, across

K — pull down, pull in, pull out

L — pull down, across

M — pull down, up, in, up and down

N — pull down, up, in and up

O — pull back and around

P — pull down, up and around

Q — pull back and around, and cross

R — pull down, up, around, in and down

S — pull back, in, around, down, and back

T — pull down, across

U — pull down, over, up and down

V — down up

W — down up, down up

X — down, down

Y — pull in, pull in and down

Z — across, pull in, across

FIGURE 16-6. Pages From a Handwriting Book

LOOK FOR IMPROVEMENT

The improvement you are looking for is in the efficiency of the process and the control exhibited by the writer. Both will lead to greater legibility and writing fluency. It will be worthwhile to take a few minutes to walk around and notice the movements that children are using as they write. Also, you can examine the products for increasing control.

In Figure 16-7, you see three writing samples from Kyra. In Sample 1, she demonstrated good understanding of the distinctive features of letters, but her production was slow and a bit shaky. She took several strokes to make some of the letters, for example, *a* and *f*. It is almost as if she was "drawing" the letters. She showed that she knew that letters have to be together in a word, however, and her spacing was good. In Sample 2, made about two weeks later, her spacing was not evident; however, she did self-correct the placement of the *u* over the *s*. She demonstrated some directional problems, and some letters were made with more strokes than necessary. About six weeks later (Sample 3), we can see considerable improvement in legibility, spacing, and the smooth production of letters. Most letters were made with efficient movement. In all three of the samples, Kyra was not necessarily practicing handwriting. In fact, she was writing about reading as part of a small group lesson. But she was having handwriting instruction a couple of times a week for short periods. Her teacher had taught children to use a verbal path even during reading group instruction.

Figure 16-8 contains two writing samples from Ryan. In producing Sample 1, Ryan wrote quickly and fluently; some let-

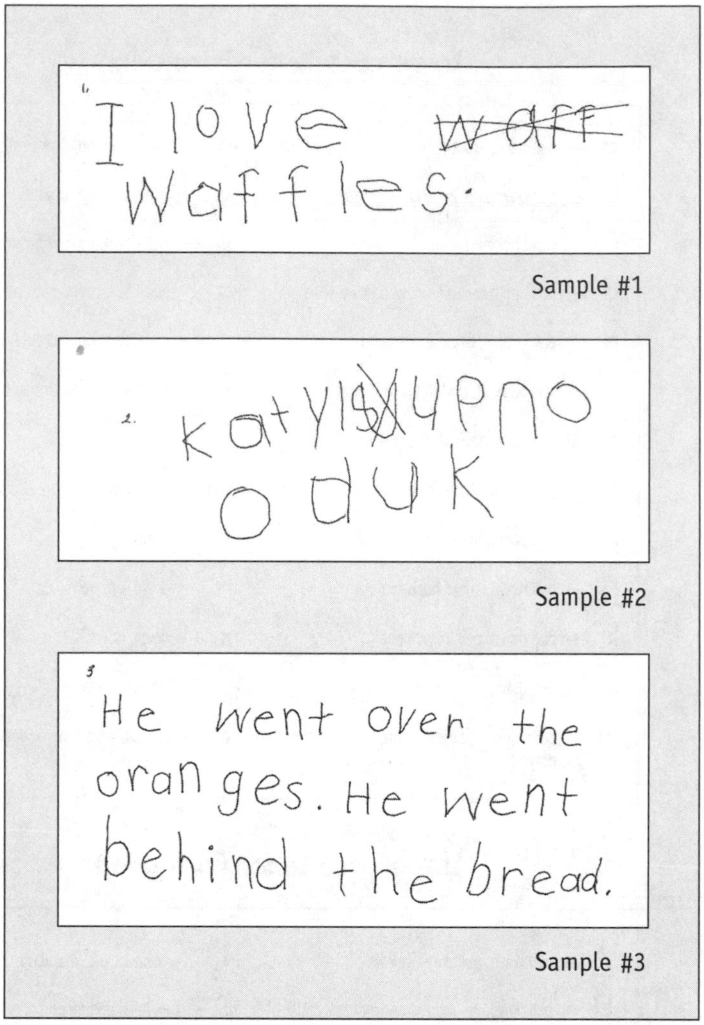

FIGURE 16-7. Kyra's Writing Samples

FIGURE 16-8. Ryan's Writing Samples

ters he made from bottom to top, others with a different motion. The problem here is that Ryan's print was not legible enough, and he was going so quickly that he ignored reversals so his handwriting is hard to read. Within about five weeks, he was producing writing like that in Sample 2. He had not sacrificed fluency in writing, but had incorporated more efficient movements, and the piece is much more legible. This more legible handwriting will make it easier for Ryan to proofread his work for spelling and punctuation.

At the beginning of first grade, Katie was already well underway as a writer. In the first sample in Figure 16-9 you see evidence that she could produce very accurate letters that clearly show the distinctive features. (She wrote this sentence to describe the results of a class survey.) Some of her letters, however, were produced with inconsistent motions, as if looking at a model and drawing them. Also, her control was a little shaky and she was still learning how to appropriately size letters and place them in relation to other letters within a word.

By January, as shown in Katie's list of "what to do to be a friend," her writing is much more mature. Her words are more clearly defined by space and letters are consistent in size. More important, she has internalized efficient motions and gained a great deal of control. Her writing is clear and legible. It did not take a great deal of handwriting instruction to support Katie in this learning, but the help she received made her conscious of its importance. She is developing good habits that will help her write efficiently and legibly. As this becomes even more automatic, it will free her attention to composing the message.

FIGURE 16-9. Katie's Writing Samples

Conclusion

Yes, we advocate specific teaching of handwriting in primary classrooms. The ease and efficiency children can develop will free them to attend more to the goals you have for them as authors. Of course, you would never allow handwriting practice to consume hours of tedious copying over the year, taking the place of authentic literacy experiences.

We suggest the following:

- Provide brief lessons, perhaps twice a week, with very explicit demonstrations of the directionality of letter writing, at first using a simple, concise verbal path.
- Draw children's attention to efficient ways of forming letters and writing words across multiple contexts.
- Create opportunities for children to practice efficient directional movement for a few minutes daily.
- Link sounds to letters during the act of writing.
- Integrate letter formation with early letter learning. (Learning to *write* letters with fluent and consistent directional movement can help children learn the visual features of letters. *Name* the letter after you write it.)

You will find that investing in these brief, focused lessons has high payoff for helping young students attend to the features of print and develop ease in writing messages, informational pieces, and stories. You can do it easily!

Suggestions for Professional Development

The following activities might be planned for one longer meeting or two shorter sessions with colleagues:

1. Ask each teacher to read Chapter 16, "Learning About, From, and Through Handwriting," before coming to the session. Ask the teachers to talk in pairs about the rationale for explicit lessons for teaching handwriting. How might such lessons benefit students? Find one or two quotes from the chapter that express the rationale. Next, explore several ways you might include handwriting instruction in your literacy block and share your ideas and one of the quotes with the group.

2. Review the suggested language for teaching handwriting by demonstrating and engaging students in "a verbal path." Talk about why using a consistent method, language, and movement across classrooms is important. With a partner or in a small group, practice the movement you will use to accompany the language for each letter. Design/chart a handwriting lesson to include demonstration, guided practice, and independent practice during the week. Using the chart, share your ideas with the whole group.

3. Gather samples of students' writing by dictating two or three simple sentences. Provide a month of handwriting instruction and then dictate the same sentences. Analyze the "before and after" samples to plan future instruction. ❦

Books Worth Talking About

In this appendix, we take a closer look at a few old favorites and lots of newer ones that offer opportunities for readers and listeners to grow in their understanding and appreciation of the techniques used by authors to write a variety of genres and to apply what they learn to their own writing. For each book, there are several discussion questions that can lead to learning about a specific aspect of the writer's craft. This appendix is not intended to be an extensive list of books to discuss to study the writer's craft. Rather, thinking through the questions below may help you plan such questions for your favorite books so that every discussion is an opportunity to learn about writers and writing.

Henry's Freedom Box: A True Story From the Underground Railroad

(Scholastic, 2007)

By Ellen Levine, illustrated by Kadir Nelson

When Henry's wife and children are sold to another master, Henry enlists the help of Dr. Smith, a member of the Underground Railroad, to mail Henry to Philadelphia where he will be free. Henry's journey in the box is difficult but he arrives in Philadelphia a free man, now called Henry "Box" Brown.

Craft Question	Craft Lesson
What does Henry's mother mean when she says that the leaves blowing in the wind are like slave children torn from their families?	Using metaphor to describe
How does the author use the wind to tell the story?	Linking ideas across your writing
How does the author set up the problem in this story?	Writing to describe a problem

Lilly's Big Day

(Greenwillow, 2006)

Written and illustrated by Kevin Henkes

Lilly is disappointed when she is not asked to be the flower girl at her teacher's wedding but ends up "saving the day" when the flower girl is unable to walk down the aisle out of fright.

Craft Question	Craft Lesson
What do you know about this story from the first page?	Starting a story with an interesting lead
What do you learn about the story from the way the characters talk with each other?	Using dialogue to move the plot ahead and develop character
Why does the author sometimes use three periods (...)?	Using punctuation to make the text interesting
How does Lily feel when Mr. Slinger tells her that Ginger will be the flower girl?	Using words to convey the feelings of the characters

The Giant of Seville: A "Tall" Tale Based on a True Story

(Henry N. Abrams, 2007)

Written & illustrated by Dan Andreasen

Dan Andreasen lives about 20 minutes from Seville, the setting for this biography of Martin

Van Buren Bates, a circus performer who was born in 1845 and grew to be nearly 8 feet tall. In other towns, Bates has felt like he was too big to fit in, but the people of Seville do all that they can to make him feel at home.

Craft Question	Craft Lesson
What are you wondering about after reading or listening to the text on the first page? How did the author make you wonder about what will happen next?	Using strong leads to set up a story Establishing the setting
How did the author help you to learn more about the giant? Why is the description of what he wore so important?	Developing a character
How did the author make this story interesting?	Writing a biography—a story of a person's life or part of a person's life

My Great-Aunt Arizona

(HarperCollins, 1992)

By Gloria Houston, illustrated by Susan Condie Lamb

Using poetic lan-

guage and format, the narrator tells the life story of Great-Aunt Arizona, who was born in a log cabin in the Blue Ridge Mountains and spent her life teaching the boys and girls in the one-room schoolhouse about the faraway places they would visit some day.

Craft Question	Craft Lesson
What do you know about the setting of the book from the first page? How do the illustrations further explain the setting?	Drawing the reader into the book through the setting
How do you get to know Arizona as a little girl? As an adult? As a reader?	Developing character by describing events
What did you learn about Arizona over time?	Sequencing action to build plot and character
Why do you think the print looks like a poem?	Using poetic language
Why did the author repeat parts of the text multiple times ("pretty white apron, with her highbutton shoes, and her many petticoats, too")?	Use of repetition as a literary device

17 Things I'm Not Allowed to Do Anymore

(Schwartz & Wade, 2007)

By Jenny Offill & Nancy Carpenter

A young girl writes a first-person account of the ideas she had about things to do such as staple her brother's head to a pillow or do a cartwheel to show Joey Whipple her underpants. Each idea is followed with a similar refrain—"I am not allowed to show Joey Whipple my underpants anymore."

Craft Question	Craft Lesson
What pattern do you notice in the writing of this book?	Using refrains or repetition for emphasis
What do you learn about her character through the illustrations?	Illustrating stories to extend the text
How did the author connect several of the little girls' ideas together?	Using sequence to tell the story
What words would you use to describe the main character? How did the author develop her character without using those words?	Showing character rather than telling

Mind Your Manners, B. B. Wolf

(Alfred A. Knopf, 2007)

By Judy Sierra, illustrated by Jotto Seibold

The Big Bad Wolf has retired to the Villain Villa and is plagued with bills relative to past decisions—damage to the homes of two pigs, cleaning one granny outfit, and purchase of one Bo-Peep outfit of sheep's clothing. An invitation to come to the library for their annual storybook tea motivates him to brush up on his manners and be on his best behavior at the event, after which he promises the library that he will return another time to explain how stories about him really happened!

Craft Question	Craft Lesson
As you look over the end-papers, what characters do you notice who have been part of other "wolf" stories?	Using endpapers to build meaning for the story
Look at the illustrations closely to find connections to other fairy tales. What do you notice?	Writing new stories that "lean" on favorite stories
Listen for language you have heard before in other stories. ("What a big smile you have!" exclaimed a girl in a red cape.)	Repeating familiar language to support character development
What do you think the wolf meant when he said he'd come back to tell the librarian what really happened in those stories?	Using perspective to describe the same event

Ribbit! Flip and See Who Froggy Can Be

(HarperCollins, 2007)

Written & created by Bender & Bender Studio

Each page of this unique, spiral-bound picture book is cut into three parts—Froggy's eyes and top of the head, Froggy's mouth, and Froggy's body. Through photography and computer imagining, the Bender & Bender Studio has created hundreds of possibilities for Froggy as readers mix and match various parts of each page and the accompanying text on the back.

Craft Question	Craft Lesson
What do you notice about each of the names? (Angler Arthur, Doctor David, Royal Randy)	Using words that begin the same (alliteration)
Let's think about what these descriptions mean: "with a frog in his throat" or "with 'baited' breath" or "with a nose for news."	Using expressions and sayings
What do you learn about Froggy through the hats, clothes, and expressions?	Using illustrations to support character

This Is a Poem That Heals Fish

(Farrar, Straus & Giroux, 2007)

By Jean-Pierre Siméon, illustrated by Olivier Tallec, translated by Claudie Zoe Bedrick

First published in France in 2005, this book explores the definition of a poem through the eyes of Arthur, who believes that a poem can save the life of his lethargic fish. After not finding a poem in the kitchen cabinet or under the bed, Arthur seeks out others who provide a range of definitions for the ever-elusive poem. Although Arthur does not realize it, each reply is actually a poem. (A poem is when you hear/the heartbeat of a stone.)

Craft Question	Craft Lesson
Let's think about what we know about poetry. What do you know about a poem?	Understanding specific characteristics of a genre
The first person Arthur visits is his friend who owns the bicycle shop who is always in love. What does his definition mean? (A poem, Arthur, is when you are in love/and have the sky in your mouth.)	Using words to mean more than the literal definitions
What do you think is the "big idea" of this story?	"Showing" rather than "telling" multiple themes of a text

Whopper Cake

(Simon & Schuster, 2007)

Written & illustrated by Karma Wilson & Will Hillenbrand

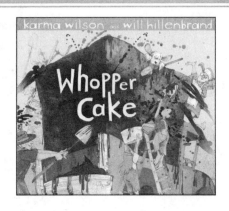

It's Grandma's birthday! As she leaves to do some errands, she warns Granddad not to make a fuss or even bake a cake. Granddad's determined to make her a cake but his attempts get bigger and bigger with each ingredient until he truly comes up with a "whopper cake" enjoyed by all.

Craft Question	Craft Lesson
How does the author make "big" events in the story?	Using exaggeration to emphasize a point
Every decision that Granddad makes causes him a problem that has to be solved. How does the author explain each problem and solution?	Using cause and effect to tell a story
Think about the words that rhyme. What is special about the way this story is written?	Rhyming and poetic text to tell a story
How does the author use punctuation to create the surprise ending?	Using ellipsis (…) to create tension

Tippy-Tippy-Tippy, Hide!

(Simon & Schuster, 2007)

By Candace Fleming, illustrated by G. Brian Karas

Mr. McGreely is ready for winter but the bunnies in his yard repeatedly find a way to get into the warmth of his house until he has finally boarded up every opening—the windows, doors, and even the chimney. When spring comes, the bunnies enjoy the flowers and Mr. McGreely can't get out of his own house!

Craft Question	Craft Lesson
How does the author help you to learn about the setting of the story on the first page?	Using repetition and actions to establish setting
What words make noises in the book?	Using words to represent sounds (onomatopoeia)
How does the author use problems and solutions to write the story?	Using multiple problems within one story
What are the ways Mr. McGreely describes the bunnies?	Using descriptive language

Frequently Asked Questions About Writing

Writing Workshop

What is writing workshop?

In writing workshop the teacher provides instructional support through mini-lessons, guided writing, conferring, and sharing. Mini-lessons focus instruction on a need relevant to the whole class. Guided writing is focused, small-group instruction based on the needs of a few students. Conferring is done one-on-one with students and takes place during time set aside for the teacher to learn about students, as writers, and their writing. While the teacher is meeting with students in guided writing groups and/or conferences, students work silently on their own writing pieces as they move the pieces through the writing process. At the end of each writing workshop, time (five to ten minutes) is devoted to sharing student work. Sharing provides constructive feedback and generates new thinking.

How much time should I plan for writing workshop?

An hour is generally recommended for writing workshop. However, young writers may need to work up to that amount of time. You may want to start with 30- to 45-minute sessions, especially at the beginning of the school year, and gradually increase the time.

Should I tell my students what to write, or have they thought of their own topics?

Having students regularly generate their own topics helps them develop a sense of ownership in their writing. They are the "experts" when it comes to writing about their lives and experiences. Assigned topics can frustrate writers if they cannot draw upon their personal knowledge to write about those subjects. Writing about topics that they choose themselves creates motivation to write and to write well. However, teachers need to prepare students for standardized tests that require writers to respond to a prompt. Therefore, it is appropriate to use a prompt when you are teaching the test-writing genre, but topics for the bulk of student writing should be self-selected.

How can I use my writing to teach the writing process?

Investing time, thought, and energy into a writing piece of your own allows you to learn more about yourself as a writer and more about the writing process itself. When you share with your students the process you go through, it provides students with a clear example of an author's initial ideas, decisions, and revisions regarding a piece. You can talk about where your idea came from, how you organized your piece, what decisions you had to make as the author, and the impact of revision on the final writing. You can also share your purpose for writing, and the message you want to leave with readers. Each draft of your work, complete with revisions, is a concrete example that you share with students to demonstrate the writing process from beginning to end.

Should I use graphic organizers during writing workshop?

Graphic organizers can be effective tools for helping young writers organize their thinking and writing. They can be used in the form of concept webs to assist writers in collecting their ideas or as simple process charts to model story development (i.e., "a beginning, a middle, and an end"). Use graphic organizers when they will serve as good models, but be cautious about using them too frequently. Too-frequent use of such organizers leads students to assume that they always have to be a part of the writing process. Writers need to experience a variety of writing tools in order to discover which tools work best for their own process of writing.

Mini-Lessons

What are the characteristics of a good mini-lesson?

A good mini-lesson focuses on one principle or skill, lasts five to ten minutes, and provides one or more clear examples of the principle stated in concise, child-friendly language. Focusing on a single principle or procedure minimizes the time spent on teacher instruction, but maximizes the time devoted by writers to applying the new information to their writing. Principles taught during mini-lessons can be revisited multiple times based on the needs of your class. Effective lessons engage students by encouraging their input and support students as they apply the principle to their own writing.

What is the teacher's role in a mini-lesson?

The teacher's role during a mini-lesson is to provide explicit teaching based on the needs of the students. The teacher provides specific instruction regarding effective writing strategies and skills or may focus writers' attention on particular elements of literature that can be applied to their writing. The teacher should also be clear about how students can apply what they have learned to their own work as writers.

What is the student's role during a mini-lesson?

During a mini-lesson, students should be attentive and prepared to engage in conversation around the instruction. They may be asked to generate additional examples or share personal experiences or connections. By the end of the mini-lesson, students should be thinking about the possibilities for applying the concepts or skills discussed to their own writing.

How will I know what kinds of mini-lessons to plan?

The teacher determines the content for mini-lessons based on student needs. Teachers are continually collecting information about their writers during the day in various settings, such as interactive writing and writing conferences. The information learned will provide "topics" for your mini-lessons. When planning mini-lessons ask yourself, "What do my students already know and what do my students need to learn next?" Mini-lessons usually fall into these categories: management, strategies and skills, and literary analysis. Management mini-lessons are provided more frequently in the beginning of the school year when new routines are being established. Mini-lessons to support the use of strategies, skills, and literary analysis should be planned throughout the year.

How do I make mini-lessons more powerful?

Mini-lessons that include student writing, teacher writing, and mentor texts as examples can have a great impact. These powerful resources cause students to consider the power of language and view the craft of writing more carefully and critically.

Do I read aloud to students as part of a mini-lesson?

Mini-lessons should be short and explicit, so as to maximize the time for students to actually write during the writing workshop. With that in mind, we advocate that children's literature be read outside of the writing workshop so that there is enough time for these great books to be enjoyed and discussed. Then, during writing workshop mini-lessons, these texts can be revisited and referred to, to show decisions the authors made about their craft. If these mentor texts are already familiar to the students when used during writing workshop mini-lessons, then students will be able to better attend to the analysis of the writer's craft.

Does it take a lot of time to use a mentor text?

The beauty of mentor texts is that, initially, they are enjoyed together in classrooms over the course of the year as interactive read-alouds. Children get to discuss meaning, hear rich language, predict events, and share their thinking in an inviting setting. The shared discussions bring added meaning to the story itself, and children make connections from the story to their own lives. Therefore, referring to the book again as a mentor text for writing is simple, yet powerful. Because students are familiar with the story line, characters, language, and structure, they can quickly learn to borrow these aspects of written text for their own writing pieces. Using

mentor texts actually preserves precious writing time in the classroom because students have heard the books previously, and are able to use them as models as they develop their own writing process.

Should I always use a mentor text for my mini-lessons?

Mentor texts can provide excellent examples of literature for mini-lessons. However, it is not necessary to use a mentor text for every mini-lesson. Student and teacher writing can contain powerful examples of the sort of writing that would serve as a strong model for writers. Sharing their own writing with students allows teachers also to share their thinking during the writing process.

Learning Writing Conventions

How can I ensure that students learn the conventions of writing—the spelling and punctuation that they need to write well?

The conventions of writing are essential standards for written communication, and as such, they need to be modeled, learned, and applied in writing workshop. Mini-lessons, guided writing, and conferences are all appropriate contexts in which to teach writers how to use conventions and the impact those conventions have on clarity and meaning.

Does it establish bad habits for students to write quickly, without spelling or punctuating correctly?

Having students write quickly is often the best way to draw out ideas. Writers need to learn that there is a portion of the writing process (i.e., "writing a draft") where writing quickly without regard for conventions is appropriate and helpful. However, during other portions of the writing process, such as editing and publishing, writers are expected to apply the conventions that they have learned.

Independent Writing

What is the role of the teacher during independent writing and conferring?

While students are working independently on their writing, teachers are freed up to meet one-on-one with students in order to conduct writing conferences. As teachers confer with the student, you are collecting information about the student as a writer and the writing piece that he is currently working on. The goal is to support the writer. You can also meet with students who have similar needs in guided writing groups.

What is guided writing?

Guided writing is an instructional context within the writing workshop when the teacher pulls together a small group of children who need assistance around a given topic or skill. Rather than the teacher meeting individually with students around the same need, guided writing is a way to maximize time by working with these students in a small group setting. Guided writing groups are pulled together based on need so group membership and objectives are constantly changing.

What is the student's role during independent writing and conferring?

The student should be generating new ideas for writing, rereading the writer's notebook to select an idea to write about, or working on a piece of writing during independent writing time. A student's role during conferring time with the teacher is to share the piece of writing that they are cur-

rently working on. They may read a portion of the writing aloud to the teacher in order to get feedback; share concerns or questions about ways to improve their piece; discuss various options for the type of genre that best suits their piece; and/or ask for support in revising or editing.

How can I plan a conferring schedule to allow me to get to all of my students?

Some conferences may take only two to three minutes; others may take longer. Preparing for conferences by reviewing students' writing folders the night before will help you keep conferences as brief as possible. The best plan for conferring with all students is to meet with three to five students a day. You can increase the number of students you confer with by balancing longer and shorter conferences. For example, if you know that three of your students require only a few minutes each, meet with those students on the same day that you meet with a student whose conference may take longer. It is also helpful to keep some sort of record of conferences, such as marking a calendar, so that none of your writers is overlooked and you can track how frequently you are meeting with each student.

What is a good conference?

A good conference is brief and focused, so as not to monopolize the writer's independent writing time, and is one from which the teacher and student walk away knowing more than when they sat down together. A teacher should have a better sense of the writer's strengths and what the writer needs to work on next; a student should leave the conference feeling like a successful writer—realizing what he or she is already doing well and what can be improved.

Sharing Time

What is sharing?

Sharing time is an opportunity for the students to come together as a community of writers. By doing so, students can learn what their fellow classmates are writing. Also, sharing can become an important instructional time because it affords the teacher an opportunity to revisit the mini-lesson and highlight some of the good decisions made by various writers during the workshop. This yields an additional opportunity for the writers to learn from each other.

What is the teacher's role during sharing?

During sharing, the teacher plays the role of facilitator and selects students to share a part of their writing by reading it aloud to the class. Often, the teacher selects writers who will share while conferring or meeting with guided writing groups. The teacher may select writing that applies the principle or skill taught during a mini-lesson, such as a strong lead. When students are faced with a difficulty, they may share their work with the class in order to get feedback in the form of suggestions for how to work through the problem.

What is the student's role during sharing?

The student who is sharing may read aloud a portion of her or his writing to get feedback from her or his peers. As the audience, other students should listen carefully while individuals share their work. Teachers can demonstrate how an audience provides constructive feedback. This teaches students to analyze writing thoughtfully and consider multiple possibilities for improving writing.

How much sharing time should I schedule?

Five to ten minutes for sharing at the conclusion of each writing workshop is usually effective.

Should every student share each day?

It is too time-consuming to have all students share every day in front of the whole class. One efficient way to let all students have an opportunity to share, however, is for students to share with a partner or within a small group of students. This also allows time for the teacher to highlight the work of various student writers to reinforce the mini-lesson.

What if I find it very difficult to reserve time for sharing?

Facilitators of a writing workshop have found that the five to ten minutes' sharing time at the end of writing workshop to be valuable in developing a positive community of writers. This time also provides a great opportunity to revisit the mini-lesson and make any needed clarifications. Scheduling sharing right into your plan book after the writing workshop can block out the time needed.

Writer's Notebook

What is a writer's notebook?

A writer's notebook is a notebook of any style that is used by writers to collect thoughts, ideas, and artifacts that might someday become writing projects. Those thoughts, ideas, and artifacts are sometimes called *seeds*, and writers are encouraged to enter seeds in their notebooks daily. The seeds take various forms such as webs, lists, sketches, questions, memories, charts, graphs, or artifacts like photos, bulletins, notes, and ticket stubs. Writers refer to the collected ideas, artifacts, and texts in the notebook to generate ideas for possible writing projects.

When is a good time to start using writer's notebooks?

Second grade is a good time to teach students to create a record of things as charts and observations about experiments, responses to read-alouds, lists, sketches, ideas for future writing pieces, or informational notes from content areas. They may use a spiral-bound notebook, sometimes called a Think Book, to organize their thinking through writing and to become familiar with the use of notebooks and journals. Using a Think Book prepares them for using a writer's notebook in grade 3 and beyond.

How do I help students get started with a writer's notebook?

Several things can be done to help students get started with a writer's notebook. First, provide a concrete model for them. Develop a notebook of your own and add to it regularly. Your notebook is a resource for demonstrating how to decide which topics to record, and for demonstrating ways to enter information and thoughts. Share information on authors and about how authors collect ideas for stories. Next, provide students with a simple spiral notebook. Have them enter some initial seeds, such as writing about how they got their name, observing and recording events of an experiment, describing a photograph of their choice, or developing a web of their favorite places. Demonstrate the kinds of seeds they can notice and collect outside of school, and encourage them to enter those ideas daily. Share often, valuing their entries and their work as authors, and begin talking about how some of their ideas could be turned into a longer writing piece.

How long should I keep students writing in their notebooks before going on to a draft?

For students who are just learning how to use a writer's notebook, it is beneficial to build the collection of ideas and artifacts for four to six weeks. Students need multiple opportunities to enter seeds both at school and at home, so that they have plenty of choices of topics to write about. As students add entries over time, encourage them to reread what they have recorded. Teach them to star or otherwise note two or three possible topics for their first writing piece then choose from those few. Students might notice that they have several entries around the same subject—this signifies high interest or appeal and could be a natural way to choose a first writing topic.

How do students go from a writer's notebook to a real piece of writing?

A writer's notebook is a tool for helping writers gather thoughts and mementos from their daily lives. Writers can then refer to their notebooks and reread their entries to look for potential writing topics that can be further developed. Some important questions for writers to ask themselves when revisiting their notebook are, "What do I really care about?" or "What would I like to spend more time on developing into a writing piece?" Once a potential idea or topic has been identified, then the writer simply closes his or her notebook and begins writing on draft paper. Closing the writer's notebook ensures that the writer will not simply copy notebook entries and instead will begin to write and shape a topic based on current thinking.

Overcoming Challenges

If I find writing difficult myself, how can I teach my students to become writers?

Most teachers would agree that we learn something best by actually doing it. Writing is no exception. One of the best ways to teach your students about becoming writers is to share your own experiences. Begin by starting a writer's notebook for yourself. Then, select an idea and take your idea through the writing process. It is okay if some parts of the process are challenging for you. Share your challenges and how you solved them with your students. Your modeling will have a tremendous impact on your students and provide you with many insights about the decisions that they will face as writers.

What about students who are not independent and always need attention?

A teacher's long-term goal is to develop independent students who manage themselves and their school responsibilities. Students in a particular class are at various stages in that growth process and need appropriate support from the teacher.

The best first step to an effective writing workshop is to approach writing with enthusiasm and create opportunities for early success. Engagement and enjoyment in what children are asked to do and learn in school often propels them toward independence and prevents the development of undesirable behaviors. After that, the use of explanation, modeling, and practice of expected behaviors helps set the procedures for the workshop; reinforcing effective behaviors holds interruptions to a minimum.

Some students will need more guidance, however, and some teachers find it helpful to check in with these learners at the beginning of every workshop to review the students' writing, set goals for the workshop time (perhaps connected to the day's mini-lesson), and monitor the students' progress. When students know the teacher will be available at specific intervals, they can sustain work for those shorter amounts of time. Including these students during sharing time, authentically

praising their work efforts, and treating them as capable authors goes a long way toward developing their independence.

Why is it necessary for the room to be quiet?

Just as reading requires quiet work time, so does writing. Students need a supportive environment to think critically and deeply about the writing choices they make. A reflective atmosphere allows students to rethink and revise during a constant flow of thoughts about the writing. This has implications for conferences as well. Students and teachers alike must use soft voices when conferring, so that other students' thinking is not interrupted.

What do I do about students who will not stop talking and moving around?

Setting expectations from the first day is crucial to the success of writing workshop. This includes modeling and practicing the behaviors the teacher wants in place. Provide time in the beginning for sharpening pencils, gathering supplies, and the like; then, state clearly that no one gets up or talks to his or her neighbor for a certain number of minutes. (Start with a manageable amount of time to ensure success and gradually increase the time on task.) Be consistent and firm, and students gradually will respond to these directions. Another way to reduce interruptions is to let students know they will have a chance to share their thoughts and their writing at the end of the writing workshop time. For students who continue to have difficulty staying seated, plan to meet with them quickly at the beginning of the writing time and help them establish a plan for their work. Some students may need a brief check-in by the teacher during the writing time as well.

Picture Books About Writers and Writing

Ada, A. F. (1994). *Dear Peter Rabbit.* Illustrated by L. Tryon. New York: Simon & Schuster.

Ada, A. F. (1998). *Yours Truly, Goldilocks.* Illustrated by L. Tryon. New York: Simon & Schuster.

Ada, A. F. (2001). *With Love, Little Red Hen.* Illustrated by L. Tryon. New York: Simon & Schuster.

Adler, D. A. (1999). *My Writing Day.* Photographs by Nina Crews. Katonah, NY: Richard C. Owen.

Cherry, L. (1994). *The Armadillo from Amarillo.* San Diego: Harcourt Brace.

Christelow, E. (1995). *What Do Authors Do?* New York: Clarion.

Cronin, D. (2003). *Diary of a Worm.* Illustrated by H. Bliss. New York: HarperCollins.

Danneberg, J. (2003). *First Year Letters.* Illustrated by J. Love. Watertown, MA: Charlesbridge.

DeCesare. (1999). *Flip's Fantastic Journal.* New York: Penguin Putnam.

Heide, F. P., & Gilliland, J. H. (1990). *The Day of Ahmed's Secret.* Illustrated by T. Lewin. New York: Lothrop, Lee & Shepard.

James, S. (1991). *Dear Mr. Blueberry.* New York: Macmillan.

Johnson, J. (1999). *My Dear Noel: The Story of a Letter From Beatrix Potter.* New York: Penguin Putnam.

Koutsky, J. D. (2002). *My Grandma, My Pen Pal.* Honesdale, PA: Boyds Mills Press.

Kvasnosky, L. M. (2006). *Zelda and Ivy: The Runaways.* Cambridge, MA: Candlewick Press.

Lowry, L. (2002). *Gooney Bird Greene.* Illustrated by M. Thomas. Boston: Houghton Mifflin.

Moss, M. (1995). *Amelia's Notebook.* Berkeley, CA: Tricycle Press.

Moss, M. (2001). *Rose's Journal: The Story of a Girl in the Great Depression.* Orlando, FL: Harcourt.

Pulver, R. (2003). *Punctuation Takes a Vacation.* Illustrated by L. R. Reed. New York: Holiday House.

Rand, G. (2005). *A Pen Pal for Max.* Illustrated by T. Rand. New York: Henry Holt & Company.

Scieszka, J. (1994). *The Book That Jack Wrote.* Illustrated by D. Adel. New York: Penguin.

Teague, M. (2002). *Dear Mrs. LaRue: Letters From Obedience School.* New York: Scholastic.

Wong, J. S. (2002). *You Have to Write.* Illustrated by T. Flavin. New York: Simon & Schuster.

Frequently Asked Questions About Interactive/Shared Writing

What is interactive writing?

During an interactive writing experience, the teacher and students jointly compose and write a message. The purpose is to develop children's understanding of the writing process, concepts about print, and functions of written language. Interactive writing also helps emerging readers and writers learn about letters and how words work.

What is shared writing?

During shared writing, the teacher and students jointly compose a message and the teacher writes it on sentence strips or chart paper so the children can easily see it to reread or revise. Its purpose is to help children understand that their messages can be written down and reread. Because the teacher writes the message, a shared writing text is typically longer than an interactive writing text written in a similar amount of time. Students are successful rereading the texts they create during shared writing because they are an integral part of the composing process.

How can I organize for interactive and shared writing?

Creating a supportive learning environment for interactive writing lessons takes planning, because you need to gather the necessary materials so they are close at hand during the lesson. This allows for a quick-paced lesson, which helps to keep the students engaged and helps them to focus on your teaching points and the print as they discuss, compose, and write their messages at the easel. Gather pointers, markers, "Fix-It" tape (correction or cover-up tape), and a MagnaDoodle®, whiteboard, or chart paper (24" x 36"). As you decide how to set up your space make sure that:

- the children sit so that everyone can see.
- the children's positioning allows for a path to the easel. It is helpful to leave a walkway down the middle of the group. This also allows the children to walk around the others sitting close to the easel.
- the name chart and alphabet charts are nearby and can be easily seen and used.
- there is easy access to the word wall for quick reference.

Why should I invite my students to write interactively if I am already engaging them in shared writing?

In shared writing, the teacher writes the text she and the children have composed while the children watch her. As she writes, the teacher engages in a "talk-aloud," drawing children's attention to specific strategies or conventions she is using as she writes. To the extent that children are listening *and* connecting to the teacher's talk with the correct letters and words, shared writing is a powerful technique. There may be times when you want to be even more explicit in your teaching and, thus, engage the children in interactive writing. When teachers share the pen with students, students often take more ownership in both the process and how writers put messages down on paper so that their audience can read it.

Do students write every letter of an interactive writing message?

Engaging children in an interactive writing lesson does not mean that the children must write the entire message. It does mean that the teacher knows what skills or strategies students need to learn next in order to move them toward more conventional writing. The teacher decides which of those strategic actions (such as hearing and recording sounds in words) or conventions (such as the use of punctuation) to teach in this lesson by slowing down the process of putting pen to paper and sharing the pen with the children.

Why is it important to involve the children in negotiating the message?

Teachers of writers are most effective if they teach children that writers go from ideas to spoken structure to printed message. In other words, once we decide what we are going to write about—our ideas—we need to choose language that clearly communicates those ideas. During the negotiation of the message, the community of writers can develop options and then choose the option that

best communicates their intent to the audience. Children who engage in the process of negotiating a text in this way may be learning to be more flexible in expressing their own ideas as they engage in a writing process during writing workshop.

What kinds of things should I teach during an interactive or shared writing lesson?

Teachers involve children in interactive and shared writing lessons because they want to support them in understanding what a writer does by engaging them in a writing process. In addition to helping children learn how words work, you are also teaching children that writers do the following:

- Write for a purpose
- Make decisions about how to convey their message to their audience (the form the message will take)
- Use a set of conventions called the printer's code because it increases the readability of the message

How will I know which child to choose to come up to the easel to write during interactive writing?

In interactive writing, the child who is writing at the chart is serving as a scribe for the entire community of writers. It is important to remember that you may be choosing that child because she has partial control of the particular strategic action of skill being taught, but it should not be used as a tutorial specifically for that child. In general, teachers choose teaching points during the writing of the message based on data they have gathered about the group of writers as a whole. For example, the teacher who notices that children are writing the "-ed" ending as a *t* in words like *jumped* may focus on "-ed" endings when possible during interactive writing. The data sources for these decisions may include the Observation Survey, writing samples from writing workshop and managed independent learning, and strategic actions for problem solving words during guided reading.

After the teacher thinks about what teaching points will be most powerful for her students, she then chooses a child who does *not* have the skill or strategy fully under control, based on her analysis of her data. For example, if Jennifer is using *t* for -*ed* in her independent writing, the teacher may ask her to write the word *liked* in the message. The teacher's rationale is that she can refer Jennifer back to her writing of the word *liked* on the easel when she asks Jennifer to check her own writing of words with the "-ed" ending that sounds like /t/ in her independent writing.

How can I teach in ways that encourage independence?

Teachers can teach for independence during interactive and shared writing lessons in at least three ways.

First, teachers can teach for a writing process so that whatever the particular form the piece of writing takes (e.g., a letter, a recipe, a retelling of a story), the writers are still involved in a process that goes from ideas based on experience, to the following:

- Crafting a message that communicates the idea to the readers (intended audience)
- Getting the spoken message into print
- Rereading the message to determine if it is necessary to either edit or revise

A second way teachers teach for independence in community writing is to teach for strategic action rather than for item knowledge. This means that we teach children ways to solve words they cannot write by using the strategic action of hearing and recording sounds in words or how to use a word they know to write a word they do not know. Teachers can also teach children why we use punctuation and how to use the meaning of a sentence to decide on the appropriate punctuation mark.

Lastly, teachers can teach for independence by helping children check on themselves rather than relying on the teacher to check or monitor their use of craft and conventions. For example, children can be taught to reread their writing to see whether it makes sense or if it needs to be revised. They can also learn that they need to initiate checking for the proper use of conventions such as spelling, use of upper- and lowercase letters, and appropriate use of punctuation.

How can I engage my students more fully when they get distracted and restless?

Some students may need extra support in learning the writing process and focusing their attention during interactive or shared writing lessons. One way to provide this support is by using interactive writing with a small group of these students who have similar instructional needs. This provides more opportunities for them to talk and problem solve the composition and writing of the message in a small group, and enables you to assess their learning easily as the lesson unfolds. When children are writing something that is important to them, they become highly engaged in the task, and when children are engaged, they are more focused and there are fewer management concerns and more learning.

Why should the purpose of writing be established during an interactive or shared writing lesson?

The teacher and students need to collaborate in establishing an authentic reason to write. The opening conversation of the interactive or shared writing lesson sets the stage for writing and informs children about the authentic forms of writing (lists, logs, letters, surveys, retellings, etc.). The teacher and students may decide to write a letter to thank the librarian for a new set of books or to create a list of ingredients they will need for a baking project. Once the purpose and form are determined, the rest of the work of generating the text and thinking about letters and words makes sense to the children because they are creating a meaningful message. When the purpose of the task makes sense to the children, it is easier for them to attend to the visual features of the print while constructing a meaningful message. Also, it is easier to involve students and maintain their attention if there is an authentic reason for writing.

What reference charts will support learning?

Teachers and children can use a variety of reference charts during interactive and shared writing lessons. For example, you can place within arm's reach a name chart with the children's names listed in alphabetic order, an alphabet chart with pictures of items that begin with the corresponding initial letter, and a pocket chart filled with high-frequency words. In addition, small charts of word families may help children learn to problem solve the spelling of unknown words by analogy.

Children's Books Supporting Community Writing

Predictable Patterns

Kindergarten teachers, first-grade teachers at the beginning of the year, and teachers of English Speakers of Other Languages (ESOL) often use books with predictable patterns or songs and rhymes as the basis of community writing lessons. Some of teachers' favorite books for community writing are listed below in this section and the next.

Carter, D. (1988). *How Many Bugs in a Box?* New York: Little Simon.

Hill, E. (1980). *Where's Spot?* New York: G. P. Putnam's Sons.

Martin, B. (2007). *Brown Bear, Brown Bear, What Do You See?* New York: Henry Holt.

Martin, B. (2007). *Polar Bear, Polar Bear, What Do You Hear?* New York: Henry Holt.

Miller, M. (1991). *Whose Shoes?* New York: Greenwillow.

Miller, M. (1997). *Whose Hat?* New York: HarperTrophy.

Tafuri, N. (1988). *Spots, Feathers and Curly Tails.* New York: Greenwillow.

Wildsmith, B. (1987). *Cat on the Mat.* New York: Oxford University Press.

Williams, S. (1989). *I Went Walking.* San Diego: Gulliver Books.

Rhymes and Songs

Baker, K. (1994). *Big Fat Hen.* New York: Harcourt Brace.

Christelow, E. (1989). *Five Little Monkeys Jumping on the Bed.* New York: Clarion.

Hale, S. (1984). *Mary Had a Little Lamb.* New York: Holiday House.

Hort, L. (2000). *Seals on the Bus.* New York: Henry Holt.

Karas, G. (1960). *I Know an Old Lady.* New York: Scholastic.

Marshall, J. (1991). *Old Mother Hubbard and Her Wonderful Dog.* New York: Farrar, Straus & Giroux.

Raffi. (1976). *Spider on the Floor.* New York: Crown.

Taback, S. (1997). *There Was an Old Lady Who Swallowed a Fly.* New York: Penguin.

Trapani, I. (1993). *The Itsy Bitsy Spider.* Boston: Whispering Coyote.

Whippo, W. (2000). *Little White Duck.* Boston: Little Brown.

Wickstrom, S. (1988). *Wheels on the Bus.* New York: Crown.

Domestic Cats

Many primary-grade children have had personal experiences with cats. Some children may even have a cat as a pet. Your class may choose to write a retelling or alternative version of the *Three Little Kittens* or *Cookie's Week* or read aloud the other books in this collection to support other writing sessions.

Stories

Ehlert, L. (1998) *Top Cat*. New York: Harcourt Brace.

Ehlert, L. (1990). *Feathers for Lunch*. New York: Harcourt Brace.

Fleming, D. (1998). *Mama Cat Has Three Kittens*. New York: Henry Holt.

Galdone, P. (1999). *Three Little Kittens*. New York: Clarion.

Halpern, S. (1994). *Little Robin Redbreast*. New York: North-South Books.

Henkes, K. (2004). *Kitten's First Full Moon*. New York: Scholastic.

Hillenbrand, W. (2002). *Fiddle-I Fee*. New York: Gulliver Books.

Pinnell, G. (2006). *Mugs Indoors and Outdoors*. Columbus, OH: KEEP BOOKS.

Rylant, C. (1999). *The Cookie-Store Cat*. New York: Blue Sky Press.

Sweet, M. (1992). *Fiddle-I-Fee*. Boston: Little Brown.

Wahl, J. (1992). *My Cat Ginger*. New York: Tambourine.

Ward, C. (1997). *Cookie's Week*. New York: Putnam Juvenile.

Nonfiction

Gibbons, G. (1996). *Cats*. New York: Holiday House.

Pinnell, G. (2006). *Cats Are Hunters*. Columbus, OH: KEEP BOOKS.

Penguins

Whereas many children have personal experience with cats, they most likely develop their knowledge of penguins through watching television or movies, visiting zoos, or reading about them. This collection of books represents the kinds of books a teacher might read along with the *Tacky in Trouble* stories described in Chapter 5.

Stories

Fromental, J., & Jolivet, J. (2006). *365 Penguins*. New York: Abrams.

Lester, H. (1988/2005). *Tacky in Trouble*. Boston: Houghton Mifflin.

Lester, H. (2005). *Tacky and the Winter Games*. Boston: Houghton Mifflin.

Lester, H. (1994). *Three Cheers for Tacky*. Boston: Houghton Mifflin.

Weeks, S., & Duranceau, S. (2003). *Without You*. New York: HarperCollins.

Nonfiction

Fletcher, N. (1993). *Penguins, See How They Grow*. New York: DK Publishing.

Jenkins, J. (2002). *The Emperor's Egg*. Cambridge: Candlewick.

Jeunesse, G., & Mettler, R. (1995). *Penguins*. New York: Scholastic.

Patent, D. (1993). *Looking for Penguins*. New York: Holiday House.

Salmansohn, P. (1997). *Project Puffin*. Gardiner: Tilbury House.

Sierra, J. (1998). *Antarctic Antics*. New York: Harcourt.

Folktales and Fairy Tales

Children always enjoy talking and writing about folktales and fairy tales. There are also three poetry collections in this section. Other folktales and legends can be found as part of the integrated curriculum collection in the next part of this appendix.

Cinderella

Bateman, T. (2002). *The Princesses Have a Ball*. Morton Grove: Albert Whitman.

Climo, S. (1993). *The Korean Cinderella*. New York: HarperCollins.

dePaola, T. (2002). *Adelita*. New York: G.P. Putnam's Sons.

Louie, A. (1982). *Yeh-Shen*. New York: Philomel.

Martin, R. (1992). *The Rough-Face Girl*. New York: G.P. Putnam's Sons.

Minters, F. (1994). *Cinder-Elly*. New York: Viking.

Onyefuly, O. (1994). *Chinye: A West African Folk Tale*. New York: Viking.

Perlman, J. (1992). *Cinderella Penguin*. New York: Viking.

San Souci, R. (2000). *Little Gold Star*. New York: HarperCollins.

San Souci, R. (2002). *Cendrillon*. New York: Simon & Schuster.

Schroeder, A. (1997). *Smoky Mountain Rose*. New York: Dial.

Steptoe, J. (1987). *Mufaro's Beautiful Daughters*. New York: Lothrop, Lee, & Shepard.

Little Red Hen

Galdone, P. (1979). *The Little Red Hen*. New York: Clarion.

Paye, W., & Lippert, M. (2006). *The Talking Vegetables*. New York: Henry Holt.

Pinkney, J. (2006). *The Little Red Hen*. New York: Dial.

Stevens, J., & Crummel, S. (2005). *Cook-a-Doodle-Doo*. New York: Voyager.

Sturges, P., & Walrod, A. (2002). *The Little Red Hen (Makes a Pizza)*. New York: Puffin.

Little Red Riding Hood

Daly, N. (2006). *Pretty Salma*. New York: Clarion.

Ernst, L. (1995). *Little Red Riding Hood*. New York: Simon & Schuster.

Marshall, J. (1987). *Red Riding Hood*. New York: Dial.

Sweet, M. (2005). *Carmine, A Little More Red*. Boston: Houghton Mifflin.

Young, E. (1989). *Lon Po Po*. New York: Philomel.

Integrated Curriculum

This section contains categories of books that integrate language arts with content area studies. You may choose to read some of these books aloud for enjoyment or as resources for deepening children's knowledge of a topic. Books suggested below may be selected as springboards for community writing lessons.

Grow, Grow, Grow

Stories

Cooper, H. (1998). *Pumpkin Soup*. New York: Farrar, Straus.

Ford, M., & Noll, S. (1995). *Sunflower*. New York: Greenwillow.

George, L. (2006). *In the Garden: Who's Been Here?* New York: Greenwillow.

Hall, Z. (1994). *It's Pumpkin Time!* New York: Scholastic.

Hicks, K. (2006). *Garden Giant*. Columbus, OH: KEEP BOOKS.

Titherington, J. (1986). *Pumpkin Pumpkin*. New York: Greenwillow.

Van Rynbach, I. (1995). *Five Little Pumpkins*. Honesdale, PA: Boyds Mills.

"Giant" Tales

Davis, A. (1997). *The Enormous Potato*. Buffalo, NY: Kids Can Press.

Peck, J. (1998). *The Giant Carrot*. New York: Penguin Putnam.

Stevens, J. (1995). *Tops & Bottoms*. New York: Harcourt Brace.

Tolstoy, A., & Sharkey, N. (1998). *The Gigantic Turnip*. Brooklyn: Barefoot Books.

Vladimir, V. (1998). *The Enormous Carrot*. New York: Scholastic Press.

Wilson, K., & Hillenbrand, W. (2007). *Whopper Cake*. New York: Simon & Schuster.

Nonfiction

De Bourgoing, P. (1989). *Vegetables in the Garden*. New York: Scholastic.

Eclare, M. (2000). *A Handful of Sunshine*. Brooklyn, NY: Ragged Bears.

Ehlert, L. (1997). *Hands*. New York: Harcourt Brace.

Gibbons, G. (1991). *From Seed to Plant*. New York: Holiday House.

Hicks, K. (2006). *A Sunflower Plant Life Cycle*. Columbus, OH: KEEP BOOKS.

King, E. (1990). *The Pumpkin Patch*. New York: Dutton Children's Books.

King, E. (1993). *Backyard Sunflower*. New York: Dutton Children's Books.

Levenson, G. (1999). *Pumpkin Circle*. Berkeley, CA: Tricycle.

Maass, R. (1998). *Garden*. New York: Henry Holt.

Peterson, C. (1996). *Harvest Year*. Honesdale, PA: Boyds Mills Press.

Robbins, K. (2005). *Seeds!* New York: Atheneum.

Robbins, K. (2006). *Pumpkins*. New Milford, CT: Roaring Books.

Schaefer, L. (2003). *Pick, Pull, Snap*. New York: Greenwillow.

Sloat, T. (1999). *Patty's Pumpkin Patch*. New York: G.P. Putnam's Sons.

Tomecek, S. (2002). *Dirt*. Washington, DC: National Geographic.

Water, Water, Water

Stories

Climo, S. (1994). *Stolen Thunder*. New York: Clarion.

Cowan, C., & Buehner, M. (1997). *My Life With the Wave*. New York: Lothrop, Lee, & Shepard.

Fried, M. (2006). *Beach Days*. Columbus, OH: KEEP BOOKS.

Germein, K. (1999). *Big Rain Coming*. New York: Clarion.

Hooper, M. (2000). *River Story*. Cambridge, MA: Candlewick.

McCarrier, A. (2006). *Reece to the Rescue*. Columbus, OH: KEEP BOOKS.

Polacco, P. (1997). *Thunder Cake*. New York: Putnam.

Rumford, J. (1996). *The Cloudmakers*. Boston: Houghton Mifflin.

Stojic, M. (2000). *Rain*. New York: Crown.

Wisniewski, D. (1991). *Rain Player*. New York: Clarion.

Wolfson, M. (1996). *Marriage of the Rain Goddess*. New York: Barefoot.

Yeh, C., & Baillie, A. (1991). *Bawshou Rescues the Sun*. New York: Scholastic.

Poetry

Locker, T. (1997). *Water Dance*. New York: Harcourt Brace.

Singer, M. (2005). *Monday on the Mississippi*. New York: Henry Holt.

Nonfiction

Asch, F. (1995). *Water*. New York: Gulliver Green.

Cicola, A. (2006). *Here Comes a Thunderstorm*. Columbus, OH: KEEP BOOKS.

Dorros, A. (1991). *Follow the Water From Brook to Ocean*. New York: HarperCollins.

Fried, M. (2006). *Oceans All Around Us*. Columbus, OH: KEEP BOOKS.

Harrison, D. (2002). *Rivers, Nature's Wondrous Waterways*. Honesdale, PA: Boyds Mills.

Kalan, R. (1978). *Rain*. New York: Greenwillow.

Morrison, G. (2006). *A Drop of Water*. New York: Houghton Mifflin.

Schaefer, L. (2001). *This Is the Rain*. New York: Greenwillow.

Simon, S. (1989). *Storms*. New York: Morrow Junior Books.

Tripp, N. (1994). *Thunderstorm!* New York: Dial.

Waldman, N. (2003). *The Snowflake*. Minneapolis: Millbrook.

Walker, S. (1992). *Water Up, Water Down*. Minneapolis: Carolrhoda.

Wick, W. (1997). *A Drop of Water*. New York: Scholastic.

Change, Change, Change: Autumn

Stories

Ehlert, L, (2005). *Leaf Man*. New York: Harcourt.

Moore, E. (1995). *Grandma's Smile*. New York: Lothrop, Lee, & Shepard.

Rylant, C. (2000). *In November*. New York: Harcourt.

Poetry

Florian, D. (2006). *Handsprings*. New York: Greenwillow.

Gerber, C. (2004). *Leaf Jumpers*. Watertown, PA: Charlesbridge.

Plourde, L. (1999). *Wild Child*. New York: Simon & Schuster.

Rogasky, B. (2001). *Leaf by Leaf: Autumn Poems.* New York: Scholastic.

Schnur, S. (1997). *Autumn: An Alphabet Acrostic.* New York: Clarion.

Nonfiction

Allen, M., & Rotner, S. (1991). *Changes.* New York: McMillan.

Ehlert, L. (1991). *Red Leaf, Yellow Leaf.* New York: Scholastic.

Maass, R. (1990). *When Autumn Comes.* New York: Henry Holt.

Robbins, K. (1998). *Autumn Leaves.* New York: Scholastic.

Brrr, Brrr, Brrr: Winter

Snowmen

Cuyler, M. (1998). *The Biggest, Best Snowman.* New York: Scholastic Press.

Ehlert, L. (1995). *Snowballs.* New York: Harcourt Brace.

Fleming, D. (2005). *The First Day of Winter.* New York: Henry Holt.

Sams, C., & Stoick, J. (2000). *Stranger in the Woods.* Milford, MI: Carl R. Sams II Photography.

Schertle, A. (2002). *All You Need for a Snowman.* New York: Harcourt.

Stories

Brett, J. (1997). *The Hat.* New York: G. P. Putnam's Sons.

Hader, B., & Hader, E. (1948). *The Big Snow.* New York: Simon & Schuster.

Johnson, A. (1990). *Do Like Kyla.* New York: Orchard Books.

Keats, E. J. (1962). *The Snowy Day.* New York: Scholastic Book Services.

London, J. (1992). *Froggy Gets Dressed.* New York: Penguin Group.

San Souci, D. (1990). *North Country Night.* New York: Doubleday.

Tresselt, A. (1947). *White Snow, Bright Snow.* New York: Lothrop, Lee & Shepard.

Yolen, J. (1987). *Owl Moon.* New York: Putnam.

Folktales

Brett, J. (1989). *The Mitten.* New York: G. P. Putnam's Sons.

Poems

Carlstrom, N. (1992). *Northern Lullaby.* New York: Philomel.

Denslow, S. (2005). *In the Snow.* New York: Greenwillow.

Prelutsky, J. (1984). *It's Snowing! It's Snowing!* New York: Greenwillow.

Rogasky, B. (1994). *Winter Poems.* New York: Scholastic.

Van Laan, N. (2000). *When Winter Comes.* New York: Atheneum.

Yolen, J. (1997). *Once Upon Ice.* Honesdale, PA: Boyds Mills.

Nonfiction

Martin, J. (1998). *Snowflake Bentley.* Boston: Houghton Mifflin.

Maass, R. (1993). *When Winter Comes.* New York: Henry Holt.

Waldman, N. (2003). *The Snowflake.* Minneapolis: Millbrook.

Courage

This collection of books shows how an individual's courage can make a positive difference. This set of books all celebrate the life of Rosa Parks:

Edwards, P. (2005). *The Bus Ride That Changed History*. Boston: Houghton Mifflin.

Giovanni, N. (2005). *Rosa*. New York: Henry Holt.

Rappaport, D. (2005). *The School Is Not White!* New York: Hyperion.

Ringgold, F. (1999). *If a Bus Could Talk*. New York: Simon & Schuster.

KEEP BOOKS

In addition to the KEEP BOOKS listed above, others are available that fit into the themes above. These books have been designed by literacy experts at The Ohio State University to support young children as they begin to learn to read and write. KEEP BOOKS are sold in sets because they are intended to not only be used in a classroom setting, but also to go home with children to read again and again. They provide a wonderful way to supplement the titles listed in the bibliography above. For more information about the many uses and benefits of KEEP BOOKS, please see Chapter 11. For ordering information, please see Appendix F.

The following KEEP BOOKS sets of rhymes, songs, and poetry serve as a starting point for children in community writing:

- *Nursery Rhymes*
- *Rhymes & Songs 1*
- *Going & Doing Poems*
- *Critter Poems*
- *Silly Poems*
- *Silly Animal Poems*
- *Spanish Nursery Rhymes*

Additionally, Fact & Fiction 1 covers several of the themes listed in the bibliography above in a very entertaining and educational manner.

Grow, Grow, Grow
- *Garden Giant*
- *A Sunflower Plant Life Cycle*

Domestic Cats
- *Cats Are Hunters*
- *Mugs Indoors and Outdoors*

Water, Water, Water
- *Oceans All Around Us*
- *Beach Days*
- *Reece to the Rescue*
- *Here Comes a Thunderstorm*

KEEP BOOKS Set Information and Order Form

KEEP BOOKS is a research-based, nonprofit program that addresses the need for inexpensive but appropriate books in the home (as little as 25 cents per book). The books are written and developed by educators at the Ohio State University to create positive communications with parents and caregivers and to enhance achievement. KEEP BOOKS are leveled for Guided Reading (Fountas & Pinnell) and Reading Recovery. This allows teachers to choose a level at which children can read the books themselves, helping to build confidence in their reading abilities and to foster a joy of learning to read.

As described in Chapter 11, KEEP BOOKS create a bridge not only between school and home, but also between reading and writing. KEEP BOOKS can be used to inspire children to write their own stories using blank My Own KEEP BOOKS

Order using the included form, visit us at **www.keepbooks.org**, or contact us with questions or to receive a full catalog and sample KEEP BOOKS.

EMERGENT READER
pre-kindergarten, kindergarten, beginning first grade

- **Caption Books (CB):** The Caption Book format encourages beginning readers to interact with the print. (levels A–B, 1–2)

Dinosaurs	*Look at Me!*
Trucks	*Balloons*
What Do I See?	*The Farm*
Traffic!	*Watch Me!*

- **Emergent Reader 1 (ER1):** Eight more engaging stories similar to those in Caption Books. (levels A–B, 1–2)

Playing	*The Swimming Pool*
Boo-boos!	*Scrub-a-dub-dub!*
Zoo Animals	*Getting Dressed*
Building a House	*My Cat*

- **Nursery Rhymes (NR):** This set consists of 8 traditional nursery rhymes formatted with clear print text. (not leveled)

Itsy Bitsy Spider	*Humpty Dumpty*
Mary Had a Little Lamb	*One, Two, Buckle My Shoe*
Jack and Jill	*Little Boy Blue*
Old Mother Hubbard	*Little Miss Muffet*

- Rhymes & Songs 1 (RS1): This set encourages emergent readers to attend to the print as they read classic rhymes and songs again and again. (not leveled)

To Market, To Market	*Teddy Bear, Teddy Bear*
Hey! Diddle, Diddle	*Five Little Ducks*
Fuzzy Wuzzy	*Five Little Monkeys*
Hickory, Dickory, Dock!	*This Little Pig*

LETTERS, SOUNDS & WORDS SETS
kindergarten, beginning first grade

Each of these sets offers 16 engaging stories for beginning readers and places emphasis on learning lowercase letter forms, a core of high-frequency words, and common spelling patterns.

- **Letters, Sounds, & Words 1 (LSW1):** (levels A–E, 2–7)

Baby Animals	*The Tree, a Bee and Me*
Patty	*Patty's Cat*
Up in the Sky	*Billy Loves Baseball*
What Will I Eat?	*Betsy and Her Bug*
The Zoo	*Always Listen to Mother*

My Room *Jake's Day*
I Like to Go *Don't Break the Eggs!*
Mole's Nice Hole *Will You Play With Me?*

- **Letters, Sounds, & Words 2 (LSW2):**
(levels A–E, 1-8)

Up, Up, Up *My Dump Truck*
Field Day *A Good Place to Hide*
Growing Up *Brad's Tooth*
Going to the Farm *Mother Bird*
Eating Breakfast *Watching TV*
BIG and little *My Little Brother*
My New Bike *James Goes to the Hospital*
Can I? *My Seed*

EARLY READER SETS

kindergarten, first grade

- **Letters, Words, & Numbers Caption Books (LWNCB):** The books in this set introduce numbers to young children by showing how they are used in everyday activities. (levels B–C, 2–4)

Making a Mask *How Old Are You?*
School Times *What Do I See in the Tree?*
The Garage Sale *Vegetable Soup*
Sandwich Shapes *Pigs at the Pool*

- **Set 1 (SET1):** Each book in this set has pages with one to three lines of text. The text is supported by pictures and predictable patterns.
(levels C–D, 3–5)

Gingerbread Girl *My Backpack*
Keeping Warm *Our Van*
The New Baby *My Map*
My Mom Likes Blue
Making a Peanut Butter and Jelly Sandwich

- **Set 2 (SET2):** This set uses similar techniques to those in Set 1. (levels C–D, 3–5)

Lunch Box *Max's Birthday*
Let's Pretend *Together*
Good Morning *Going Places*
My Snowman *Party Time!*

- **Health & Safety 1 (HS1):** Learning about health and safety becomes fun in this set.
(levels C–E, 4–8)

Gym Class *Just Like Me*
Shopping for Lunch *Staying Safe*
Good for You *Always Brush Your Teeth*
My Happy Heart *A Visit to the Doctor*

POETRY SETS

pre-kindergarten, kindergarten, first grade

Children will enjoy these poetry books as they become aware of the sounds of the language, helping them to become readers.

- **Going & Doing Poems (GDP):** (not leveled)

Zoom, Zoom, Zoom *Here Is the Sea*
Lunar Lars *Hippity Hop*
I Have a Little Wagon *Window Watching*
Chickery, Chickery, Cranny, Crow
This Is the Way We Go to School

- **Critter Poems (CP):** (not leveled)

Little Snail *My Dog Rags*
Baby Mice *Hickety, Pickety*
Gray Squirrel *If I Were a Bird*
Here Is a Bunny *The Elephant Goes Like This*

- **Silly Poems (SP):** (not leveled)

Lickety Splicket *The Lady and the Crocodile*
Old Dan Tucker *On Top of Spaghetti*
The Clever Hen *Three Elephants*
Way Down South *I've Got a Dog as Thin as a Rail*

- **Silly Animal Poems (SAP):** (not leveled)

Crocodile *Five Little Froggies*
The Donkey *Little Bird*
Quincy
The Elephant Who Jumped a Fence
I Never Had a Dog That Could Talk
A Horse and a Flea and Three Blind Mice

TRANSITIONAL READER SETS
first grade

- **Set 3 (SET3):** The text is supported by pictures as the vocabulary and language patterns increase in complexity. (levels D–E, 6–8)

The Zoo Trip	*The Three Little Pigs*
Lunch Time	*Feeding the Birds*
Come Over	*The Soccer Game*
Our Favorite Snowman	*Growing a Pumpkin*

- **Set 4 (SET4):** This set helps to ease beginning readers through the transition to longer, more complex story books. (levels F–G, 8–11)

Notes to Me	*Max and Mutt*
Burnt Cookies!	*Reading at Home*
Almost Ready	*My Messy Sister*
My Brother's Motorcycle	*Goldilocks and Baby Bear*

- **Health & Safety 2 (HS2):** Readers learn about staying healthy and safe through the experiences of children like them. (levels E–G, 7–12)

Safety First	*Time Out*
Don't Be a Couch Potato	*Home Sick*
Birthday Shots	*The Eye Doctor*
Just in Case	*The Big Race*

SELF-EXTENDING READER SETS
first grade, second grade

- **Raccoon Family Adventures 1 (RAC1):** Take children on 8 delightful adventures with this colorful family as they explore the world around them. (levels E–H, 7–14)

The New House	*The Best Birthday Present*
Scary Noises	*Be Careful!*
Night Games	*Trapped*
Digging for Dinner	*Where's Papa?*

- **Set 5 (SET5):** Full pages of text with less support from the pictures and enriched vocabulary increase the level of text difficulty. (levels G–H, 12–14)

The Smoke Detector	*The Birthday Present*
Mugs	*Mutt Goes to School*
Hold On!	*The Mystery of the Chocolate Chips*
Monkey Tricks	*The Gingerbread Man*

- **Letters, Words, & Numbers (LWN):** Through a lively story format, children are shown how numbers are used in everyday activities. (levels F–I, 10–15)

"That's Not Fair!"	*Is It Lunch Time?*
Wait for the Change	*Too Many Pets*
The Contest	*What a Night*
The Treasure Hunt	*Clickety-Clack*

- **Fact & Fiction 1 Chapter Books (FF1):** This set includes 8 paired chapter books—4 fictional titles and 4 factual titles. The books are larger and have 16 pages of text to challenge a self-extending reader. (levels K–L, 18–20)

Here Comes a Thunderstorm	*Reece to the Rescue*
Oceans All Around Us	*Beach Days*
A Sunflower Plant Life Cycle	*Garden Giant*
Cats Are Hunters	*Mugs Indoors and Outdoors*

LIBRITOS MÍOS SETS:
SPANISH KEEP BOOKS
pre-kindergarten, kindergarten, beginning first

- **Spanish Language Caption Books (sCB):** Translation of English Caption Books. (levels A, 1–2)

Dinosaurios	*¡Mírame a mí!*
Camiones	*Globos*
¿Qué es lo que veo?	*La Granja*
El Tráfico	*¡Mírame!*

- **Spanish Language Emergent Reader 1 (sER1):** Translation of English Emergent Reader 1. (levels A–B, 1–2)

Mira como juego	*La alberca*
¡Curitas!	*¡Agua y jabón!*
Los animales del zoológico	*Me visto*
Construyendo una casa	*Mi gato*

- **Spanish Language Nursery Rhymes (sNR):** Based on Spanish culture, these eight books offer Spanish language rhymes, songs, and games. (not leveled)

Al Juego Chirimbolo   Los Pollitos
Cinco Pollitos   Naranja Dulce
Un Elefante Se Balanceaba Tengo, Tengo, Tengo
Los Maderos de San Juan   Los Animalitos

OTHER KEEP BOOKS PRODUCTS

- **My Own KEEP BOOKS:** Eight-page booklets with blank pages that are twice the size of regular KEEP BOOKS. Children can personalize their books to make them their own. Full grade level sets of 300 blank books are $100 and individual sets of 30 blank books and 12 colored pencils are $20.

- **BIG My Own KEEP BOOKS:** Twelve-page booklets with blank pages that are twice the size of regular My Own KEEP BOOKS, allowing your student to maximize his/her creative experience. Sets of 15 blank books are $30.

- **KB Boxes:** These boxes are open at the top and sturdy enough to sit upright. They are designed to loosely hold 16 KEEP BOOKS, but can hold up to 32. A pack of 25 boxes is only $25. Each box sold individually is $1.25.

- **BIG KEEP BOOKS:** These 8½-by-11-inch books with laminated covers are perfect for teachers to use when introducing Emergent Reader and Libritos Míos sets. Each set of 8 books is $20.
  - Caption Books (BIGCB)
  - Rhymes and Songs 1 (BIGRS1)
  - Nursery Rhymes (BIGNR)
  - Emergent Reader 1 (BIGER1)
  - Spanish Caption Books (BIGsCB)
  - Spanish Nursery Rhymes (BIGsNR)
  - Spanish Emergent Reader 1 (BIGsER1)

QUANTITIES AND PRICING*

The first step is to choose a set above that is the perfect level for your students. KEEP BOOKS can then be ordered in the following quantities:

- **Grade-Level Sets of 400 books:** These consist of 50 copies of 8 different titles for most sets. Letters, Sounds, & Words sets contain 25 copies of 16 different titles. Fact & Fiction 1 set includes 25 copies of 8 titles. *Grade-Level Sets are only $120.*

- **Classroom Sets of 200 books:** These consist of 25 copies of the 8 titles in each set. Letters, Sounds, & Words and Fact & Fiction 1 sets are not available as Classroom Sets. *Classroom Sets are only $75.*

- **Tutoring Sets of 80 books:** Tutoring sets offer flexibility when working with small groups of students. Choose 1 set and get 10 copies of 8 titles. Choose 2 sets and get 5 copies of 16 titles. Choose a Letters, Sounds, & Words set and get 5 copies of 16 titles. Choose Fact & Fiction 1 and get 5 copies of 8 titles. Specify your set or set combination on your order form. *Tutoring Sets are only $30.*

* Prices are subject to change without notice.

Visit us at www.keepbooks.org for special promotions.

KEEP BOOKS®
ORDER FORM

Name of Set	Type of Set	Qty	Price	Total
sNR	Grade-Level	1	$120	$120
CB	Classroom	2	$75	$150
ER1 + CB	Tutoring	1	$30	$30
			Subtotal	
		*Add Shipping 10%, minimum $4.95		
		Tax Non-exempt Ohio customers only, 6.75%.		
		Grand Total		

For help placing your order, please visit www.keepbooks.org/ordering_help or call 1-800-678-6484.

Bill to: Name _____
School _____
Address _____
City, State, Zip _____
E-Mail Address _____
Would you like to receive notice of special offers via e-mail? Y N (circle one)
Phone _____ Fax _____
P.O./Check No. _____

Ship to: Name _____
Address _____
_____
City, State, Zip _____
Phone _____ Fax _____

Payment
All orders must be accompanied by a check, purchase order, or a credit card number.

☐ Payment Enclosed
  Check or P.O. payable to
  The Ohio State University

○ Visa   ○ MasterCard

Name on Credit Card _____
Credit Card # _____
Exp. Date _____
Signature _____

KEEP BOOKS Info:
800-678-6484
614-292-2869
keepbooks@osu.edu

Fax or mail orders to:
614-688-3452
KEEP BOOKS
807 Kinnear Road
Columbus, OH 43212

GWI

ABOUT THE AUTHORS

Patricia L. Scharer is a professor in the College of Education and Human Ecology at the Ohio State University. Her research interests include early literacy development, phonics and word study, and the role of children's literature to foster both literary development and literacy achievement. Her research has been published in *Reading Research Quarterly, Research in the Teaching of English, Educational Leadership, Language Arts, The Reading Teacher, Reading Research and Instruction,* and the yearbooks of the National Reading Conference and the College Reading Association.

She has served as co-editor of the *Journal of Children's Literature, Bookbird: A Journal of International Children's Literature,* and the Children's Books column of *The Reading Teacher.* Professor Scharer is also co-editor of *Extending Our Reach: Teaching for Comprehension in Reading, Grades K–2* and co-author of *Rethinking Phonics: Making the Best Teaching Decisions.* Currently, she is a member of the national Literacy Collaborative Trademark Committee and is conducting federally funded research in partnership with University of Chicago, Lesley University, and Stanford University.

Gay Su Pinnell is Professor Emeritus in the School of Teaching and Learning at the Ohio State University. She has extensive experience in classroom teaching and field-based research, and has developed and implemented comprehensive approaches to literacy education. She received her Ph.D. in literacy education from the Ohio State University in 1975. She has worked extensively in clinical tutoring and early intervention for young struggling readers.

She has been principle investigator for two large-scale research projects, one utilizing a randomized design. She received the International Reading Association's Albert J. Harris Award for research in reading difficulties. She also received the Ohio Governor's Award for contributions to literacy education. She received the Charles A. Dana Foundation Award, given for pioneering contributions in the fields of health and education. She is a member of the Reading Hall of Fame. With Irene Fountas, she is co-author of *Guided Reading: Good First Teaching for All Children* (1996), *Matching Books to Readers: Using Leveled Books in Guided Reading, K–3* (1999), *Word Matters: Teaching Phonics and Spelling in the Reading/Writing Classroom* (1998), *Help America Read: A Handbook for Volunteers* (1997), and *Guiding Readers & Writers, Grades 3–6* (2000). She also has co-authored *Systems for Change: A Guide to Professional Development,* with Carol Lyons. Recently, she has published a four-volume set, *Phonics Lessons: Letters, Words, and How They Work,* for kindergarten, first, second, and third grades. Her most recent publication, with Irene Fountas, is *Teaching for Comprehending and Fluency, Grades K–8: Thinking, Talking, and Writing About Reading.*

AUTHORS

LAURIE DESAI is a lecturer at the Ohio State University where she teaches courses in literacy and children's literature. Her interests include the role of writing in thinking and learning, school-university collaboration, and issues related to culture and its impact on learning. She is a strong believer in the value of diversity for our schools and for our society.

IRENE C. FOUNTAS, a professor in the School of Education at Lesley University in Cambridge, Massachusetts, has been a classroom teacher, language arts specialist, and consultant in school districts across the nation and abroad. She has co-authored numerous books and articles with Gay Su Pinnell, including *Teaching for Comprehending and Fluency: Thinking, Talking, and Writing About Reading, K–8; Fountas and Pinnell Benchmark Assessment Systems 1 and 2;* and *The Continuum of Literacy Learning K–8.*

JUSTINA HENRY earned a Ph.D. at Kent State University, Kent, Ohio. She has been a Head Start, kindergarten, and first-grade teacher, worked as a Title I reading teacher and later was a Reading Recovery Teacher Leader. She served as an associate editor for *The Reading Teacher*, a journal of the International Reading Association (IRA), and received the Literacy Award of the Ohio Council of the IRA in 1993. Currently, she is a program coordinator and trainer for Literacy Collaborative at the Ohio State University. Her work is published in *Extending Our Reach: Teaching for Comprehension in Reading, Grades K–2.*

KECIA HICKS is a trainer for Intermediate Literacy Collaborative at the Ohio State University and has extensive classroom experience in elementary settings. She is an Ohio State football fanatic and enjoys playing with her miniature dachshund, Sloopy.

SHERRY KINZEL is an intermediate university trainer for the Literacy Collaborative at the Ohio State University. She has a range of teaching experiences in primary and intermediate classrooms, as well as Reading Recovery and Title I. Sherry strives to empower teachers and literacy leaders by helping them to improve their practices and increase student achievement. She places a high value on the work done daily in America's classrooms by teachers—still America's greatest heroes.

MARSHA LEVERING is currently an intermediate trainer for Literacy Collaborative at the Ohio State University. Her 14 years in public education include being a Reading Recovery teacher, elementary classroom teacher, and working as a literacy coordinator.

ANDREA MCCARRIER received her Ph.D. from the Ohio State University. Formerly a classroom teacher and research associate, she has been involved in implementing intensive long-term professional development programs in elementary schools throughout the country. She has conducted research on interactive writing, children's literature, and language learning in primary grade classrooms, and is the author of articles and chapters on early literacy. She is a co-author, along with Gay Su Pinnell and Irene Fountas, of the book *Interactive Writing, How Language and Literacy Come Together, K–2*.

JOHN MCCARRIER is a research associate with the Literacy Collaborative at the Ohio State University. He is the author of several KEEP BOOKS for primary grade readers. He has made presentations as a guest author to children in more than 520 classrooms in 65 schools, primarily in the Midwest.

RAULINE MORRIS was trained as a primary and intermediate Literacy Collaborative literacy coordinator and later as an intermediate district trainer. She trained classroom teachers and assisted them in establishing full implementation of the Literacy Collaborative framework within the classroom setting. Rauline is committed to helping teachers use their time more effectively and efficiently to raise student achievement.

LYNDA HAMILTON MUDRE is a former university trainer at the Ohio State University. She worked with Literacy Collaborative as a doctoral student in its formative years. Her research interests include teacher learning and literacy coaching, guided reading, writing, and early literacy. Lynda enjoys all types of writing, jogging, and other outdoor activities. Publications are found in *Reading and Writing—Where It All Begins: Helping Your Children at Home, The Whole Idea, Literacy Matters, Running Record,* and *Extending Our Reach: Teaching for Comprehension in Reading, Grades K–2*.

EMILY RODGERS is an associate professor in the College of Education and Human Ecology at the Ohio State University. She has worked in schools as a reading specialist and special education teacher and now teaches graduate courses in early literacy and reading development at OSU. Her research focuses on the professional development of teachers and scaffolding literacy learning particularly for young children having great difficulty learning to read and write. She is co-author of *The Effective Literacy Coach*.

BARBARA JOAN WILEY is a university trainer for the Literacy Collaborative at the Ohio State University, where she works with teachers as they train to become literacy coordinators in their school. She feels that the best part of her job is visiting teachers in their schools and writing about what she learns. She has been a classroom teacher and reading specialist in school districts across the nation and abroad and is published in *Extending Our Reach: Teaching for Comprehension in Reading, Grades K–2*.

REFERENCES

Professional Resources

Anderson, R. C., Wilson, P. T., & Fielding, L. C. (1998). Growth in reading and how children spend their time outside of school. *Reading Research Quarterly, 23*(3), 285–303.

Anderson, C. (2000). *How's it going? A practical guide to conferring with student writers.* Portsmouth, NH: Heinemann.

Anderson, C. (2005). *Assessing writers.* Portsmouth, NH: Heinemann Publishing.

Askov, E., Otto, W., & Askov, W. (1970). A decade of research in handwriting: Progress and prospect. *Journal of Educational Research, 64,* 100–111.

Barbe, W., & Lucas, V. (1974). Instruction in Handwriting a New Look. *Childhood Education,* 207–09.

Berninger, V., Mizokawa, D. T., & Bragg, R. (1991). Theory-based diagnosis and remediation of writing disabilities. *Journal of School Psychology, 29,* 57–79.

Berninger, V., Vaughn, K., Abbott, R., Abbott, S., Rogan, L., Brooks, A., Reed, E., & Graham, S. (1998). Early intervention for spelling problems: Teaching spelling units of varying size within a multiple connections framework. *Journal of Educational Psychology, 90,* 587–605.

Bodrova, E., & Leong, D. (1995). *Tools of the mind: The Vygotskian approach to early childhood education.* Englewood Cliffs, NJ: Merrill.

Bomer, R. (1994). *Time for meaning: Crafting literate lives in middle & high school.* Portsmouth, NH: Heinemann.

Bomer, R., & Bomer, K. (2001). *Reading and writing for social action.* Portsmouth, NH: Heinemann.

Britton, J. (1973). *Language and learning.* Harmondsworth, England: Pelican Books.

Burroway, J. (2003). *Writing fiction: A guide to narrative craft.* New York: Longman.

Calkins, L. M. (1983) *Lessons from a child: On the teaching and learning of writing.* Portsmouth, NH: Heinemann.

Calkins, L. M. (1986). *The art of teaching writing.* Portsmouth, NH: Heinemann.

Calkins, L. (1994). *The art of teaching writing.* Portsmouth, NH: Heinemann.

Calkins, L. (2003). *The nuts and bolts of teaching writing.* Portsmouth, NH: Heinemann.

Calkins, L. (2003). *Small moments: Personal narrative writing.* Portsmouth, NH: Heinemann.

Calkins, L., & Bleichman, P. (2003). *Units of study for primary writing: A yearlong curriculum.* Portsmouth, NH: Heinemann.

Clay, M. M. (1975). *What did I write?* Auckland, New Zealand: Heinemann Educational.

Clay, M. M. (1975, 2000). *What did I write? Beginning writing behaviour.* Portsmouth, NH: Heinemann.

Clay, M. M. (1998). *By different paths to common outcomes.* York, ME: Stenhouse.

Clay, M. M. (1991). *Becoming literate: The construction of inner control.* Portsmouth, NH: Heinemann.

Clay, M. M. (2001). *Change over time in children's literacy development.* Portsmouth, NH: Heinemann.

Clay, M. M. (2002a). *An observation survey of early literacy achievement.* Auckland, New Zealand: Heinemann.

Clay, M. M. (2002b). *Change over time in children's literacy development.* Auckland, New Zealand: Heinemann.

Clay, M. M. (2005). *Literacy lessons designed for individuals: Part two, teaching procedures.* Auckland, New Zealand: Heinemann Educational.

Culham, R. (2005). *6 + 1 traits of writing: The complete guide for the primary grades.* New York: Scholastic.

Cunningham, P. M. (1995). *Phonics they use.* New York: HarperCollins.

DeFord, D. (1994). Early writing: Teachers and children in Reading Recovery. *Literacy Teaching and Learning, 1,* 32–56.

Early, G. (1973). The case for cursive writing. *Academic Therapy, 9,* 105–109.

Fisher, C. J., & Terry, C. A. (1990). *Children's language and the language arts.* Needham Heights, MA: Allyn & Bacon.

Fletcher, R. (1993). *What a writer needs.* Portsmouth, NH: Heinemann.

Fountas, I. C., & Pinnell, G. S. (1996). *Guided reading: Good first teaching for all children.* Portsmouth, NH: Heinemann.

Fountas, I. C., & Pinnell, G. S. (2001). *Guiding readers and writers, grades 3–6: Teaching comprehension, genre, and content literacy.* Portsmouth, NH: Heinemann.

Fountas, I. C., & Pinnell, G. S. (2003). *Phonics lessons, K & 1.* Portsmouth, NH: Heinemann.

Fountas, I. C., & Pinnell, G. S. (2006). *Teaching for comprehending and fluency: Thinking, talking, and writing about reading, K–8.* Portsmouth, NH: Heinemann.

Fountas, I. C., & Pinnell, G. S. (2007). *The continuum of literacy learning: A guide for teaching, K–8.* Portsmouth, NH: Heinemann.

Fox, M. (1992). *Dear Mem Fox, I have read all your books even the pathetic ones: And other incidents in the life of a children's book author.* San Diego: Harcourt Brace Jovanovich.

Gibson, S. A., & Scharer, P. L. (2001). "She can read them by herself!": Parents and teachers respond to a kindergarten school-home literacy project. In J. V. Hoffman, D. L. Schallert, C. M. Fairbanks, J. Worthy, & B. Maloch (eds.), *50th Yearbook of the National Reading Conference* (pp. 238–247). Chicago, IL: National Reading Conference.

Graham, S. (1990). The role of production factors in learning disabled students' compositions. *Journal of Educational Psychology, 82,* 781–791.

Graham, S., & Weintraub, N. (1996). A review of handwriting research: Progress and prospect from 1980 to 1993. *Educational Psychology Review, 8,* 7–87.

Graham, S., Berninger, V., Abbott, R., Abbott, S., & Whitaker, D. (1997). The role of mechanics in composing of elementary school students: A new methodological approach. *Journal of Educational Psychology, 89,* 170–182.

Graham, S., Berninger, V., Weintraub, N, & Schafer, W. (1998). Development of handwriting speed and legibility in grades 1–9. *Journal of Educational Research, 92,* 42–57.

Graves, D. (2004). "What I've learned from teachers of writing." *Language Arts 82* (2): 88–94.

Harris, T. L., & Hodges, R. E. (1995). *Literacy dictionary.* Newark, DE: International Reading Association.

Harwayne, S. (2001). *Writing through childhood: Rethinking process and product.* Portsmouth, NH: Heinemann.

Heard, G. (2002). *The revision toolbox.* Portsmouth, NH: Heinemann.

Hildreth, G. (1963). Simplified handwriting for today. *Journal of Educational Research, 56,* 330–333.

Hobsbaum, A., Peters, S., & Sylva, K. (1996). Scaffolding in Reading Recovery. *Oxford Review of Education, 22*(1), 17–35.

Lindfors, J. (1987). *Children's language and learning.* 2nd ed. Englewood Cliffs, NJ: Prentice-Hall.

Lose, M. K. (2007). Applying Wood's levels of contingent support for learning in reading recovery. *Literacy Teaching and Learning, 6,* 17–30.

McCarrier, A. M., Pinnell, G. S., & Fountas, I. C. (2000). *Interactive writing: How language & literacy come together, K–2.* Portsmouth, NH: Heinemann.

New Zealand Ministry of Education. (1992). *Dancing with the pen: The learner as writer.* Katonah, NY: Richard C. Owen.

Northwest Regional Educational Laboratory. (1999). *Seeing with new eyes.* Portland, OR: Author.

Peck, M., Askov, E., & Fairchild, S. (1980). Another decade of research in handwriting: Progress and prospect in the 1970s. *Journal of Educational Research, 73,* 283–297.

Pinnell, G. S., & Scharer, P. L. (Eds.). (2005). *Extending our reach: Teaching for comprehension in reading, grades K–2.* Columbus, OH: Literacy Collaborative at the Ohio State University.

Ray, K. W. (1999). *Wondrous words: Writers and writing in the elementary classroom.* Urbana, IL: National Council of Teachers of English.

Ray, K. W. (2004). *About the authors: Writing workshop with our youngest writers.* Portsmouth, NH: Heinemann.

Read, C. (1971). Preschool children's knowledge of English phonology. *Harvard Educational Review, 41,* no. 1.

Rodgers, E. (2004). Interactions that scaffold reading performance. *Journal of Literacy Research, 36,* 501–532.

Roorbach, B.(1998). *Writing life stories.* Cincinnati, OH: Story Press.

Selling, B. (1998). *Writing from within.* Alameda, CA: Hunter House.

Sipe, L. R. (1998). Transitions to the conventional: An examination of a first grader's composing process. *Journal of Literacy Research, 30*(3), 357–388.

Stiggins, R. (1996). *Student-centered classroom assessments.* 2d ed. Columbus, OH: Merrill Education/Prentice Hall.

Vygotsky, L. (1934/1986). *Thought and language.* Cambridge, MA: MIT Press.

Vygotsky, L. (1962). *Thought and language.* Cambridge, MA: MIT Press.

Vygotsky, L. (1978). *Mind in society: The development of higher psychological processes.* Cambridge, MA: Harvard University Press.

Wells, G. (1986). *The meaning makers: Children learning language and using language to learn.* Portsmouth, NH: Heinemann.

Wong, S., Groth, L., O'Flahavan, J., Gale, S., Kelley, G., Leeds, S., Regetz, J., & O'Malley-Steiner, J. (1994). *Characterizing teacher-student interaction in reading recovery lessons.* (Reading Research Report No. 17). Athens, GA: National Reading Research Center. (ERIC Document Reproduction Service No. ED 375 392).

Wood, D., Bruner, J., & Ross, G. (1976). The role of tutoring in problem-solving. *Journal of Child Psychology, 17,* 89–100.

Children's Books Cited

Agard, J., & Nichols, G. (1995). *No hickory no dickory no dock: Caribbean nursery rhymes.* Cambridge, MA: Candlewick.

Animals at the zoo. Berkeley, CA: Children's Press (Rookie Readers).

Animal babies. Ontario, Canada: Troll Company (First Start).

Aylesworth, J. (1992). *Old black fly.* New York: Henry Holt.

Banks, K. (2006). *Max's words.* New York: Farrar, Straus.

Barraclough, S. (1999). *The little lost duckling.* New York: Parragon.

Berger, M. (1992). *Look out for turtles.* New York: HarperCollins.

Bloome, S. (2005). *A splendid friend indeed.* Honesdale, PA: Boyds Mills.

Blos, J. (1987). *Old Henry.* New York: William Morrow.

Brett, J. (1989). *The mitten.* New York: G. P. Putnam's Sons.

Browne, A. (2006). *Silly Billy.* Cambridge, MA: Candlewick.

Bunting, E. (1999). *Butterfly house.* New York: Scholastic.

Bunting, E. (2000). *The memory string.* New York: Clarion.

Cannon, J. (1993). *Stellaluna.* San Diego: Harcourt.

Cole, H. (1995). *Jack's garden.* New York: Greenwillow.

Cooney, B. (1982). *Miss Rumphius.* New York: Penguin Putnam.

Cowley, J. (1980). *The hungry giant.* Bothell, WA: The Wright Group.

Cowley, J. (1999). *Red-eyed tree frog.* New York: Scholastic.

Crews, D. (1996). *Shortcut.* New York: HarperTrophy.

Cullinan, B. E. (Ed.). (1996). *A jar of tiny stars: Poems by NCTE award-winning poets.* Honesdale, PA: Boyds Mills.

Curtis, J. L. (2000). *Tell me again about the night I was born*. New York: HarperTrophy.

Dorros, A. (1997). *A tree is growing*. New York: Scholastic.

Doubilet, A. (1991). *Under the sea from a to z*. New York: Crown, Random House.

Esbensen, B. J. (1986). *Words with wrinkled knees*. New York: Thomas Y. Crowell.

Falconer, I. (2006). *Olivia forms a band*. New York: Atheneum.

Fox, M. (1984). *Wilfrid Gordon McDonald Partridge*. New York: Scholastic.

Fox, M. (1990). *Possum magic*. San Diego: Harcourt Brace.

Fraustino, L. R. (2001). *The hickory chair*. New York: Scholastic.

Frazee, M. (2006). *Walk on! A guide for babies of all ages*. Orlando, FL: Harcourt.

Gibbons, G. (1993). *From seed to plant*. New York: Holiday House.

Giblin, J. C. (1992). *George Washington: A picture book biography*. Jefferson City, MO: Scholastic Books.

Grimes, N. (1997). *It's raining laughter*. Honesdale, PA: Boyds Mills.

Henkes, K. (1996). *Chrysanthemum*. New York: Harper Trophy.

Henkes, K. (2004). *Kitten's first full moon*. New York: Greenwillow.

Hillenbrand, J., & Hillenbrand, W. (2006). *What a treasure!* New York: Holiday House.

Howe, J. (1998). *Pinky and Rex and the school play*. New York: Scholastic.

Hutchins, P. (1969). *Rosie's walk*. New York: Macmillan.

Hutchins, P. (1986). *The doorbell rang*. New York: Scholastic.

King, E. (1990). *The pumpkin patch*. New York: Dutton Children's Books.

Laminack, L. (2004). *Saturdays and teacakes*. Atlanta, GA: Peachtree Publishing.

Lester, H. (1998). *Tacky in trouble*. New York: Houghton Mifflin.

Lester, A. (2005). *Are we there yet?: A journey around Australia*. LaJolla, CA: Kane Miller.

Lorbiecki, M. (1998). *Sister Anne's hands*. New York: Puffin Books.

McMahon, P., & McCarthy, C. C. (2005). *Just add one Chinese sister: An adoption story*. Honesdale, PA: Boyds Mills.

Micklos, J. (2006). *No boys allowed: Poems about brothers and sisters*. Honesdale, PA: Boyds Mills.

Modesitt, J. (1996). *Sometimes I feel like a mouse: A book about feelings*. New York: Scholastic.

Mora, P. (1997). *Tomás and the library lady*. New York: Alfred A. Knopf.

Numeroff, L. J. (1985). *If you give a mouse a cookie*. New York: Scholastic.

Numeroff, L. J. (1991). *If you give a moose a muffin*. New York: Scholastic.

Nye, N. S. (2003). *Baby radar*. New York: HarperCollins.

Polacco, P. (1987). *Meteor!* New York: Putnam & Grosset.

Polacco, P. (1994). *My rotten redheaded older brother*. New York: Simon & Schuster.

Polacco, P. (1995). *My ol' man*. New York: Putnam & Grosset.

Pope, J. (1986). *Do animals dream?* New York: Viking.

Randell, B. (1994). *The clever penguins*. New York: Harcourt Achieve.

Randell, B. (1994). *Wake up, Dad!* New York: Harcourt Achieve.

Randell, B. (1996). *Baby bear's present*. New York: Rigby.

Raven, M. T. (2005). *Let them play*. Chelsea, MI: Sleeping Bear Press.

Ringgold, F. (1988). *Tar beach*. New York: Crown.

Ringgold, F. (1992). *Aunt Harriet's underground railroad in the sky*. New York: Crown.

Ringgold, F. (1993). *Dinner at Aunt Connie's house*. New York: Hyperion.

Robberecht, T. (2006). *Sam is never scared*. New York: Clarion.

Robbins, Ken. (2005). *Seeds*. New York: Atheneum Books.

Rocks. Northborough, Maine: Newbridge (Discovery Links).

Rollins, C. (1971). *Tent in the yard*. New York: Scott Foresman & Company.

Rylant, C. (1982). *When I was young in the mountains*. New York: E. P. Dutton.

Rylant, C. (1985). *The relatives came*. New York: Macmillan.

Rylant, Cynthia. (2002). *Let's go home: The wonderful things about a house*. New York: Aladdin Paperbacks.

Seeds, seeds, seeds. Northborough, Maine: Wright Group (Sunshine).

Sierra, J. (2004). *Wild about books*. New York: Knopf.

Shannon, D. (1998). *No, David!* New York: Scholastic.

Shannon, D. (1999). *David goes to school*. New York: Scholastic.

Shannon, D. (2002). *David gets in trouble!* New York: Scholastic.

Snicket, L. (2001). *The hostile hospital*. New York: HarperCollins.

Swinburne, S. R. (2000). *What's opposite?* Honesdale, PA: Boyds Mills Press.

The pot of gold (An Irish folk tale). New York: Scott Foresman & Company. (1971).

Young, E. (2006). *My Mei Mei*. New York: Penguin.

Voirst, J. (1972). *Alexander and the terrible, horrible, no good, very bad day*. New York: Atheneum.

Waddell, M. (1992). *The pig in the pond*. Cambridge, MA: Candlewick.

Waddell, M. (2002). *Owl babies*. Cambridge, MA: Candlewick.

KEEP BOOKS

Brand, M. (1995). *Trucks*. Columbus, OH: The Ohio State University.

Cicola, A. (2005). *Home sick*. Columbus, OH: The Ohio State University.

Fountas, I. (1995). *Look at me!* Columbus, OH: The Ohio State University.

Francis, J. (illustrator). (1995). *A retold tale: The three little pigs*. Columbus, OH: The Ohio State University.

Fried, M. D. (1999). *Zoo animals*. Columbus, OH: The Ohio State University.

Fried, M. (2007). *Be careful!* Columbus, OH: The Ohio State University.

Hicks, K. (2006). *Garden giant*. Columbus, OH: The Ohio State University

Hicks, K. (2006). *A sunflower plant life cycle*. Columbus, OH: The Ohio State University

Mann, C. (1996). *The smoke detector*. Columbus, OH: The Ohio State University.

McCarrier, A. (1995). *Growing a pumpkin*. Columbus, OH: The Ohio State University.

McCarrier, A. (1996). *Clickety-clack*. Columbus, OH: The Ohio State University.

McCarrier, A. (1996). *Goldilocks and baby bear*. Columbus, OH: The Ohio State University.

McCarrier, J. (1995). *Feeding the birds*. Columbus, OH: The Ohio State University.

McCarrier, J. (1996). *My brother's motorcycle*. Columbus, OH: The Ohio State University.

McCarrier, M. (1995). *Our favorite snowman*. Columbus, OH: The Ohio State University.

Pinnell, G. S. (1995). *My backpack*. Columbus, OH: The Ohio State University.

Pinnell, G. S. (1996). *Mugs*. Columbus, OH: The Ohio State University.

Pinnell, G. S. (2006). *Mugs indoors and outdoors*. Columbus, OH: The Ohio State University.

Pinnell, G. S. (2006). *Cats are hunters*. Columbus, OH: The Ohio State University.

INDEX